Azure Integration Guide for Business

Master effective architecture strategies for business innovation

Joshua Garverick

Jack Lee

Mélony Qin

Trevoir Williams

‹packt›

BIRMINGHAM—MUMBAI

Azure Integration Guide for Business

First Edition

Acquisition Editors: Mamta Yadav & Sathya Mohan

Lead Development Editor: Alex Patterson

Development Editor: Siddhant Jain

Content Development Editor: Afzal Shaikh

Project Coordinator: Yash Basil

Copy Editor: Safis Editing

Proofreader: Safis Editing

Production Designer: Deepak Chavan

Production reference: 1260923

Published by Packt Publishing Ltd.

Grosvenor House, 11 St Paul's Square, Birmingham, B3 1RB, UK.

ISBN 978-1-83763-914-4

www.packtpub.com

Contributors

About the authors

Joshua Garverick is a Microsoft **Most Valuable Professional** (**MVP**) and a seasoned IT professional with nearly two decades of enterprise experience working in several large industries (finance, healthcare, transportation, and logistics). He specializes in Azure application and platform architecture and is currently involved with application modernization and digital transformation projects. Josh is a **Microsoft Certified Solution Expert** (**MCSE**) in Cloud Platform and Infrastructure, as well as a certified Microsoft Azure Solution Architect Expert and a Microsoft DevOps Engineer Expert.

Jack Lee is a Microsoft MVP and an Azure Certified Solutions Architect with a passion for software development, cloud, and DevOps innovations. He is an active Microsoft tech community contributor and has presented at various user groups and conferences, among them the Global Azure Bootcamp at Microsoft Canada.

Jack is an experienced mentor and judge at hackathons and is also the president of a user group that focuses on Azure, DevOps, and software development. He has authored numerous books published by Packt, notably *Azure or Architects*, *Azure Strategy and Implementation Guide*, and *Cloud Analytics with Microsoft Azure*. In addition, he has earned multiple certifications including Microsoft Azure Solutions Architect Expert and Microsoft DevOps Engineer Expert. You can follow Jack on Twitter at `jlee_consulting`.

Mélony Y. Qin, also known as CloudMelon, is the founder of CloudMelon Vis, a tech media and educational platform for technopreneurs in the cloud-native and serverless space, and a former product manager at Microsoft. With a passion for cloud-native technologies, OSS, DevOps, Kubernetes, serverless, data, and AI, Mélony has authored multiple books, including the *Certified Kubernetes Administrator (CKA) Exam Guide*, the *Kubernetes Workshop*, and *Microsoft Azure Infrastructure*, all published by Packt Publishing. Mélony is a member of the **Association for Computing Machinery** (**ACM**) and the **Project Management Institute** (**PMI**), leveraging her extensive experience with diverse cloud technologies to drive innovation in the cloud-native, serverless, and generative AI space. She runs the `@CloudMelonVis YouTube` channel and *Cloud-Native Innovators* newsletter, read by professionals from top tech companies such as Microsoft, Google, Amazon, Dell, and Carrefour.

Trevoir Williams is a software engineer, lecturer, and author. With a master's degree in computer science, he has spent over a decade teaching web, software, and database development courses. He also has extensive industry experience in web application development, Azure cloud services, and server administration. He enjoys teaching IT and development courses and hopes to impart knowledge of the latest developments in industry standards and techniques to his students.

About the reviewers

Jetro Wils is a cloud and information security advisor who posts daily on LinkedIn. He's a certified Azure expert and an MCT. He's currently pursuing the Cybersecurity Architect Expert certification.

He helps organizations stay relevant and grow by securely applying cloud technology. He is active at Proximus NXT, one of Belgium's biggest ICT service providers, with an international footprint, where he focuses on providing secure and sovereign cloud solutions for the enterprise market.

Since 2016, the rise in cloud technology has fundamentally changed business operations. However, many businesses and IT professionals struggle to stay relevant and are falling behind. Jetro offers training and coaching to help them adapt to this new reality without overwhelming them so that they feel confident and can grow their value.

Peter De Tender has an extensive background in architecting, deploying, managing and training Microsoft technologies, dating back to Windows NT4 Server in 1996, all the way to the latest and modern cloud solutions available in Azure today. With a passion for cloud architecture, DevOps, and security, Peter always has a story to share on how to optimize clients' enterprise-ready cloud workloads. When he's not providing a technical Azure workshop in his role as an Azure technical trainer at Microsoft Corp, for which he relocated from Belgium to Seattle in early 2022, he's developing some new apps on .NET Blazor as a new hobby.

Peter was an Azure MVP for 5 years. He has been an MCT for over 13 years and is still actively involved in the community as a public speaker, technical writer, book author, and publisher.

You can follow Peter on twitter `@pdtit` and read his technical blog adventures on `http://www.007ffflearning.com`.

Vaibhav Gujral is based out of Omaha, Nebraska. He is a thought leader and a seasoned cloud professional with over 17 years of extensive experience working with several global clients spanning multiple industries. He specializes in cloud strategy and governance with deep technical expertise in cloud security, cloud architecture, microservices architecture, and DevOps practices. He helps organizations adopt the cloud the right way by clearly understanding the business drivers and developing a cost-effective solution utilizing suitable architectural patterns and design principles. Vaibhav holds a bachelor of engineering degree and is a Microsoft Azure MVP. He runs the Omaha Azure user group and regularly blogs at `https://vaibhavgujral.com/`.

Vaibhav shares the following dedication:

"I'd like to thank my wife and our two children for their daily support and patience. I'd like to thank my parents, siblings, relatives, friends, and mentors for their guidance and continued support. Finally, I'd also like to thank Packt Publishing for the opportunity to review this book."

Table of Contents

3

Cloud Architecture Design Patterns   41

4

Azure Network Infrastructure and Design   63

5

Automating Architecture on Azure   81

6

Optimize Performance with Azure OLTP Solutions   109

7

Designing Serverless Architecture Solutions in Azure   135

8

Deploying, Managing, and Scaling Containers with Azure Kubernetes Service   161

9

Designing Big Data Solutions with Azure   185

10

Architecting Secure Applications on a Trusted Platform   201

11

Cost Governance on Azure   223

12

Conclusion   237

Preface

Azure Integration Guide for Business covers different solutions to help architects and business decision-makers thrive in the face of limited resources and showcase the power of Microsoft Azure as a transformative tool for achieving remarkable results. This book highlights the key features and functionalities provided by Azure, enabling architects and business decision-makers to harness the limitless potential of the cloud. It also examines how Azure can enhance operational efficiency, scale businesses seamlessly, strengthen security measures, and stimulate innovation across organizations.

Who this book is for

This book is for business decision-makers, IT decision-makers, and solution architects who are considering a migration to the cloud as part of their organization's modernization strategy.

What this book covers

Chapter 1, *Unlock New Opportunities with Azure*, highlights some of the compelling reasons why Azure has become the preferred choice for many decision-makers. It gives a walk-through of different cloud models, shared responsibilities between Microsoft and customers, and various Azure subscription models.

Chapter 2, *Achieve Availability, Scalability, and Monitoring with Azure*, lets you explore how high availability, scalability, and monitoring play significant roles in modern cloud-based architectures. You'll see how they are essential in ensuring seamless operations, optimal performance, and ultimately, the success of businesses in the digital landscape.

Chapter 3, *Cloud Architecture Design Patterns*, focuses on design patterns related to **virtual networks** (**VNets**), storage accounts, performance, and messaging. These constructs affect how you implement your solution and, with enough attention to detail, can help you gauge costs, efficiencies, and overall productivity properly. This chapter also outlines some design best practices.

Chapter 4, *Azure Network Infrastructure and Design*, gives a walk-through of the various networking services Azure offers, from base networking to advanced traffic control. You'll get to review several standard design patterns used when configuring and provisioning networking components, a list of the many different Azure cloud networking services that are currently available, and a collection of common problem spaces that you may encounter when designing networks in the wild.

Chapter 5, *Automating Architecture on Azure*, shows how automation and **Infrastructure as Code** (**IaC**) play a crucial role in streamlining the provisioning and management of resources. You'll get to know the various tools available for implementing IaC in Azure, including ARM templates, Bicep, and Terraform.

Chapter 6, Optimize Performance with Azure OLTP Solutions, highlights the various aspects of using transactional data stores, such as Azure SQL Database and other open source databases that are typically used in **online transaction processing** (**OLTP**) systems. With these Azure services, you'll learn how to achieve performance and cost optimization.

Chapter 7, Designing Serverless Architecture Solutions in Azure, gives a comprehensive understanding of developing serverless applications utilizing Azure Functions, as well as implementing event-driven architectural solutions through the effective utilization of various Azure services on the Azure serverless platform.

Chapter 8, Deploying, Managing, and Scaling Containers with Azure Kubernetes Service, delves into various aspects, including the upstream Kubernetes and **Azure Kubernetes Service** (**AKS**) cluster architecture and the use of add-ons, extensions, and third-party integrations with AKS. It provides the knowledge and skills required to build and scale applications on AKS clusters and Azure Container Apps.

Chapter 9, Designing Big Data Solutions with Azure, discusses big data in the context of data warehousing and advanced analytics and talks about solutions that allow the use of large amounts of data. It shares insight into the best Azure tools and services that can be used to design big data and intelligent solutions.

Chapter 10, Architecting Secure Applications on a Trusted Platform, outlines the Azure tools, services, and best practices for building resilient and secure applications. It will help you navigate the complex security landscape in Azure, ensuring your applications stand against evolving threats in the digital landscape. It will provide invaluable insights into secure application architecture on Azure.

Chapter 11, Cost Governance on Azure, gives you insights into the significance of cost management and optimization on Azure. You'll be able to investigate the various pricing options, and the services and tools offered by Azure for managing costs.

Chapter 12, Conclusion, covers the key takeaways from each chapter. It summarizes the book and delivers guidance for further action.

To get the most out of this book

You do not require any existing knowledge of Azure or cloud computing.

Get in touch

Feedback from our readers is always welcome.

General feedback: If you have questions about any aspect of this book, email us at customercare@ packtpub.com and mention the book title in the subject of your message.

Errata: Although we have taken every care to ensure the accuracy of our content, mistakes do happen. If you find a mistake in this book, we would be grateful to you for sending the report to us. Please visit www.packtpub.com/support/errata and fill in the form.

Piracy: If you come across any illegal copies of our works in any form on the internet, we would be grateful if you would provide us with the location address or website name. Please contact us at copyright@packt.com with a link to the material.

Becoming an author: If there is a topic that you have expertise in and you are interested in either writing or contributing to a book, please visit authors.packtpub.com.

Download a free PDF copy of this book

Thanks for purchasing this book!

Do you like to read on the go but are unable to carry your print books everywhere?

Is your eBook purchase not compatible with the device of your choice?

Don't worry, now with every Packt book you get a DRM-free PDF version of that book at no cost.

Read anywhere, any place, on any device. Search, copy, and paste code from your favorite technical books directly into your application.

The perks don't stop there, you can get exclusive access to discounts, newsletters, and great free content in your inbox daily

Follow these simple steps to get the benefits:

1. Scan the QR code or visit the link below

https://packt.link/free-ebook/9781837639144

2. Submit your proof of purchase
3. That's it! We'll send your free PDF and other benefits to your email directly

1
Unlock New Opportunities with Azure

In recent years, a remarkable transformation has taken place in the business landscape as organizations of all sizes and industries are increasingly embracing cloud technology. Cloud computing has emerged as a game changer, reshaping the way companies operate, make decisions, and design their architectural frameworks. This paradigm shift is driven by many factors, with two prominent reasons standing out: cost savings and the ability to accomplish more with fewer resources. At the forefront of this cloud revolution is Microsoft Azure.

One of the primary drivers compelling business decision makers and architects to adopt cloud solutions is the potential for substantial cost savings. Traditional on-premises infrastructure demands substantial upfront investments in hardware, software licenses, and dedicated IT staff to maintain and manage the infrastructure. With Azure, organizations can opt for a pay-as-you-go model, where they only pay for the resources and services they use. We will learn more about this in *Chapter 11, Cost governance on Azure*.

Azure enables companies to do more with less, amplifying the impact of their resources. Businesses can tap into virtually unlimited computing power and storage capacity, allowing them to scale their operations seamlessly. We will learn more about this in *Chapter 2, Achieve availability, scalability, and monitoring with Azure*.

Beyond cost savings and resource optimization, Azure offers additional benefits that drive its adoption among business decision makers and architects. These advantages include enhanced data security, improved disaster recovery capabilities, simplified software updates and maintenance, and the ability to access data and applications from anywhere at any time. Azure's advanced security measures and compliance certifications meet the highest industry standards, providing organizations with peace of mind as they embrace the cloud. We will learn more about this in *Chapter 10, Architecting secure applications on a trusted platform*.

Azure has become a catalyst for business transformation, revolutionizing the decision-making processes and architectural practices of organizations worldwide. With cost savings, improved resource utilization, and a wealth of additional benefits, it is no surprise that business decision makers and architects are enthusiastically embracing the cloud. Azure is supporting companies in unlocking new opportunities, driving efficiency, and gaining a competitive edge in today's rapidly evolving business landscape.

In the next section, we will highlight some of the compelling reasons why Azure has become the preferred choice for many decision makers.

Why many decision makers choose Azure

Azure is an excellent choice for businesses looking to take advantage of cloud computing technology. Many decision makers choose Azure for the following reasons:

- **Cost-effectiveness**: By using Azure, businesses can reduce their IT infrastructure costs significantly, as they only pay for the resources they use. This eliminates the expenses associated with maintaining on-premises datacenters or investing in costly hardware.

- **Security and governance**: Azure is built with security in mind by offering robust features such as built-in encryption, access controls, and recommendations through Azure Advisor's security baseline. Businesses can trust Azure to safeguard their data from unauthorized access and cyber threats.

- **Scalability**: Azure allows businesses to scale their operations up or down as needed, providing them with access to resources on demand without the need to invest in expensive hardware.

- **Reliability**: Backed by Microsoft's extensive infrastructure, Azure is designed to deliver high **service-level agreements (SLAs)** and ensure uptime. Businesses can rely on Azure to provide uninterrupted access to their data and applications.

- **High availability**: Azure is built with high availability and resilience in mind. With multiple zones within a region, robust backup and recovery capabilities, and built-in disaster recovery options, businesses can trust that their applications and data are safe and accessible.

- **Comprehensive services**: Azure offers a variety of services that cater to diverse business needs, spanning from storage and networking to artificial intelligence and machine learning.

- **Seamless integration**: Azure is designed to seamlessly integrate with Microsoft tools, services, and other cloud providers. This makes it easy for businesses to incorporate Azure into their existing workflows and systems without disruption.

- **Global reach**: Azure has a global presence, with datacenters in over 60 regions worldwide, providing businesses with a highly available and scalable infrastructure. This global presence ensures reliable access to services regardless of geographical location.

- **Flexibility**: Azure supports a wide range of programming languages, platforms, and tools, granting businesses the flexibility to choose the technologies that align with their specific needs, skills, and preferences.

- **Customizable**: Azure enables businesses to select and customize the services they require, allowing for tailored solutions that integrate seamlessly with existing workflows and systems.

- **Analytical assistance**: Azure Synapse Analytics offers a unified platform for architects and data professionals to unlock the full potential of their data. By leveraging powerful analytical capabilities and integrating data from various sources, businesses can derive valuable insights for analytics and reporting purposes.

Within the realm of cloud computing, Microsoft Azure provides three distinct cloud models, each defining the level of control and maintenance responsibilities for customers. These cloud models facilitate the segregation of responsibility. In the upcoming section, we will examine each of these models, exploring how they help businesses to effectively manage their cloud resources.

Understanding segregation of responsibility in different Azure cloud models

Segregation of responsibility is an important concept in cloud computing, particularly in environments where multiple teams or individuals have access to shared resources. Understanding how segregation of responsibility works in different Azure cloud models can help ensure that your organization's data and resources are protected and managed effectively.

There are three different deployment patterns that are available in Azure:

- **Infrastructure as a service (IaaS)**
- **Platform as a service (PaaS)**
- **Software as a service (SaaS)**

The differentiation among these three deployment patterns is the level of control customers have over their resources through Azure.

IaaS

IaaS is a type of deployment model that allows customers to provision their own infrastructure on Azure. Azure provides several infrastructure resources and customers can provision them on demand. Customers are responsible for maintaining and governing their own infrastructure, while Azure takes care of the maintenance of the physical infrastructure on which the virtual infrastructure resources are hosted. This approach requires customers to actively manage and operate within the Azure environment.

PaaS

PaaS eliminates the need for customers to handle infrastructure deployment and control, offering a higher-level abstraction compared to IaaS. In this approach, customers bring their own application, code, and data, and deploy them on the platform provided by Azure. These platforms are managed and governed by Azure, while customers retain sole responsibility for their applications. Since Azure manages the underlying infrastructure, customers can focus solely on activities related to their application deployment. This model facilitates faster and simpler options for application deployment when compared to IaaS.

SaaS

SaaS represents a higher-level abstraction in comparison to PaaS. In this approach, customers have access to software and its associated services for their consumption. The services are fully managed by the provider. Customers only need to bring their data into the SaaS environment without any control over the underlying infrastructure or services.

Figure 1.1 illustrates the areas of responsibility between customers and Microsoft, spanning SaaS, PaaS, IaaS, and on-premises.

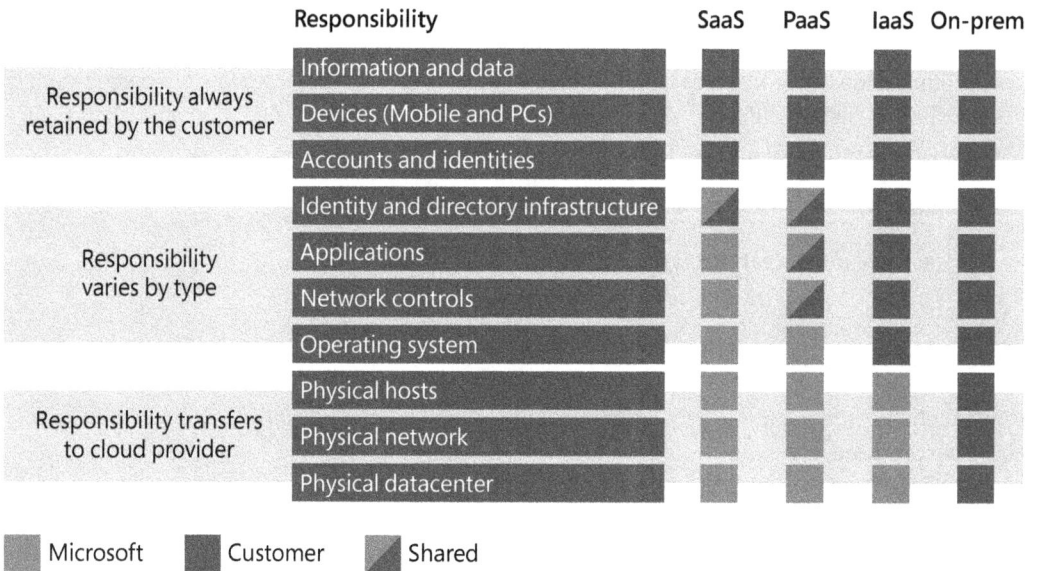

	Responsibility	SaaS	PaaS	IaaS	On-prem
Responsibility always retained by the customer	Information and data				
	Devices (Mobile and PCs)				
	Accounts and identities				
Responsibility varies by type	Identity and directory infrastructure				
	Applications				
	Network controls				
	Operating system				
Responsibility transfers to cloud provider	Physical hosts				
	Physical network				
	Physical datacenter				

■ Microsoft   ■ Customer   ◸ Shared

Figure 1.1: Segregation of responsibilities

Regardless of the deployment type or cloud model, you retain ownership of your data and identities. It is your responsibility to protect the security of your data, identities, on-premises resources, and the components within your control in the cloud.

The following responsibilities are always retained by you regardless of deployment type:

- Information and data
- Devices (mobile and PCs)
- Accounts and identities

Understanding the segregation of responsibility across different Azure cloud models is crucial for ensuring the security and integrity of your organization's data and resources. With the robust security and compliance features of Azure and the implementation of best practices for managing and securing your Azure environments, organizations can effectively protect and manage their data and applications.

In the next section, we will provide guidance on how to get started with Azure.

How to get started with Azure

For business decision makers seeking to help their organizations engage with the advantages of cloud computing, embarking on the Azure journey is a straightforward process that can be simplified into a few essential steps.

Step 1: Understand your business needs

Before diving into Azure, it is important to understand your business needs and goals. This will help you determine which Azure services and solutions are the best fit for your organization.

Consider questions such as:

- What are the current pain points or challenges within your organization?
- What business processes could benefit from cloud computing?
- What are the specific goals you hope to achieve by using Azure?

Identifying the current pain points or challenges within your organization is crucial when considering Azure as a cloud computing solution. By recognizing areas where your current IT infrastructure or processes are inefficient or ineffective, you can begin to evaluate how Azure can help as a cloud computing solution.

For example, if your organization struggles with managing and maintaining on-premises hardware that requires frequent updates, moving to Azure could help alleviate the burden of physical hardware management. Alternatively, if data security or backup is a concern, Azure's built-in security features and automated backup solutions can help address these issues.

Furthermore, evaluating which business processes could benefit from cloud computing can help determine the most suitable Azure services and solutions for your organization. For example, if your goal is to modernize legacy applications or develop new ones, Azure App Service provides a platform for building and deploying web and mobile apps in the cloud. If storing large volumes of data is a priority, Azure Blob Storage or Azure SQL Database may be the right fit.

Lastly, identifying specific goals that you hope to achieve by using Azure can help ensure that you make the most effective use of the platform. Some organizations may aim to reduce costs by migrating to the cloud, while others may be looking to improve scalability and flexibility. By defining these goals, you can choose the Azure services and solutions that align with your organization's needs and objectives, enabling you to track progress toward achieving those goals over time.

Overall, understanding the pain points and challenges within your organization, identifying processes that can benefit from cloud computing, and setting specific goals for Azure adoption are key steps in getting started with the platform. These steps will help maximize the benefits of cloud computing, driving growth and innovation for your organization.

Step 2: Create an Azure account

Once you have a clear understanding of your business needs, the next step is to create an Azure account. Creating an Azure account will grant you access to the Azure portal, where you can explore and utilize the wide range of services and solutions offered by Azure.

To create an Azure account, follow these steps:

1. Go to `https://azure.microsoft.com/free/` and click on **Start free** (see *Figure 1.2*).

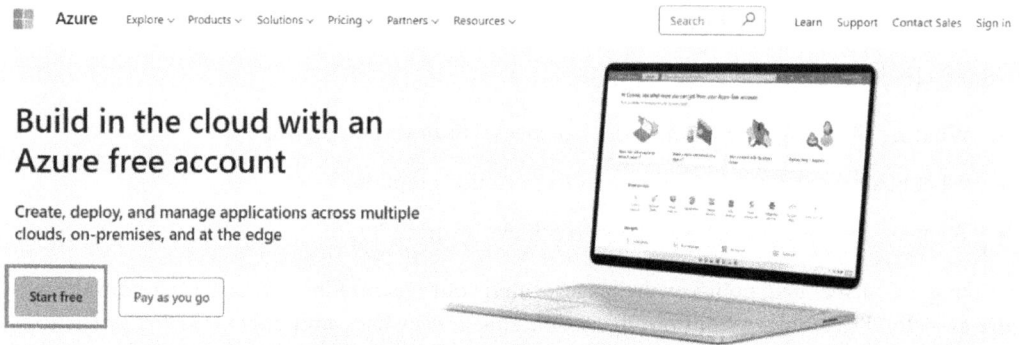

Figure 1.2: Azure free account

2. Sign in with your Microsoft account or create a new one if you don't have an existing account.
3. Provide your basic information, such as name, email address, and phone number.
4. Verify your identity through the required verification process.
5. Choose a subscription type and provide payment information if necessary.
6. Verify your account by following the instructions in the confirmation email.

Step 3: Familiarize yourself with the Azure portal

The Azure portal serves as the central hub for managing your Azure resources. It is important to familiarize yourself with the portal and the different services and solutions available.

Here are some tips to get started:

- **Take the Azure portal tour**: The Azure portal tour provides an overview of the portal and its features. It is a great way to get familiar with the platform.
- **Use the search bar**: The search bar at the top of the portal can be used to find specific services and resources.
- **Pin frequently used resources**: You can pin frequently used resources to the dashboard for easy access.

Step 4: Choose your services and solutions

Azure offers a wide range of services and solutions to meet the needs of businesses of all sizes.

Here are some common Azure services that you can use in your architecture design:

- **Azure App Service**:

  Azure App Service is a versatile HTTP-based service designed to host a wide range of web applications, REST APIs, and mobile backends. With the flexibility to develop in your preferred programming language, such as .NET, .NET Core, Java, Ruby, Node.js, PHP, or Python, Azure App Service ensures compatibility and ease of use. It enables seamless deployment and scaling of applications on both Windows and Linux-based environments, providing developers with a unified and efficient platform for building and running their applications. https://learn.microsoft.com/azure/app-service/overview

- **Azure Storage**:

  Azure Storage serves as Microsoft's advanced cloud storage solution, tailored to meet the requirements of modern data storage scenarios. With Azure Storage, businesses gain access to a highly available, immensely scalable, and securely managed storage infrastructure in the cloud. This comprehensive storage platform accommodates a wide range of data objects, ensuring durability and security while offering unparalleled flexibility and reliability for storing and accessing data in various formats. https://learn.microsoft.com/azure/storage/common/storage-introduction

- **Azure Virtual Machines**:

  Azure Virtual Machines provide businesses with the flexibility of virtualization without the need to invest in and manage physical hardware. With Azure Virtual Machines, organizations can create and run virtual machines in the cloud, eliminating the hassle of hardware procurement, maintenance, and infrastructure management. This allows businesses to focus on their core objectives and quickly deploy virtual machines tailored to their specific needs, with the ability to scale resources up or down as required. Azure Virtual Machines offer a cost-effective and efficient solution for running a wide range of applications and workloads in a flexible and scalable environment. `https://learn.microsoft.com/azure/virtual-machines/overview`

- **Azure SQL Database**:

  Azure SQL is a suite of managed, secure, and intelligent products that use the trusted SQL Server database engine within the Azure cloud environment. This family of products offers businesses a range of options for storing, managing, and analyzing data using the familiar SQL Server technology they are already familiar with. Azure SQL provides a seamless and scalable solution for organizations to build and deploy applications, store and retrieve data, and gain valuable insights from their data assets. With its robust security features, Azure SQL ensures data protection and compliance, while its intelligent capabilities enable advanced analytics, machine learning, and AI-driven insights. By leveraging Azure SQL, businesses can harness the power of SQL Server in a cloud-based environment, unlocking new possibilities for data-driven decision-making and innovation. `https://learn.microsoft.com/azure/azure-sql/azure-sql-iaas-vs-paas-what-is-overview`

- **Azure Kubernetes Service (AKS)**:

  AKS streamlines the process of deploying and managing a Kubernetes cluster in Azure by shifting the operational responsibilities to the Azure platform. With AKS, businesses can take advantage of the benefits of Kubernetes, such as containerization, scalability, and orchestration, without the need to handle the underlying infrastructure and administrative tasks. AKS abstracts away the complexities of setting up and maintaining a Kubernetes environment, allowing organizations to focus on deploying and running their applications seamlessly. By offloading the operational overhead to Azure, AKS provides a hassle-free experience, ensuring that businesses can engage with the full potential of Kubernetes for their containerized workloads, without being burdened by the underlying infrastructure management. `https://learn.microsoft.com/azure/aks/intro-kubernetes`

- **Azure Synapse Analytics**:

  Azure Synapse Analytics is a comprehensive enterprise analytics service designed to expedite the time it takes to gain valuable insights from data warehouses and big data systems. By combining the strengths of various SQL technologies commonly utilized in enterprise data warehousing, Spark technologies used for handling big data, Data Explorer for log and time series analytics, Azure Pipelines for efficient data integration and ETL/ELT processes, and seamless integration with other Azure services such as Power BI, Cosmos DB, and Azure ML, Azure Synapse Analytics provides a unified platform for end-to-end analytics. With Azure Synapse Analytics, organizations can accelerate their data analytics workflows, enabling them to extract valuable insights and make informed business decisions efficiently.
  `https://learn.microsoft.com/azure/synapse-analytics/overview-what-is`

To get started, choose the services and solutions that align with your business needs and goals.

Step 5: Monitor and optimize your usage

Once you have chosen your Azure services and solutions, it is important to monitor and optimize your usage to ensure you are getting the most out of the platform.

Azure provides a range of tools and features to help you monitor and optimize your usage, including the following:

- **Azure Monitor**:

  This tool provides monitoring and analytics for your Azure resources.
  `https://learn.microsoft.com/azure/azure-monitor/overview`

- **Azure Advisor**:

  This tool provides personalized recommendations to help optimize your Azure resources.
  `https://learn.microsoft.com/azure/advisor/advisor-overview`

- **Microsoft Cost Management**:

  This tool helps you monitor and manage your Azure spending.
  `https://learn.microsoft.com/azure/cost-management-billing/cost-management-billing-overview`

By following these steps, you can initiate your journey with Azure and gain the benefits of cloud computing for your organization. As you gain proficiency with Azure, you can engage with the more advanced features and solutions that the platform offers. For instance, you may choose to use Azure to store and manage large volumes of multimedia content or to develop and deploy sophisticated AI applications that require robust computing resources.

With the right tools and resources at your disposal, you can accomplish your business objectives and foster growth and innovation within your organization.

In the next section, we will discuss various Azure subscription models, enabling you to better understand and choose the most suitable option for your organization.

Understanding the Azure subscription models

Azure offers a range of subscription models tailored to accommodate businesses of all sizes. Familiarizing yourself with these subscription models will assist you in selecting the most suitable option for your organization's requirements.

When making your choice, take into account factors such as your organization's usage patterns, budget constraints, and specific business needs. It is also important to understand the cost structure associated with each subscription model, as pricing can fluctuate based on factors such as usage, geographical location, and service type.

To effectively manage costs and optimize resource utilization, Azure provides helpful tools such as the Microsoft **Cost Management + Billing** portal. This portal enables you to monitor and track your usage and spending across multiple Azure subscriptions. Additionally, Azure Advisor offers personalized recommendations tailored to optimize your Azure resources based on your unique usage patterns and business requirements.

The following is an overview of the different Azure subscription models, each designed to cater to specific business needs and circumstances:

Free tier

The free tier is an excellent choice for individuals or small businesses embarking on their Azure journey. It grants free access to a wide range of Azure services, albeit with specific usage limits. This tier is particularly suitable for those who wish to experiment with Azure or test small workloads without incurring costs. It offers a risk-free environment to explore the capabilities and benefits of Azure.

Pay-as-you-go

The pay-as-you-go subscription model provides the flexibility to pay for Azure services based on your actual usage, without any upfront costs or long-term commitments. This model is well suited for businesses with unpredictable or fluctuating usage patterns. With pay-as-you-go, you have the freedom to scale your usage up or down as needed, ensuring that you only pay for the services you actually use. This allows for greater cost control and agility, making it an ideal choice for organizations that require flexibility in their Azure consumption.

Azure for Students

Azure for Students is a no-cost subscription model designed specifically for students, providing them with access to a wide range of Azure services for educational and experimental purposes. This subscription model is tailored to support students in their learning journey by offering hands-on experience with cloud technologies. With Azure for Students, students can explore and experiment with various Azure services, gaining practical knowledge and skills that are in high demand in today's digital landscape. It is an excellent opportunity for students to delve into cloud computing, develop their technical expertise, and unlock the potential of Azure for their academic and personal projects.

Enterprise Agreement (EA)

EA is a customized agreement designed for larger organizations that have substantial Azure usage. This agreement provides customized pricing discounts and additional benefits that are specifically based on the organization's size and usage patterns. The EA offers a flexible and scalable solution for organizations to optimize their Azure usage and streamline their cloud operations. By entering into an EA, organizations can unlock cost savings and gain access to specialized support, enabling them to maximize the value and efficiency of their Azure deployment. It is an ideal option for enterprises that require a comprehensive and personalized approach to managing their Azure services and resources.

Cloud Solution Provider (CSP)

The CSP subscription model is a collaborative partnership between Microsoft and chosen cloud solution providers. Through the CSP program, customers gain access to customized Azure solutions, specialized support, and flexible billing options. This model allows customers to work closely with their CSP partner to design, deploy, and manage their Azure environment according to their specific requirements. The CSP subscription model offers a comprehensive solution for organizations seeking a more personalized and hands-on approach to utilizing Azure services.

Microsoft Partner Network (MPN)

The MPN subscription model is specifically tailored for Microsoft partners, providing them with a range of valuable benefits to support their business operations. With an MPN subscription, partners gain access to internal-use licenses, enabling them to utilize Microsoft products and services within their own organization for demonstration, development, and testing purposes. Additionally, partners receive training resources, technical support, and valuable insights into the latest Microsoft technologies and solutions. The MPN subscription model helps Microsoft partners enhance their expertise, expand their capabilities, and deliver innovative solutions to their customers.

Having a clear understanding of the various Azure subscription models enables you to select the most suitable option for your organization, aligning with your specific requirements and budget. Azure's cost management and optimization tools play a crucial role in maximizing the value of your subscription by helping you monitor and control costs effectively. These tools ensure that your Azure resources are utilized efficiently, enabling you to achieve the best return on investment while maintaining cost control. Making informed decisions about your Azure subscription and utilizing cost management tools will give your organization the ability to optimize its cloud resources and drive business success.

Summary

Architects and business decision makers constantly encounter the task of achieving greater results with limited resources. As discussed in this chapter, Microsoft Azure provides a wide range of solutions to tackle these challenges effectively. By leveraging the capabilities of the cloud and adopting hybrid environments, architects can enhance efficiency, exercise greater control over expenditure, and surpass their business requirements.

Azure gives architects the tools to optimize their operations by leveraging the scalability, flexibility, and cost-effectiveness of cloud technology. With Azure's comprehensive suite of tools and services, architects can streamline workflows, enhance productivity, and achieve more with the resources at hand. By adopting a hybrid approach, architects can strike a balance between on-premises infrastructure and cloud-based solutions, enabling them to enjoy the benefits of both environments.

Furthermore, Azure offers robust cost management tools, allowing architects to monitor and control spending on cloud resources. This helps organizations maximize their return on investment and make informed decisions regarding resource allocation. With Azure's pay-as-you-go model and flexible pricing options, architects can effectively manage costs while ensuring that their business needs are met.

In the upcoming chapters, our focus will be on exploring the precise features and functionalities offered by Azure that enable architects and business decision makers to harness the full potential of the cloud. We will examine various ways in which Azure can optimize operations, deliver scalability, fortify security, and foster innovation within organizations.

2

Achieve Availability, Scalability, and Monitoring with Azure

In designing a robust and successful cloud architecture, three key elements play a pivotal role: high availability, scalability, and effective monitoring. These elements are essential for businesses striving to meet their objectives and cater to evolving customer demands.

High availability ensures uninterrupted access to applications, guaranteeing seamless service delivery and safeguarding business continuity. By eliminating single points of failure and implementing redundant systems, organizations can minimize downtime and maintain consistent availability, bolstering customer satisfaction and trust.

Scalability is another critical factor that businesses seek in their cloud architecture. It empowers organizations to efficiently handle fluctuations in user traffic and resource requirements. With scalable solutions, businesses can dynamically adjust their resources to match the demands of peak periods, ensuring optimal performance. Additionally, during periods of low demand, scaling down resources helps minimize costs, promoting cost efficiency without compromising performance.

Effective monitoring is a vital component for businesses aiming to maintain the health, performance, and security of their applications and infrastructure. By continuously monitoring system behavior, organizations gain valuable insights and visibility into potential issues before they impact users. Proactive detection and resolution of performance bottlenecks, resource utilization tracking, and swift response to risks or anomalies become possible with comprehensive monitoring. Such measures enhance overall system reliability and enable businesses to deliver a seamless user experience.

In this chapter, we will examine the significant roles that high availability, scalability, and monitoring play in modern cloud-based architectures. They are essential in ensuring seamless operations, optimal performance, and ultimately, the success of businesses in the digital landscape. We will also explore the comprehensive suite of services and features offered by Azure, empowering businesses to achieve and sustain high availability, scalability, and effective monitoring across their cloud environments.

Importance of achieving high availability with Azure

Achieving high availability in Azure enables businesses to safeguard against the potential risks and detrimental impact of downtime. Downtime can lead to significant consequences, including financial losses, damage to reputation, and dissatisfaction among customers. The inability to access critical applications and services in a timely fashion can disrupt business operations, impede productivity, and erode customer trust.

Organizations can proactively mitigate these risks and ensure uninterrupted operations by prioritizing high-availability measures in Azure. High availability allows businesses to maintain continuous access to their applications and services, even in the face of unexpected events or system failures. This resilience not only minimizes the financial impact of downtime but also helps preserve the reputation of the business and instills confidence in customers.

Understanding high availability with Azure

High availability refers to an important aspect of a service or application that ensures uninterrupted operations by meeting or surpassing its promised **service-level agreement** (**SLA**). Users are guaranteed a certain SLA based on the service type. For instance, an SLA might guarantee 99% availability for an application over the course of a year. This means the service should be accessible to users for a minimum of 361.35 days out of the 365-day period. Failure to meet this availability requirement would be considered a breach of the SLA.

In the case of mission-critical applications, the high-availability SLA is often up to 99.999% for the year. This means the application is expected to run continuously and remain accessible throughout the entire year, with a maximum allowable downtime of only 5.2 hours. If the actual downtime exceeds the defined SLA threshold, users may be eligible for credit, which is calculated based on the overall uptime percentage.

Some of the key factors affecting the high availability of an application include the following:

- Planned maintenance
- Unplanned maintenance
- Application deployment architecture

Within the Azure ecosystem, maintaining high availability involves implementing strategies that minimize disruptions caused by planned and unplanned maintenance events.

Planned maintenance

Planned maintenance refers to scheduled updates, upgrades, or maintenance activities performed by Azure to enhance the platform's performance, security, or reliability. By effectively managing planned maintenance, Azure aims to minimize any impact on the availability of customer applications. This is achieved through careful scheduling, communication, and coordination to ensure that deployments experience minimal downtime or service interruptions during these planned events.

Unplanned maintenance

Unplanned maintenance, on the other hand, refers to unforeseen incidents or issues that may arise, such as hardware failures, network disruptions, or software glitches. Azure employs various mechanisms to mitigate the impact of such events and maintain high availability. These mechanisms include redundancy, fault tolerance, and failover capabilities. Businesses can use Azure's distributed infrastructure, data replication, and automatic failover mechanisms to ensure that their applications remain accessible even in the face of unexpected disruptions.

Application deployment architecture

Another critical aspect of high availability is the application's deployment architecture. Azure provides a wide range of architectural options that enable businesses to design and implement resilient and highly available deployments. These include load balancing, autoscaling, and data replication across multiple regions. By distributing application components across multiple servers, virtual machines, or even geographic regions, businesses can minimize the risk of a single point of failure and enhance the availability and performance of their applications.

In the next section, we will look at the features and services that Azure offers to enable businesses to achieve and maintain high availability for their deployments.

Achieving high availability on Azure

Azure offers a wide array of features that empower architects to achieve high availability for their applications, spanning from the host and guest operating system to utilizing **platform as a service (PaaS)** capabilities. Using these native Azure features, architects can configure their applications for high availability without having to build such capabilities from scratch or rely on third-party tools.

In this section, we will look at features and capabilities provided by Azure to make applications highly available.

Load balancing options in Azure

Load balancing ensures the efficient distribution of the workload across multiple virtual machines and applications. When a single virtual machine is handling the workload, there is no need for load balancing as the entire load is concentrated on that one virtual machine without any sharing. However, in scenarios where multiple virtual machines are hosting the same application or service, load balancing becomes essential to evenly distribute the load among them.

By employing load balancing, businesses can optimize resource utilization, enhance application performance, and improve overall system reliability. The load balancer acts as a central orchestrator, intelligently directing incoming requests or traffic to the appropriate virtual machines in a balanced manner. This distribution of workload prevents any single virtual machine from becoming overwhelmed or experiencing performance bottlenecks, ensuring the smooth and efficient operation of the application.

Azure provides the following load balancing capabilities that can be seamlessly integrated into your solution.

Azure Load Balancer

Azure Load Balancer efficiently distributes incoming network traffic across multiple resources within the Azure ecosystem. Whether it is virtual machines, virtual machine scale sets, or availability sets, Load Balancer ensures that traffic is evenly distributed, thereby enhancing the availability and responsiveness of applications.

Operating at Layer 4 (TCP/UDP) of the network stack, Azure Load Balancer is capable of intelligently load balancing incoming traffic across multiple instances or virtual machines. This load balancing capability applies to both public-facing and private applications and services, making it a versatile solution for various deployment scenarios.

One of the key features of Azure Load Balancer is its ability to perform health probes. Health probes allow businesses to regularly check the health and status of their resources. If a resource is identified as unhealthy, it can be automatically removed from the load balancer pool, ensuring that incoming traffic is only directed to healthy and operational resources. This proactive approach to monitoring and managing resource health enhances the reliability and availability of applications.

To learn more about Azure Load Balancer, check the following resource: `https://learn.microsoft.com/azure/load-balancer/load-balancer-overview`

Azure Application Gateway

Azure Application Gateway is a versatile and secure web traffic load balancer that empowers businesses to effectively manage and protect the flow of web traffic to their applications. With its comprehensive set of features, Application Gateway ensures high performance and enhanced security for web applications.

Operating at Layer 7 (HTTP/HTTPS) of the network stack, Azure Application Gateway offers advanced functionalities for load balancing web traffic. It can intelligently distribute incoming traffic across multiple instances of web applications, optimizing resource utilization and providing a smooth user experience.

One of the key capabilities of Application Gateway is SSL termination, which allows businesses to offload SSL/TLS encryption and decryption processes. This not only lightens the load on the backend servers but also enables efficient handling of secure web traffic. Additionally, URL-based routing provides the flexibility to direct traffic to different backend servers based on specific URLs, enabling sophisticated traffic management and routing configurations.

Session affinity, also referred to as sticky sessions, is a significant capability offered by Application Gateway. This feature guarantees that subsequent requests from a client are consistently directed to the same backend server, preserving the session state. By maintaining the session state, Application Gateway ensures that users are presented with accurate data even if they are routed to different backend servers in the Azure infrastructure. This seamless continuity enhances the user experience by providing consistent interactions and avoiding disruptions caused by server switches.

Azure Application Gateway also supports autoscaling, enabling businesses to dynamically adjust the number of instances based on traffic demand. This ensures that Application Gateway can handle varying levels of traffic without compromising performance or availability.

To learn more about Azure Application Gateway, visit the following documentation: `https://learn.microsoft.com/azure/application-gateway/overview`

Azure Traffic Manager

Azure Traffic Manager is a dynamic DNS-based traffic load balancer that optimizes the delivery of incoming traffic to applications or resources. Businesses can ensure optimal user experiences and high availability for their applications by utilizing its intelligent routing capabilities.

Operating at the DNS level (a specific component within the OSI Layer 7), Azure Traffic Manager utilizes various routing methods to direct traffic to the most suitable resource based on factors such as proximity, application performance, and user-defined preferences. This enables businesses to efficiently distribute traffic across multiple regions or data centers, enhancing the responsiveness and scalability of their applications.

One key feature of Azure Traffic Manager is its support for health probes. By regularly monitoring the health of resources, it can detect any unresponsive or degraded instances and automatically remove them from the traffic-routing pool. This proactive approach helps ensure that only healthy resources receive traffic, minimizing disruptions and maximizing application availability.

Additionally, Azure Traffic Manager offers the following routing methods to meet diverse business needs:

- **The Priority traffic-routing method** enables you to define primary and secondary endpoints. Traffic is directed to the primary endpoint as long as it is available. If the primary endpoint becomes unavailable, Traffic Manager automatically switches traffic to the secondary endpoint.

- **The Weighted traffic-routing method** allows you to assign relative weights to different endpoints. You can allocate a higher weight to endpoints that can handle more traffic or have better performance, influencing the proportion of traffic each endpoint receives.

- **The Performance traffic-routing method** lets you route traffic based on the endpoint's performance by measuring the round-trip time between the client and each endpoint. It directs traffic to the endpoint with the lowest latency or highest throughput, improving the user experience.

- **The Geographic traffic-routing method** enables you to direct traffic based on the geographic location of the client. Traffic Manager uses the DNS resolution location of the client to determine the nearest endpoint or endpoints based on defined geographic rules.

- **The Multivalue traffic-routing method** allows you to associate multiple IP addresses with a single endpoint. When DNS queries are made, Traffic Manager returns multiple IP addresses in the DNS response, allowing the client to select an IP address from the available options.

- **The Subnet traffic-routing method** lets you direct traffic based on the client's IP address subnet. You can define routing rules that match specific IP address ranges or subnets and route traffic accordingly.

Furthermore, Azure Traffic Manager can be configured to support failover scenarios. In the event of a primary region outage or unavailability, Traffic Manager can automatically redirect traffic to a secondary region, ensuring uninterrupted service and business continuity.

To learn more about Azure Traffic Manager, read the following article: `https://learn.microsoft.com/azure/traffic-manager/traffic-manager-overview`

How to choose between Azure Application Gateway and Azure Traffic Manager

When it comes to distributing traffic across multiple regions or data centers for high availability and disaster recovery purposes, Azure Traffic Manager is generally a more suitable choice compared to Azure Application Gateway. Azure Traffic Manager provides global load balancing capabilities and allows you to route traffic to different endpoints based on various routing methods, such as performance and geographic location. It ensures that your applications are highly available and can withstand failures by directing traffic to alternative endpoints if necessary.

On the other hand, Azure Application Gateway is more appropriate for regional load balancing scenarios where the focus is on distributing traffic across multiple instances of your application within a single region. It operates at the application layer and provides advanced application delivery features such as SSL termination, URL-based routing, and session affinity. Application Gateway is designed to optimize the performance and scalability of your applications within a specific region.

As a rule of thumb, if you require traffic distribution across multiple regions or data centers for high availability and disaster recovery, Azure Traffic Manager is the preferred option. For regional load balancing within a single region, Azure Application Gateway is a better fit.

Azure Front Door

Azure Front Door is an advanced Layer 7 load balancer and **application delivery network (ADN)** service designed to streamline and enhance the management of global web application traffic. Businesses can ensure optimized performance, increased availability, and improved user experiences.

As a Layer 7 load balancer, Azure Front Door operates at the application layer, enabling granular control and efficient routing of HTTP and HTTPS traffic. It provides robust capabilities such as SSL offloading, allowing the decryption of SSL/TLS traffic at the network edge, reducing the processing load on backend servers, and improving overall performance.

URL-based routing is another key feature of Azure Front Door, enabling businesses to define routing rules based on specific URLs or path patterns. This allows for the efficient distribution of incoming traffic to different backend services or regions, optimizing workload management and resource utilization.

Similar to Azure Application Gateway, Azure Front Door also supports session affinity. This ensures that subsequent requests from the same client are consistently routed to the same backend instance. This is particularly useful for applications that require session state persistence or need to maintain user-specific data throughout a session.

In addition to load balancing and routing capabilities, Azure Front Door acts as an ADN service. It uses its global network of **points of presence** (**PoPs**) strategically distributed around the world to bring the application closer to users, reducing latency and improving responsiveness.

Azure Front Door also provides advanced security features, including **distributed denial-of-service** (**DDoS**) protection, **Web Application Firewall** (**WAF**), and SSL/TLS certificate management, ensuring robust protection for web applications against malicious attacks and unauthorized access.

To learn more about Azure Front Door, check the following resource: `https://learn.microsoft.com/azure/frontdoor/front-door-overview`

How to choose the most suitable load balancing option in Azure

In the previous sections, we learned about the four load balancing options: Azure Load Balancer, Azure Application Gateway, Azure Traffic Manager, and Azure Front Door.

Here are some factors to help decide which load balancing option is the most suitable for your business scenario:

- **Traffic type**: Is it a web (HTTP/HTTPS) application? Is it public facing or a private application?
- **Global versus regional**: Do you require load balancing virtual machines or containers within a virtual network, load balancing scale units/deployments across regions, or both?
- **Availability**: What is the SLA of the service that you are providing?
- **Cost**: In addition to the cost of the service itself, consider the operational cost of managing a solution built on that service.
- **Features and limitations**: What are the overall limitations of each service?

The following decision tree (see *Figure 2.1: Load balancing decision tree*) will further help you choose a suitable load balancing solution for your application. It guides you through a set of key decision criteria to reach a recommendation.

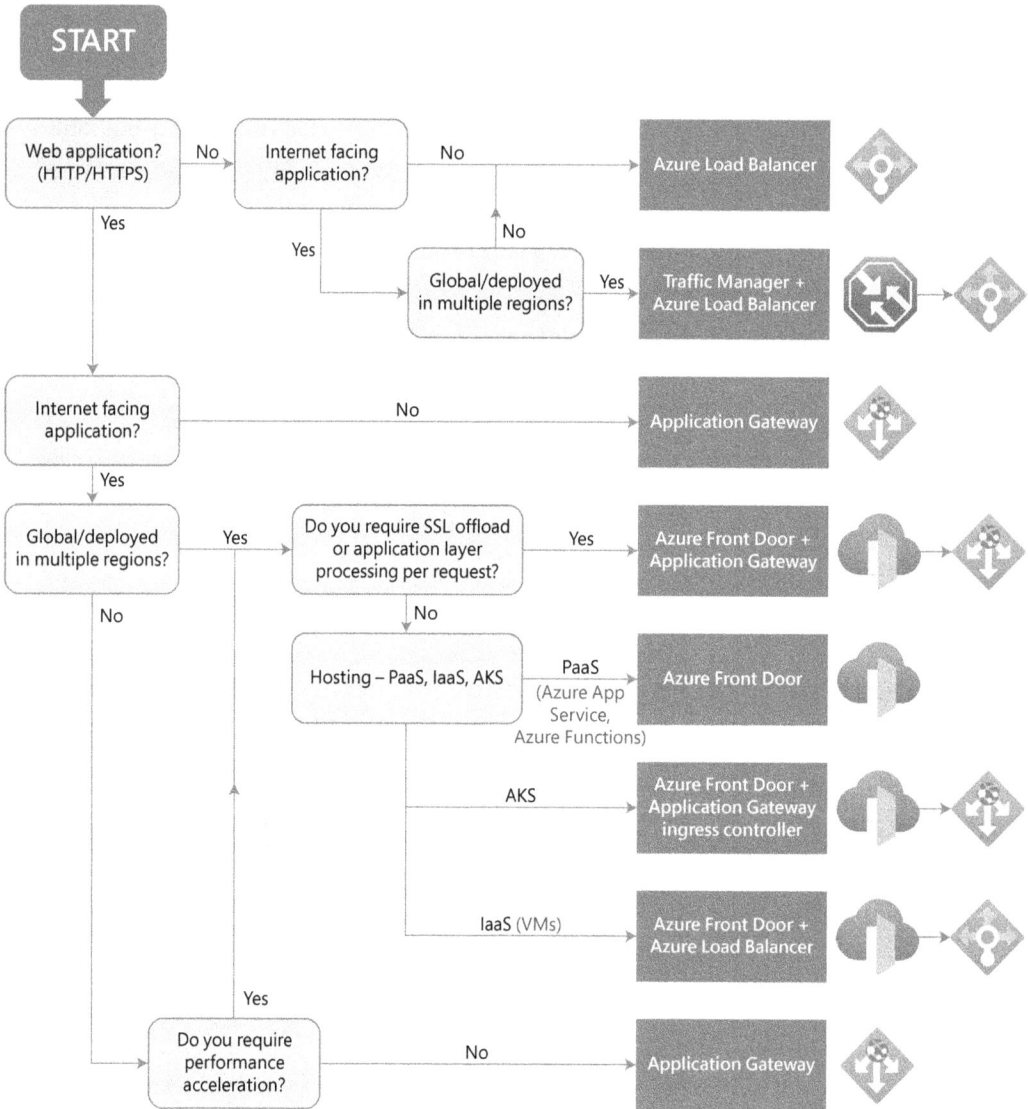

Figure 2.1: Load balancing decision tree

You should treat this decision tree as a starting point because every application has unique requirements. Use the recommendation as a starting point, then perform a further detailed evaluation. If your application consists of multiple workloads, evaluate each workload individually. A complete solution may consist of two or more load balancing solutions.

Availability sets and availability zones

Redundancy is a key strategy employed in Azure to ensure high availability. By having multiple instances of the same resource type, Azure can ensure that there is always a backup option available in case the primary resource fails. This redundancy approach forms the basis of achieving high availability in Azure.

In this section, we will explore two important concepts:

- Availability sets
- Availability zones

These features further enhance the redundancy and fault tolerance capabilities of Azure, providing businesses with additional options to ensure their applications remain available even in the face of hardware failures, infrastructure maintenance, or other unforeseen events.

Availability sets

An Azure availability set is a logical grouping of virtual machines designed to ensure redundancy and high availability for your application. By placing your virtual machines within an availability set, Azure understands the architectural needs of your application and can provide the necessary redundancy and availability features.

To achieve high availability, it is recommended to have a minimum of two virtual machines within an availability set. This configuration ensures that your application meets the 99.95% Azure SLA for availability. It is important to note that there is no additional cost for creating an availability set itself; you only pay for each virtual machine instance within the set.

When virtual machines are placed in an availability set, Azure distributes them across separate physical racks within the data center. This physical separation helps to minimize the risk of a single point of failure and provides resilience at the data center level. In the event of updates or maintenance activities, Azure updates the virtual machines within the availability set one at a time, rather than simultaneously. This approach ensures that your application remains accessible and minimizes the potential impact of maintenance activities on availability.

By utilizing availability sets, you can achieve redundancy and high availability for your application in a similar manner to how locally redundant storage operates. This means that even if one virtual machine or physical rack experiences issues, the remaining virtual machines in the availability set continue to serve your application, maintaining its availability.

To learn more about Azure availability sets, read the following article: https://learn.microsoft.com/en-us/azure/virtual-machines/availability-set-overview

While availability sets offer high availability within a data center, it is important to note that if an entire data center becomes unavailable, the application's availability will be affected. To address this scenario and ensure continued availability, Azure offers a feature called availability zones, which we will discuss next.

Availability zones

Azure availability zones are purpose-built physical locations within an Azure region that offer robust fault tolerance and high availability. They are designed to provide resilience against various types of failures, including hardware and software issues, as well as natural disasters such as earthquakes, floods, and fires. As of the time of writing, there are 60+ regions worldwide. There are three availability zones per supported Azure region.

The key to achieving this resiliency is the combination of redundancy and logical isolation of Azure services across multiple availability zones. Azure ensures that each enabled region has a minimum of three separate availability zones, creating a distributed infrastructure that significantly reduces the risk of service disruptions.

By deploying resources across multiple availability zones, businesses can enhance the fault tolerance of their applications and services. In the event of a failure in one availability zone, the workload seamlessly fails over to another zone without impacting the overall availability or performance of the application. This redundancy and isolation at the zone level help ensure continuous operation and protect against single points of failure.

Having three or more availability zones within a region also enables businesses to implement resilient architectures for disaster recovery purposes. They can replicate and distribute their applications and data across different zones, allowing for business continuity even in the face of catastrophic events or widespread outages (as shown in *Figure 2.2: To ensure resiliency, a minimum of three separate availability zones are present in all enabled regions*).

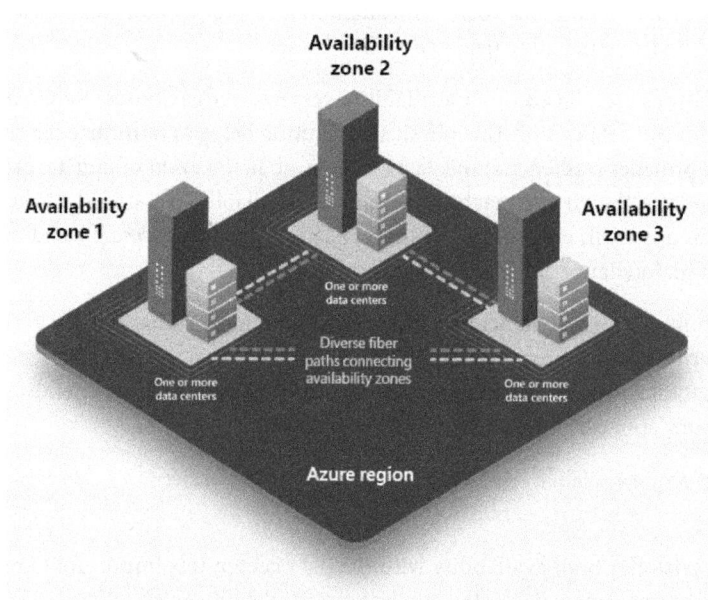

Figure 2.2: To ensure resiliency, a minimum of three separate
availability zones are present in all enabled regions

Businesses can enhance the reliability and availability of their applications and services with availability zones. The presence of multiple physically separate zones within each region ensures that applications remain operational, even in the face of unforeseen failures or disruptive events.

Availability zones support a variety of Azure resources, including virtual machines, managed disks, virtual machine scale sets, and load balancers. For a full list of resources supported by availability zones, check the following resource: `https://learn.microsoft.com/en-us/azure/reliability/availability-zones-service-support`

To learn more about Azure availability zones, read this article: `https://learn.microsoft.com/azure/reliability/availability-zones-overview`

Replica sets

Within the scope of Azure regions and availability zones, replica sets play an important role in the context of **Azure Active Directory Domain Services** (**Azure AD DS**) managed domains. When creating an Azure AD DS managed domain, a unique namespace is specified, representing the chosen domain name (e.g., mydomain.com). Subsequently, a replica set is established by deploying two **domain controllers** (**DCs**) within the designated Azure region.

The purpose of the replica set is to ensure the continuous availability of authentication services within regions where such a configuration is implemented. By having multiple DCs within the replica set, redundancy is achieved. In the event of a failure or maintenance activity affecting one DC, the other DC in the replica set can seamlessly handle authentication requests, maintaining uninterrupted access to the managed domain's services. This high-availability design enhances the reliability and resilience of Azure AD DS managed domains, minimizing potential disruptions and providing a dependable authentication infrastructure.

To learn more about replica sets, read the following article: `https://learn.microsoft.com/azure/active-directory-domain-services/concepts-replica-sets`

When architects design business-critical applications, achieving high availability is a top concern. However, scalability also holds significant importance in the minds of architects. We will look at scalability in the next section.

Why achieving scalability with Azure is important

Scalability on Azure is important for ensuring that your applications can effectively handle a growing user base while maintaining consistent performance levels. It enables your application to efficiently utilize resources for processes and deployment regardless of user load demands.

Consider a scenario where an application exhibits excellent performance and availability while catering to a small user base. However, as the user count begins to surge, the application's performance and availability gradually decline. It struggles to handle the heightened load and demand, leading to noticeable performance degradation and availability challenges. This situation is commonplace in many businesses, emphasizing the critical importance of scalability.

Understanding scalability and harnessing Azure's capabilities are essential for architects to ensure the seamless growth and adaptability of their applications.

By designing for scalability on Azure, an architect can address the following key points:

- **Capacity planning and sizing**: Scalability should be a consideration from the early stages of application development. Architectural decisions and capacity planning exercises help determine the required resources and infrastructure to support scalability. By properly sizing and provisioning resources, you can accommodate future growth and prevent performance bottlenecks.

- **Performance optimization**: Scalability allows your application to serve more user requests without experiencing performance degradation. It ensures that as your user base expands, your application can handle increased traffic and workload, delivering a smooth and responsive experience to all users. It prevents situations where increased user load leads to slower response times, errors, or even service outages. As a result, scalability contributes to customer satisfaction and retention.

- **Handling variable demands**: Some applications experience varying demands, with unpredictable spikes or fluctuations in user activity. Scalability ensures that your application can dynamically adjust its resources to meet these variable demands. Autoscaling is particularly useful for applications with unpredictable workload patterns. We will cover this in more detail later in this chapter.

So far, we have emphasized the importance of scalability and its impact on application performance. However, it is essential to recognize that while scalability and performance are interconnected, they represent distinct aspects of an application's behavior. In the upcoming section, we will clarify the differences between scalability and performance.

Scalability versus performance

Scalability encompasses the ability to expand resources to accommodate a larger user base without compromising performance.

Performance, on the other hand, relates to ensuring an application caters to a predefined response time and throughput.

To illustrate these concepts, consider a railway network where the speed of a train correlates to **performance**. However, the **scalability** of the railway network is demonstrated by the ability to operate more trains simultaneously at equal or higher speeds.

Autoscaling plays an important role in achieving both performance and scalability. We will learn more about autoscaling in the next section.

Autoscaling

Scaling involves adjusting the number of resources utilized to handle user requests, and it can be achieved through either manual or automatic means. Manual scaling entails an administrator manually modifying the resource scale, whereas autoscaling involves resources dynamically increasing or decreasing based on environmental and ecosystem events, such as CPU and memory availability.

Scaling can be achieved in various ways, including scaling up/down and scaling in/out, each serving different purposes:

- **Scaling up**: Scaling up refers to increasing the capacity of individual resources. It involves upgrading the hardware or configurations of existing resources to handle higher workloads, such as adding more memory or processing power to a virtual machine. Scaling up is suitable when applications require enhanced performance or require more resources within a single instance.

- **Scaling down**: Scaling down involves reducing the capacity of resources to optimize costs or adjust to lower demands. It can include downsizing virtual machines, reducing storage capacity, or lowering the number of instances. Scaling down allows businesses to allocate resources efficiently and save costs when the workload decreases.

- **Scaling out**: Scaling out focuses on increasing the number of instances or resources available to handle a growing workload. It involves adding more virtual machines, containers, or database replicas to distribute the load. Scaling out enhances application availability, improves performance, and ensures the system can handle higher user demands.

- **Scaling in**: Scaling in involves decreasing the number of instances or resources used by an application. This can include shutting down virtual machines, terminating containers, or reducing the number of database replicas. Scaling in optimizes resource utilization by removing unnecessary instances when the workload decreases or consolidating resources to free up capacity.

Autoscaling can handle all of the previous scaling methods dynamically and automatically based on application demands. This intelligent capability ensures that a deployment always maintains an optimal number of resource instances. Let's consider an example of an e-commerce website hosted on Azure. During peak periods, such as holiday sales, the website experiences a significant increase in user traffic. Azure autoscaling monitors the incoming traffic and dynamically scales up the resources, such as virtual machines or containers, to handle the higher workload. This ensures that the website remains responsive and provides a seamless shopping experience for users. Once the peak period ends and the traffic subsides, Azure autoscaling automatically scales down the resources, removing unnecessary instances. This helps to optimize resource utilization and reduces costs by avoiding the allocation of resources that are not required.

Another benefit of autoscaling is its impact on cost management. Many organizations often allocate more resources than they actually need, leading to wastage and higher expenses. This excessive allocation, commonly referred to as "over-provisioning," is mitigated by autoscaling. By adjusting resource levels according to demand, autoscaling prevents over-provisioning and the squandering of resources, enabling businesses to optimize their cost management.

To learn more about autoscaling, read the following article: `https://learn.microsoft.com/azure/architecture/best-practices/auto-scaling`

Azure offers scalability options for most of its services. In the next section, we will explore scalability for IaaS and PaaS.

IaaS scalability

Infrastructure as a service (**IaaS**) is a type of deployment model that empowers customers to provision their own infrastructure on Azure.

Businesses seeking full control over their underlying infrastructure often opt for IaaS solutions. With IaaS, customers have the flexibility to create and manage virtual machines according to their specific needs. However, this also means they bear the responsibility of capacity sizing and scaling.

To streamline this process and alleviate the burden of manual management, Azure offers a solution known as virtual machine scale sets.

Azure virtual machine scale sets

Azure virtual machine scale sets provide businesses with a powerful capability to automatically scale the number of virtual machines running their applications in response to demand fluctuations. With virtual machine scale sets, businesses can efficiently manage a group of virtual machines that share the same configuration and work collectively to support application requirements.

One of the quintessential features of virtual machine scale sets is their built-in support for autoscaling. This allows businesses to seamlessly scale the number of virtual machines based on demand patterns. When there is an increase in workload or user traffic, the virtual machine scale sets automatically provision additional virtual machines to handle the load, ensuring optimal performance and responsiveness. Conversely, during periods of low demand, the number of virtual machines can be automatically scaled down to avoid unnecessary resource consumption, thus reducing cost.

Businesses can effortlessly handle capacity scaling for their virtual machines using virtual machine scale sets. This feature empowers them to dynamically increase or decrease the number of virtual machine instances based on demand, ensuring optimal resource utilization and cost efficiency.

To learn more about Azure virtual machine scale sets, check the following documentation: `https://learn.microsoft.com/azure/virtual-machine-scale-sets/overview`

PaaS scalability

PaaS revolutionizes the way applications are deployed and managed by freeing customers from the responsibility of infrastructure management while retaining control over their applications.

Azure provides a comprehensive suite of fully managed PaaS offerings that streamline development and deployment for businesses. By abstracting the underlying infrastructure, developers can focus solely on application development, boosting productivity and accelerating time to market.

To ensure applications can efficiently handle growing workloads and adapt to fluctuating demands, scalability is an important capability in PaaS. In the upcoming sections, we will explore the scalability features of various Azure PaaS offerings.

Azure App Service autoscaling

Azure App Service is a comprehensive, fully managed platform designed to facilitate the development, deployment, and scaling of web apps and APIs. With support for multiple programming languages and frameworks, App Service simplifies the process of deploying and managing applications for businesses.

One of the notable features of App Service is its built-in support for autoscaling. Autoscaling empowers businesses to automatically adjust the number of application instances based on demand. This capability ensures that the application environment dynamically scales up or down to efficiently handle varying levels of user traffic and workload.

To learn more about Azure App Service autoscaling, visit the following link: `https://learn.microsoft.com/azure/app-service/manage-automatic-scaling`

Azure Functions

Serverless computing allows developers to build and deploy applications without the need to manage or provision underlying infrastructure. In a serverless architecture, the cloud provider takes care of resource allocation, scaling, and maintenance, while developers focus solely on writing code to implement the desired functionality.

Azure Functions is a powerful serverless computing service that enables businesses to execute event-driven code within a fully managed environment. Functions can be used to execute code in response to events such as HTTP requests, messages from a queue, or updates to a database.

One of the key advantages of Azure Functions is its built-in support for automatic scaling. This means that businesses can rely on the platform to dynamically adjust the number of function instances based on workload demands. When there is a surge in events or requests, Azure Functions automatically scales up, provisioning additional resources to ensure timely processing and optimal performance. Conversely, during periods of low demand, Azure Functions scales down, reducing resources to avoid unnecessary costs.

To learn more about Azure Functions, check out this resource: `https://learn.microsoft.com/azure/azure-functions/functions-overview`

Azure Kubernetes Service (AKS)

Azure Kubernetes Service (AKS) is a comprehensive and fully managed Kubernetes service designed to facilitate the seamless deployment and management of containerized applications at scale. With AKS, businesses can harness the power of Kubernetes while abstracting away the complexities of infrastructure management.

One of the key advantages of AKS is its built-in support for autoscaling. This means that businesses can use AKS to automatically scale the number of Pods running their application in response to demand fluctuations. As user traffic increases, AKS dynamically provisions additional pods to handle the workload, ensuring optimal performance and responsiveness. Conversely, during periods of low demand, AKS scales down the number of pods to minimize resource consumption and optimize cost efficiency.

To learn more about AKS, read the following article: `https://learn.microsoft.com/azure/aks/intro-kubernetes`

Azure Container Apps

Azure Container Apps provides a managed service for deploying and orchestrating applications using containers. It abstracts away the complexities of infrastructure management, allowing developers to focus on building and deploying their applications quickly and easily.

Azure Container Apps supports autoscaling, allowing applications to scale based on demand. Developers can define scaling rules to automatically adjust the number of container instances, ensuring optimal resource utilization and performance.

To learn more about Azure Container Apps, read this article: `https://learn.microsoft.com/azure/container-apps/overview`

Azure Container Instances

Azure Container Instances (ACI) enables the rapid deployment and management of containers without the need for managing underlying infrastructure. With ACI, developers can run containers in the Azure cloud with ease, as it abstracts away the complexities of infrastructure management. It provides a serverless experience for containerized applications, allowing users to focus on application logic rather than infrastructure concerns.

ACI supports a wide range of containerized workloads, from single containers to multicontainer applications. It offers fast startup times, autoscaling capabilities, and flexible pricing options based on the resources consumed. ACI integrates seamlessly with other Azure services, allowing developers to build scalable and resilient applications using a combination of containerized and serverless technologies.

ACI offers a convenient and efficient way to deploy and manage containers in the Azure ecosystem.

To learn more about ACI, read the following article: `https://learn.microsoft.com/azure/container-instances/container-instances-overview`

How to choose your IaaS and PaaS compute service

Before we wrap up this section, we'd like to share with you a decision tree (see *Figure 2.3: Decision tree for selecting your PaaS versus IaaS compute service*) to help you choose the appropriate IaaS versus PaaS compute service to meet your business requirements.

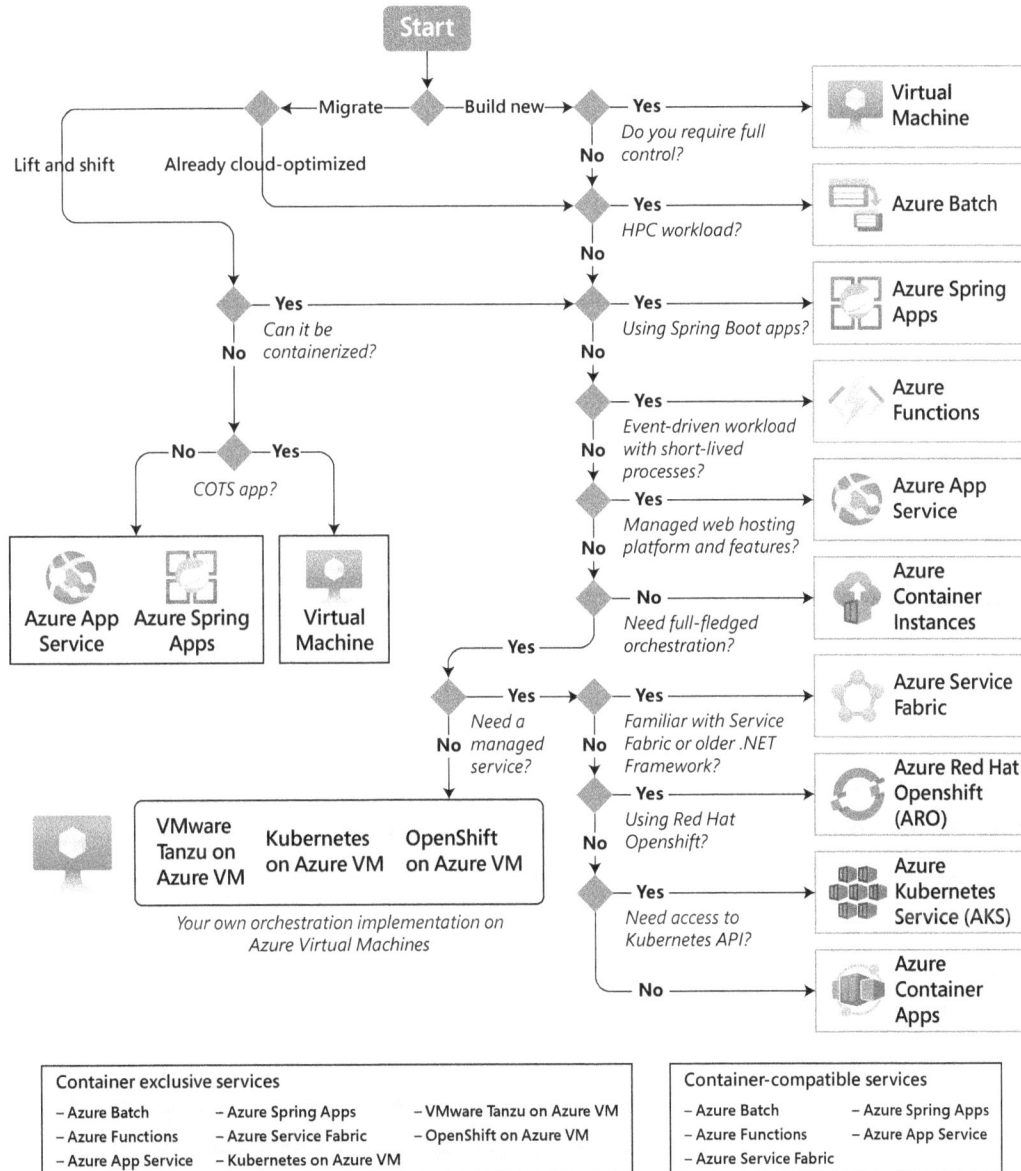

Figure 2.3: Decision tree for selecting your PaaS versus IaaS compute service

For more information on how to choose your compute services, please see the following article: `https://learn.microsoft.com/azure/architecture/guide/technology-choices/compute-decision-tree`

With that, we've covered the essential concepts and topics on scalability. In the next section, we will switch our focus to monitoring in the Azure environment.

Why do we need monitoring with Azure?

Monitoring plays a central role in ensuring the continuous and optimal operation of applications. It also serves as a proactive measure to identify and address any potential issues before they impact users, thereby minimizing disruptions and maintaining a positive experience for users.

Through effective monitoring practices, businesses can mitigate risks, improve the user experience, and maintain the desired levels of performance and availability for their applications. Furthermore, businesses can gain valuable insights into the performance, availability, and health of their applications using these monitoring tools.

In this section, we will explore the monitoring capabilities available on Azure. These tools enable businesses to proactively track and analyze metrics, logs, and other relevant data to identify performance bottlenecks, troubleshoot issues, and optimize their applications' overall efficiency.

Understanding monitoring with Azure

Azure offers a comprehensive suite of services and features specifically tailored for application monitoring. These tools enable businesses to gain valuable insights into the performance and health of their applications, empowering them to make informed decisions and take timely actions to optimize performance, troubleshoot problems, and ensure efficient resource utilization.

In this section, we will explore the various tools that empower businesses to effectively track and analyze various aspects of their applications, including performance metrics, system logs, and application diagnostics.

Azure Monitor

Azure Monitor (see *Figure 2.4: Azure Monitor*) offers comprehensive monitoring and diagnostics capabilities for applications and infrastructure hosted on the platform. It serves as a fully managed service that brings together various monitoring functionalities into a centralized location.

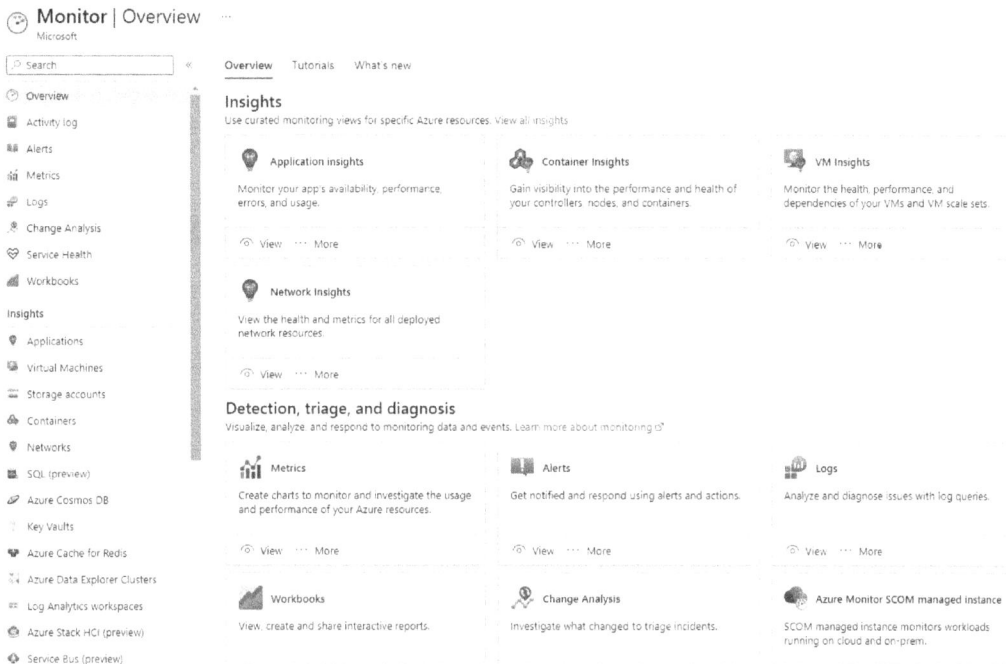

Figure 2.4: Azure Monitor

With Azure Monitor, businesses gain access to a wide range of monitoring features and tools. It enables the collection and analysis of data from diverse sources, including Azure resources, applications, and operating systems.

The key features of Azure Monitor include metrics, logs, alerts, and dashboards:

- **Metrics** offer a quantitative representation of system performance, while logs provide detailed records of events and activities.

- **Alerts** allow businesses to set up notifications for specific conditions or thresholds, enabling them to proactively respond to critical issues.

- **Dashboards** offer a visual representation of data and enable customizable views for monitoring and analysis.

Businesses can monitor their applications and infrastructure in real time, enabling them to identify and address potential issues promptly. This proactive approach helps ensure the stability, reliability, and optimal performance of their systems.

Azure Monitor is free of charge; you only pay for the data taken in. This sets it apart from third-party monitoring tools for which you pay a separate license.

To learn more about Azure Monitor, visit the following resource: `https://learn.microsoft.com/azure/azure-monitor/overview`

Azure Application Insights

Azure Application Insights (see *Figure 2.5: Azure Application Insights*) provides businesses with real-time monitoring for effective tracking and analyzing of various aspects of their applications, offering valuable insights into performance, user behavior, and usage patterns.

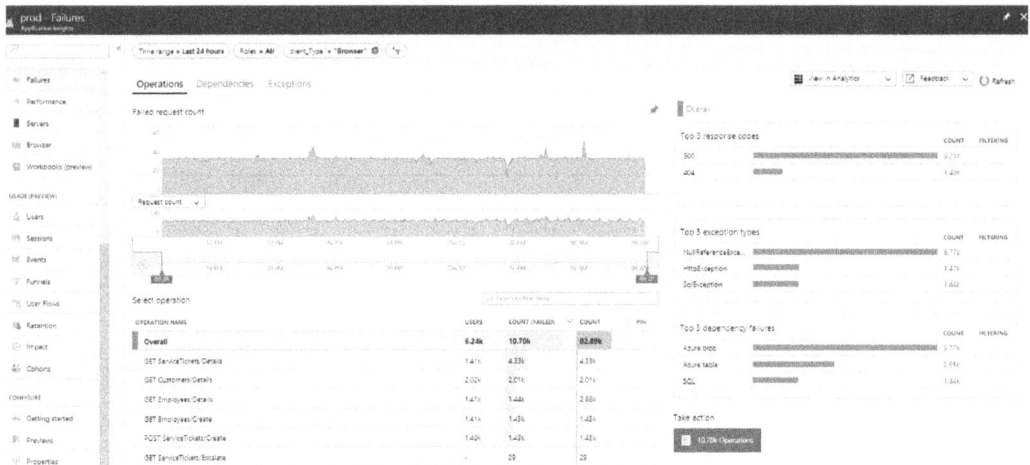

Figure 2.5: Azure Application Insights

With Azure Application Insights, businesses can effectively track and analyze various aspects of their applications. It enables the collection and analysis of telemetry data, allowing businesses to gain a deep understanding of how their applications are performing in real time. This telemetry data encompasses metrics such as response times, request rates, and resource utilization, providing valuable insights into application performance.

In addition to standard metrics, Azure Application Insights also allows businesses to define and track custom metrics specific to their application's requirements. This flexibility enables businesses to monitor and analyze key performance indicators that are relevant to their specific use case.

Another essential feature of Azure Application Insights is tracing, which enables businesses to trace and investigate the execution flow of their application code. By incorporating tracing, businesses can identify bottlenecks, diagnose issues, and optimize the performance of their applications.

Businesses can gain comprehensive visibility of their application's behavior and performance. This empowers them to make data-driven decisions, proactively detect and resolve issues, and enhance the overall user experience.

To learn more about Azure Application Insights, check out the following documentation: `https://learn.microsoft.com/azure/azure-monitor/app/app-insights-overview`

Azure Log Analytics

Azure Log Analytics (see *Figure 2.6: Azure Log Analytics*) enables businesses to effectively collect, analyze, and gain valuable insights from log and performance data across various sources.

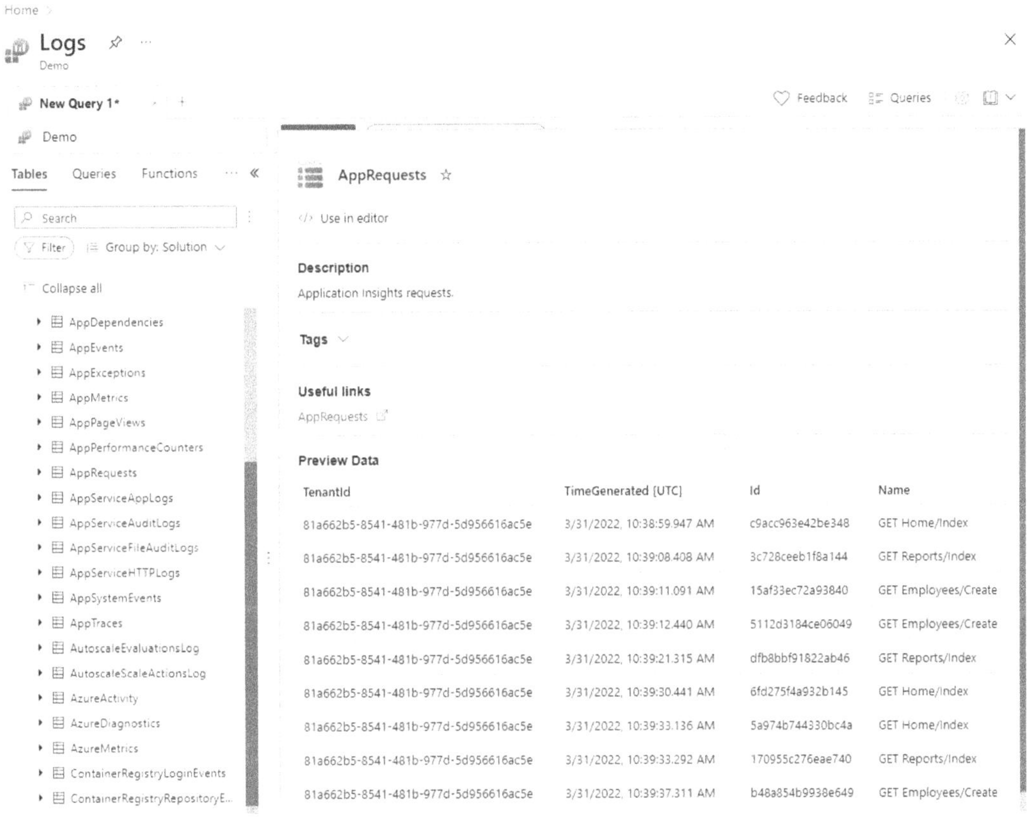

Figure 2.6: Azure Log Analytics

With Azure Log Analytics, businesses can centralize their log data from applications, operating systems, and infrastructure, allowing a comprehensive view of system behavior and performance. By collecting and analyzing this log data, businesses can identify and troubleshoot issues, track system events, and optimize the performance of their applications and infrastructure.

One of the key features of Azure Log Analytics is the ability to create custom queries. This empowers businesses to perform advanced searches and analyses on their log data, extracting specific information and gaining in-depth visibility of the behavior of their systems. These custom queries can be tailored to the unique requirements of each business, enabling them to uncover insights that are relevant and meaningful to their specific use case.

In addition to custom queries, Azure Log Analytics offers powerful alerting capabilities. Businesses can configure alerts based on specific log events or performance thresholds, ensuring that they are promptly notified of any critical issues or anomalies. This proactive approach allows businesses to take immediate action and address potential problems before they impact users or cause service disruptions.

Furthermore, Azure Log Analytics provides interactive dashboards that enable businesses to visualize and explore their log data in a user-friendly manner. These dashboards can be customized to display the most relevant information and provide a consolidated view of system performance and health. With these visualizations, businesses can easily monitor key metrics, track trends, and make data-driven decisions to optimize their applications and infrastructure.

To learn more about Azure Log Analytics, read the following article: `https://learn.microsoft.com/azure/azure-monitor/logs/log-analytics-tutorial`

Azure Network Watcher

Azure Network Watcher enables businesses to monitor and troubleshoot their network infrastructure effectively. With Azure Network Watcher, businesses can gain valuable insights into the performance and behavior of their network infrastructure.

One of the key features of Azure Network Watcher is the topology tool (see *Figure 2.7: Azure Network Watcher topology tool*). This tool offers visual representations of your Azure virtual network and its resources, interconnections, and interrelationships. It serves as a valuable aid during the initial stages of troubleshooting, enabling you to visualize all the components involved in the problem you are addressing. This visualization goes beyond the contents of resource groups in the Azure portal, revealing insights that may not be immediately apparent through conventional means.

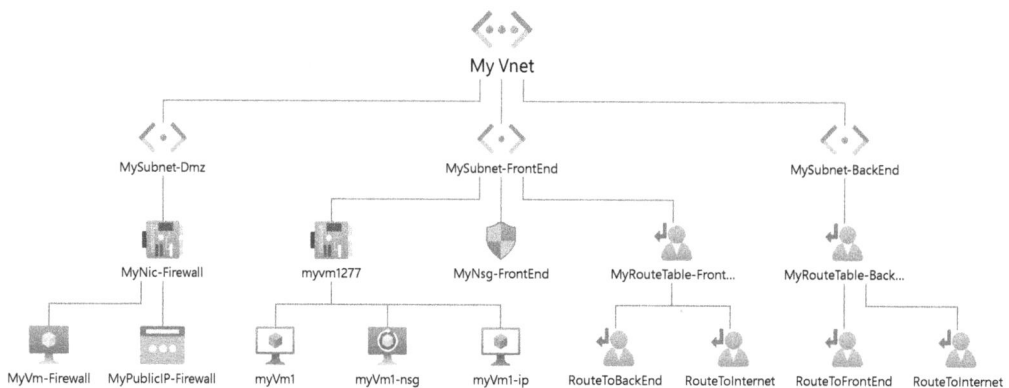

Figure 2.7: Azure Network Watcher topology tool

Packet capture is another prominent functionality offered by Azure Network Watcher. It empowers businesses to capture network packets traversing their virtual machines, facilitating in-depth analysis and troubleshooting of network-related issues. Organizations can pinpoint anomalies, diagnose connectivity problems, and optimize their network setup.

In addition to packet capture, Azure Network Watcher provides flow logs, enabling businesses to gain visibility into network traffic patterns. Flow logs allow organizations to monitor and analyze network flows within their virtual networks, detect abnormal traffic patterns, and gain insights into network performance and security.

Furthermore, Azure Network Watcher includes connection troubleshooting capabilities. This feature allows businesses to perform connectivity tests between different resources within their virtual network, aiding in the identification and resolution of network connectivity issues. Organizations can swiftly diagnose network problems and ensure smooth and reliable communication between their resources.

To learn more about Azure Network Watcher, check the following documentation: `https://learn.microsoft.com/azure/network-watcher/network-watcher-monitoring-overview`

Azure Advisor

With Azure Advisor (see *Figure 2.8: Azure Advisor*), businesses gain access to intelligent recommendations that align with best practices and industry standards. These recommendations cover various areas, including cost optimization, performance improvement, security enhancements, and considerations for high availability.

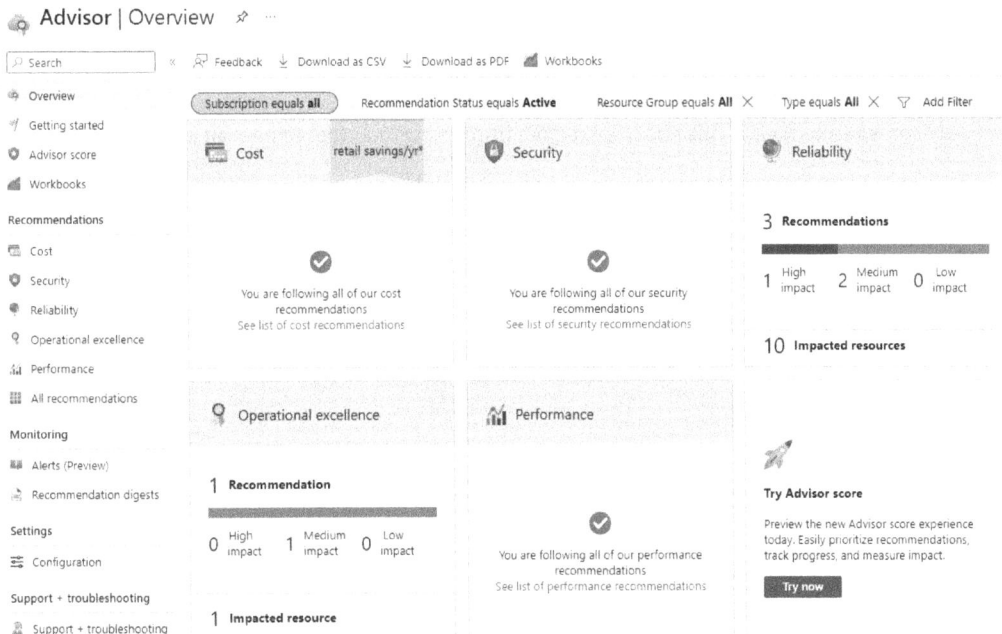

Figure 2.8: Azure Advisor

The Azure Advisor recommendations are divided into the following five categories:

- **Cost** recommendations help businesses identify potential cost-saving opportunities. Azure Advisor analyzes resource usage and configuration, highlighting areas where businesses can optimize their spending without sacrificing performance or functionality.

- **Performance** recommendations focus on enhancing the performance of applications and resources in Azure. Azure Advisor examines various factors that impact performance, such as resource utilization, networking configurations, and deployment patterns, to ensure efficient resource utilization and deliver a responsive user experience.

- **Security** recommendations help businesses strengthen the security posture of their Azure deployments. Azure Advisor assesses security configurations, access controls, and identity management practices, and suggests improvements to enhance security and mitigate potential vulnerabilities. By implementing these recommendations, businesses can safeguard their applications and data against cyber threats and comply with industry regulations.

- **Reliability** recommendations ensure businesses' applications remain accessible and resilient. Azure Advisor evaluates the deployment architecture, availability sets, and redundancy configurations, and provides guidance on enhancing availability and minimizing potential single points of failure. By following these recommendations, businesses can improve the reliability and uptime of their applications, minimizing downtime and maximizing user satisfaction.

- **Operational excellence** recommendations help businesses achieve process and workflow efficiency, resource manageability, and deployment best practices.

Azure Advisor is a free service. This sets it apart from third-party tools that require an additional license.

To learn more about Azure Advisor, check the following link: `https://learn.microsoft.com/azure/advisor/advisor-overview`

Azure status

Azure status (see *Figure 2.5*) is a status dashboard that provides businesses with real-time information regarding the health and availability of Azure services and regions.

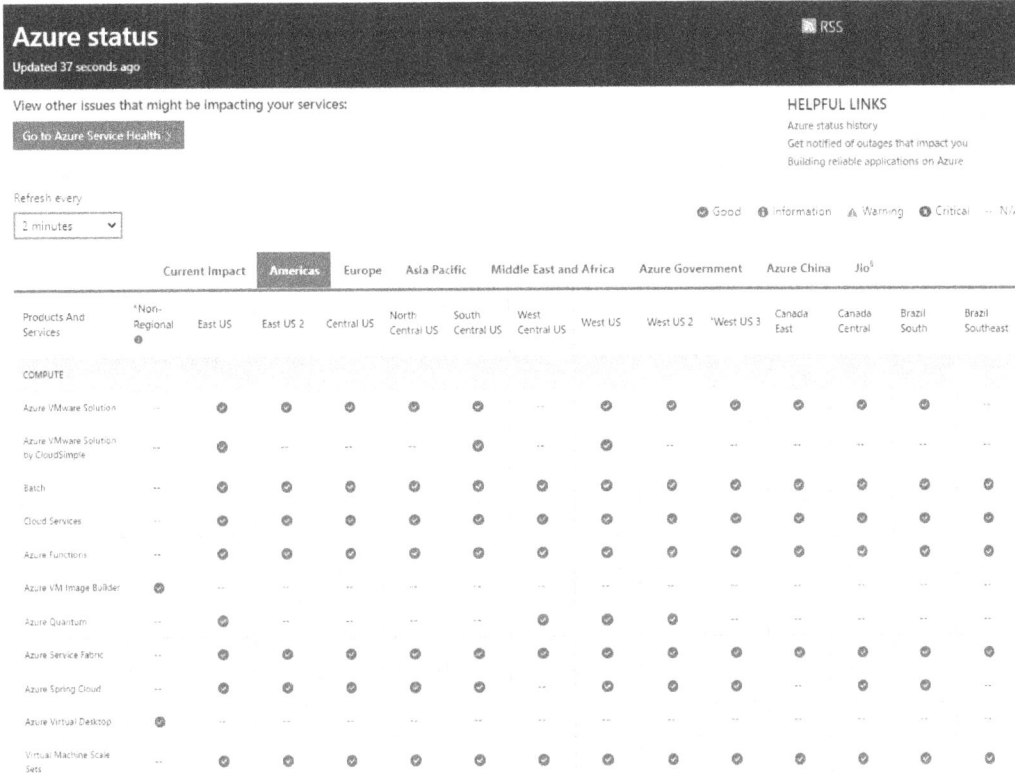

Azure status
Updated 37 seconds ago   RSS

View other issues that might be impacting your services:

Go to Azure Service Health >

HELPFUL LINKS
Azure status history
Get notified of outages that impact you
Building reliable applications on Azure

Refresh every

2 minutes

⊘ Good   ⓘ Information   ⚠ Warning   ⊗ Critical   -- N/A

	Current Impact	Americas	Europe	Asia Pacific	Middle East and Africa	Azure Government	Azure China	Jio[$]

Products And Services	*Non-Regional ⓘ	East US	East US 2	Central US	North Central US	South Central US	West Central US	West US	West US 2	*West US 3	Canada East	Canada Central	Brazil South	Brazil Southeast
COMPUTE														
Azure VMware Solution	--	⊘	⊘	⊘	⊘	⊘	--	⊘	⊘	⊘	⊘	⊘	⊘	--
Azure VMware Solution by CloudSimple	--	⊘	--	--	--	⊘	--	⊘	--	--	--	--	--	--
Batch	--	⊘	⊘	⊘	⊘	⊘	⊘	⊘	⊘	⊘	⊘	⊘	⊘	⊘
Cloud Services	--	⊘	⊘	⊘	⊘	⊘	⊘	⊘	⊘	⊘	⊘	⊘	⊘	⊘
Azure Functions	--	⊘	⊘	⊘	⊘	⊘	⊘	⊘	⊘	⊘	⊘	⊘	⊘	⊘
Azure VM Image Builder	⊘	--	--	--	--	--	--	--	--	--	--	--	--	--
Azure Quantum	--	⊘	--	--	--	--	⊘	⊘	⊘	--	--	--	--	--
Azure Service Fabric	--	⊘	⊘	⊘	⊘	⊘	⊘	⊘	⊘	⊘	⊘	⊘	⊘	⊘
Azure Spring Cloud	--	⊘	⊘	⊘	⊘	⊘	--	⊘	⊘	⊘	--	⊘	⊘	--
Azure Virtual Desktop	⊘	--	--	--	--	--	--	--	--	--	--	--	--	--
Virtual Machine Scale Sets	--	⊘	⊘	⊘	⊘	⊘	⊘	⊘	⊘	⊘	⊘	⊘	⊘	⊘

Figure 2.9: Azure status dashboard

With Azure status, businesses gain visibility into any service disruptions, planned maintenance, or other events that may impact the performance and availability of their Azure resources. This service keeps businesses informed about the current status of Azure services, allowing them to proactively manage and respond to any potential issues.

By regularly monitoring Azure status, businesses can stay updated on service incidents, outages, and maintenance activities that might affect their applications and infrastructure. This enables businesses to make informed decisions and take necessary actions to minimize the impact on their operations and end users.

To see the Azure status dashboard, simply go to `https://status.azure.com/`.

Azure Service Health

Azure Service Health (see *Figure 2.10: Azure Service Health*) notifies organizations about Azure service incidents and planned maintenance so they can take action to mitigate downtime. It provides personalized alerts and guidance to help businesses stay informed about the health and performance of their Azure resources. It offers proactive notifications, detailed incident reports, and actionable guidance to mitigate the impact of service issues.

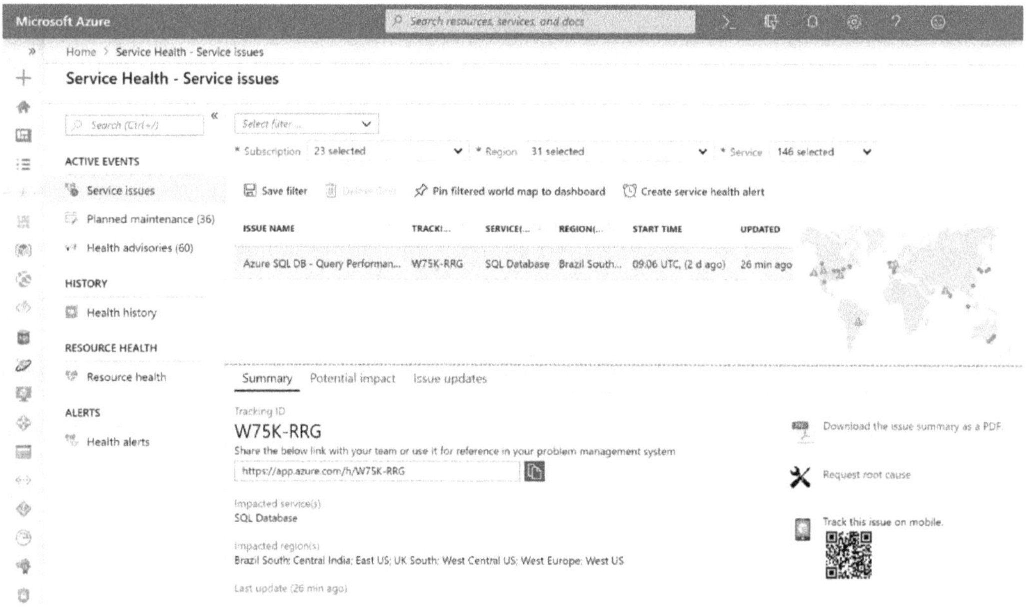

Figure 2.10: Azure Service Health

Azure Service Health provides real-time status and notifications about Azure services and regions. It helps businesses stay informed about service disruptions, planned maintenance, and other events that may impact availability.

To learn more about Azure Service Health, check out the following resource: `https://azure.microsoft.com/get-started/azure-portal/service-health/`

These Azure monitoring tools allow businesses to effectively track key metrics, monitor application dependencies, detect anomalies, and receive alerts for potential issues. This empowers them to identify performance bottlenecks, diagnose errors, and address any underlying issues promptly.

Summary

In this chapter, we have explored the extensive capabilities of Azure that empower businesses to achieve high availability, scalability, and efficient monitoring of their applications.

We have examined how Azure provides organizations with the flexibility required to handle fluctuations in traffic and demand effectively. Furthermore, we have observed how Azure equips businesses with valuable insights to proactively manage their applications and infrastructure.

By using these services, businesses can ensure the continuous maintenance of high availability, scalability, and optimal performance for their applications.

In the next chapter, our focus will shift toward discussing Azure cloud patterns pertaining to virtual networks, storage accounts, and serverless event-driven solutions.

3

Cloud Architecture Design Patterns

In the previous chapter, we looked at some key elements that make up a scalable and highly available cloud solution. In this chapter, we will focus on design patterns related to **virtual networks** (**VNets**), storage accounts, performance, and messaging. These constructs affect how you implement your solution and, with enough attention to detail, can help you to gauge costs, efficiencies, and overall productivity properly. This chapter also outlines some best practices.

In this chapter, we'll cover the following topics:

- The importance of good architectural design
- Azure Virtual Network design
- Azure Storage design
- Azure design patterns related to messaging
- Solution design practices

Let us start by exploring the importance of good architectural design in cloud systems, outlining its key benefits and the principles underpinning a robust cloud architecture.

The importance of good architectural design

As cloud computing has become an indispensable component of modern IT infrastructure, the need for good architectural design in cloud systems has become more important than ever. The complexity and scale of cloud-based services demand careful planning, strategic design, and thorough implementation to ensure optimal performance, reliability, and cost-effectiveness.

Scalability and elasticity

Cloud architectures designed with scalability and elasticity in mind enable organizations to grow or shrink their infrastructure according to the fluctuating demands of their workloads. Scalability refers to the ability to increase or decrease hardware and software resources relative to fluctuations in system resource usage. Scaling is often a pain point in implementing larger systems, as it requires manual oversight and intervention when responding to the increased load. What often happens is that we scale up and rarely scale down, so we cannot efficiently gauge the resources needed in the long run.

Elasticity, though similar, refers to automatically scaling up or down resources as needed. The key difference between scalability and elasticity is the level of automation. Elastic infrastructures will provision resources as and when needed, then downsize when they are not. This enables more cost-saving and resource efficiency for your systems.

Microsoft Azure provides several services that boast elasticity and scalability, allowing businesses to optimize resource allocation and minimize costs by only paying for their consumed resources. Microsoft Azure provides several managed services with powerful integrations. These integrations expand and contract relative to load and usage, allowing you to focus on what matters the most, and delivering the best possible user experience.

Resilience and high availability

Resiliency describes the ability of a system to recover from a transient or temporary outage and continue operating. High availability is usually achieved through redundancies to avoid a single point of failure.

A well-designed cloud architecture incorporates high availability and redundancy, ensuring the system remains functional despite hardware failures, network outages, or software bugs. This results in enhanced business continuity and reduces the risk of service disruptions. Azure offers several tools for failovers and fault-tolerant services. With a robust international network of data centers, it is possible to design a solution with little to no downtime. Most, if not all, services allow for replication across regions and countries, allowing for data to be backed up and for services to be always available.

While the exact addresses of Microsoft's data centers are not disclosed, we can rest assured that they are spread across 78 regions, and there are 164 availability zones throughout the United States, Azure Government, the Americas, Europe, Asia Pacific, the Middle East, and Africa:

- **Azure region**: Refers to a specific geographical area.
- **Availability zone**: These are physically separate locations or data centers within a region.

Some resources, specific virtual machine sizes, or storage types are not supported in some regions, so if you require an unavailable resource, you may need to choose a less-than-ideal region. Ideally, your region should be closest to you or most of your application's users.

Always verify that resources are available in the preferred region before deploying any services. An excellent source to check the list of regions and the availability of Azure products across regions is `https://azure.microsoft.com/en-us/explore/global-infrastructure/geographies/#geographies`.

Security and compliance

Security is a paramount concern for businesses operating in the cloud. Good architectural design involves strong security measures, such as data encryption, identity management, and access control, which help protect sensitive information and maintain regulatory compliance.

Alongside security is the need to adhere to each country's rules that govern data privacy and compliance. Requirements vary by country, and each country specifies how data should be stored and transported. These requirements can have legal implications and must be considered when planning an application's architecture.

When designing your application, you can consider the following Azure services that help you to implement the best possible security and compliance policies:

- **Azure Purview**: A data governance service provided by Microsoft Azure that helps organizations to create a holistic view of their data landscape and enables data discovery, classification, and lineage tracking. **Data loss prevention** (**DLP**) is a key aspect of data governance, as it helps organizations to protect sensitive data from unauthorized access and potential leaks. Azure Information Protection also uses Azure Purview to correctly classify and label sensitive data, allowing organizations to enforce policies to prevent data loss.

- **Azure Security Center**: Provides compliance baselines that allow organizations to evaluate the security posture of their Azure resources against industry best practices and regulatory requirements. It boasts a compliance scanning feature that helps to identify potential security misconfigurations and recommends remediation measures.

- **Azure Blueprints**: These are a way to automate the deployment of Azure resources and ensure that they adhere to organizational standards and compliance requirements. Organizations can define and enforce consistent policies, role-based access controls, and resource configurations across their Azure environment.

- **Landing zones**: Provide guidelines for building a well-architected and compliant foundation in Azure. They offer a standardized approach to setting up an Azure environment with the necessary security controls, network configurations, and governance mechanisms.

- **Dynamic data masking (DDM)**: This is a feature in Azure SQL Database that helps protect sensitive data by obfuscating or masking it in real time. This helps protect sensitive information while still allowing authorized users to perform their tasks.

Cost efficiency and maintainability

Using cloud-native services can optimize resource usage, and a well-designed cloud architecture can reduce infrastructure costs significantly. The initial cost-saving benefit of cloud computing is that it saves capital and operational expenditure for organizations. Instead of paying for hardware and software licenses upfront, organizations can use the pay-as-you-go pricing model offered by Microsoft. Do note that Azure costs vary from region to region, so choose the most cost-effective region to implement your solution.

Moreover, good cloud architecture is maintainable and easy for developers to update, add new features, or modify existing components. This adaptability enables organizations to keep pace with changing business requirements and technological advancements.

Loose coupling is a key principle in cloud architecture design, as it promotes modularity and separation of concerns. By dividing the system into smaller, independent components, each with a clearly defined responsibility, organizations can achieve better scalability, fault tolerance, and ease of maintenance.

Now let us discuss some key aspects of good virtual network design.

Azure Virtual Network design

Azure services often need to communicate on a private network, which is where **virtual networks** (**VNets**) come in. You can think of VNets as facilitating communication just like physical networks do, and they are very similar in concept. VNets, however, are implemented as software-defined networks on top of Azure's robust physical infrastructure.

VNets are integral to **infrastructure as a service** (**IaaS**) solutions since virtual machines cannot be provisioned without them. A virtual machine will need access to an underlying network to not only access the internet but also be discovered by other virtual machines or resources on the same VNet. The device is assigned an internal IP address on the VNet. While VNets are a foundation for IaaS implementations, **platform as a service** (**PaaS**) services can also be provisioned to communicate via VNets. For example, Azure App Service with a minimum Basic pricing tier supports TCP and UDP communication. It can communicate with other app services, functions, or logic apps via a VNet.

Apart from being a mandatory component for IaaS solutions, you can enjoy the following benefits of using VNets:

- **Isolation**: VNets allow you to restrict or facilitate traffic and communication between specific services and components. This can be accomplished through subnetting.

- **Security**: You can implement various security rules governing who can access the resource. With built-in IP whitelisting, filtering, and security group rules, you can stop access to sensitive IP addresses and ports.

- **Extensibility**: VNets can start as a local network for a set of resources, which can then be extended by connecting to other VNets in other regions and parts of the world.

There is no cost to creating a VNet, but costs will be incurred when data leaves the deployment region. Up to 50 VNets can be provisioned across all regions, and you can contact Azure Support and bid to increase this number.

It is always good to understand the allowances and limitations of services, so you may use this documentation for more guidance on Azure VNets and limits:

```
https://learn.microsoft.com/azure/azure-resource-manager/management/
azure-subscription-service-limits
```

Architecting VNets

VNets can be provisioned using ARM templates, REST APIs, PowerShell, and the Azure CLI. Although this is a software-backed network, you should take the same considerations as if you were planning a physical network. Once a network has been created and used, it is difficult to modify it without downtime.

VNets cannot span multiple regions and are provisioned within a resource group within a region. This means that the VNet can span all the data centers within a region and, thus, be implemented across multiple availability zones.

Through VNet peering, multiple VNets in the same region and subscriptions can be connected. Azure's private network backbone will facilitate the transmission of packets between the networks. You may also have a situation where the VNets are in different subscriptions but in the same region. Network peering will still work, but you can also use a VPN gateway. This provides an added benefit of communicating between an Azure virtual network and an on-premises location over the public internet. Hybrid networks can be implemented comprising on-premises data centers connected to Azure VNets. This can be done through service offerings such as **site-to-site** (**S2S**) and **point-to-site** (**P2S**) VPNs and use ExpressRoute for dedicated connectivity. Let us look at some more details.

VNet peering

With VNet peering, you can connect separate VNets on top of Azure's network infrastructure. This facilitates communication between machines and resources that are not in the same network. The assumption here is that both networks are in the same region.

Let's say you have two VNets provisioned in the East US region, and their resources need to communicate with each other. This is an ideal solution for a low-latency, high-bandwidth connection that does not use the public internet. This is useful for scenarios such as data replication or failover. *Figure 3.1* demonstrates a VNet peering implementation.

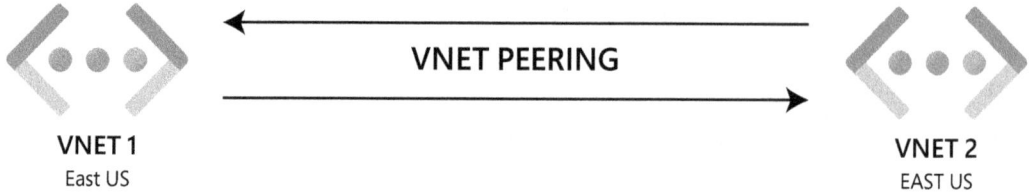

Figure 3.1: VNet peering for VNets in the same region

There's another scenario where the VNets are provisioned in separate subscriptions but in the same region. There are two implementation options in this case:

- Reuse the preceding implementation, where simple VNet peering connects the networks without needing the public internet. This is useful for data replication or failover implementations.

- Use VPN gateway resources to facilitate communication. Both VNets use a secure gateway to create a protected connection over the public internet.

Gateway resources will be required in both VNets, and traffic from either network will be routed through the VPN. This resource incurs charges when data packets are exchanged and is best used when encryption is needed and bandwidth is not a concern.

Azure VPN Gateway is a solution that employs a specialized VNet gateway to facilitate secure data transfer between an Azure VNet and on-site locations via the public internet. Additionally, this service allows for encrypted communication between Azure VNets over Microsoft's network. The VPN gateway can handle multiple connections simultaneously, with all VPN tunnels sharing the available gateway bandwidth. *Figure 3.2* shows an example of how a VPN gateway can connect two VNets in different subscriptions.

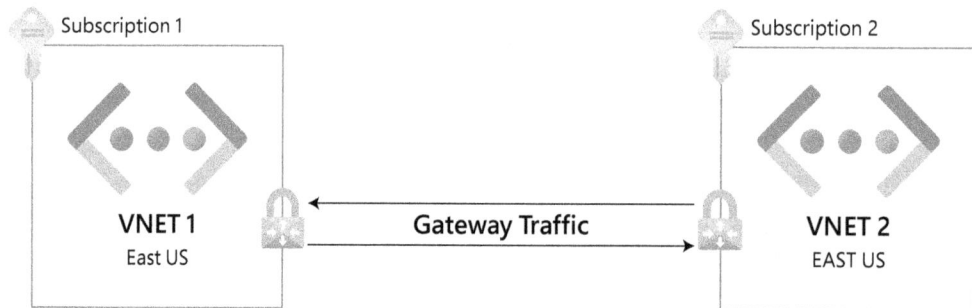

Figure 3.2: VNet peering for resources with different subscriptions using gateways

Different scenarios govern the use of VPN gateway connections. It is essential to properly scope your requirements and implement the best option that meets your needs. Now that we have seen how VNet communication can be done through a VPN, let us explore a hybrid situation where we need the VNet to share resources with an on-premises network.

Site-to-site VPN

Since we need to connect an Azure VNet to an on-site network, we will need a secure method of transmitting traffic via the public internet. For this reason, we can use a VPN gateway service in the VNet, which will assign at least one public IP address that can be used to pair with an on-site VPN device that also exposes a public IP address.

This setup is called a **site-to-site** (or **S2S** for short) connection. The VPN gateway can be configured to transmit traffic in two modes:

- **Active-standby**: In an active-standby mode, one secure tunnel works while the other is on standby. Traffic goes through the working tunnel, but if there's a problem, it switches to the standby tunnel as a backup. In this setup, one public IP address is issued.

- **Active-active**: In an active-active mode, both secure tunnels work together, and data flows through them simultaneously. This mode not only provides higher data speeds but also offers the added benefit of increased efficiency. This is the recommended setup mode, and a public IP address is assigned to each tunnel.

The following is a depiction of an S2S VPN being implemented.

Figure 3.3: Single-site S2S VPN gateway implementation

When you need multiple VPN connections from your VNet gateway to multiple on-premises locations, you can implement a **route-based VPN**. Each VNet has only one VPN gateway, and all connections share the available bandwidth. This kind of connection is often called a "multi-site" connection. Here is how this setup looks like.

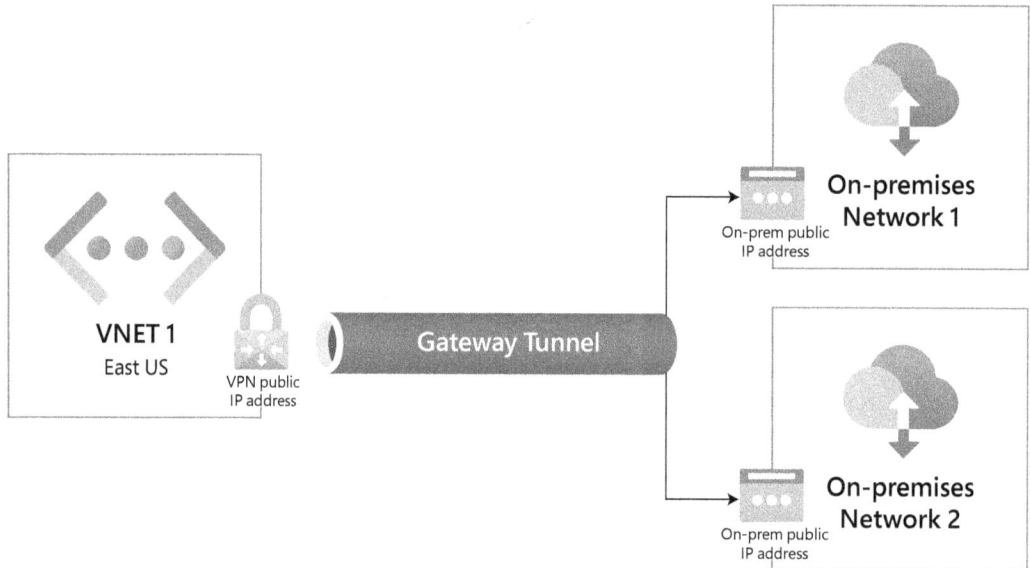

Figure 3.4: Multi-site S2S VPN gateway implementation

Now let us investigate another VPN setup where you might not be able to guarantee a static IP address from a non-Azure resource.

Point-to-site VPN

A **P2S** VPN gateway connection allows a single computer to securely connect to your VNet. This is helpful for situations where you cannot always guarantee the public IP of the non-Azure resource attempting to connect to the gateway. A P2S VPN is an excellent alternative to an S2S VPN when only a few users require access to the VNet.

For example, P2S connections resemble a standard VPN setup that could be implemented for remote workers. It differs from S2S connections in that they don't need a public-facing IP address or a VPN device at the physical location. You can use P2S connections alongside S2S connections through the same VPN gateway, provided their configurations are compatible.

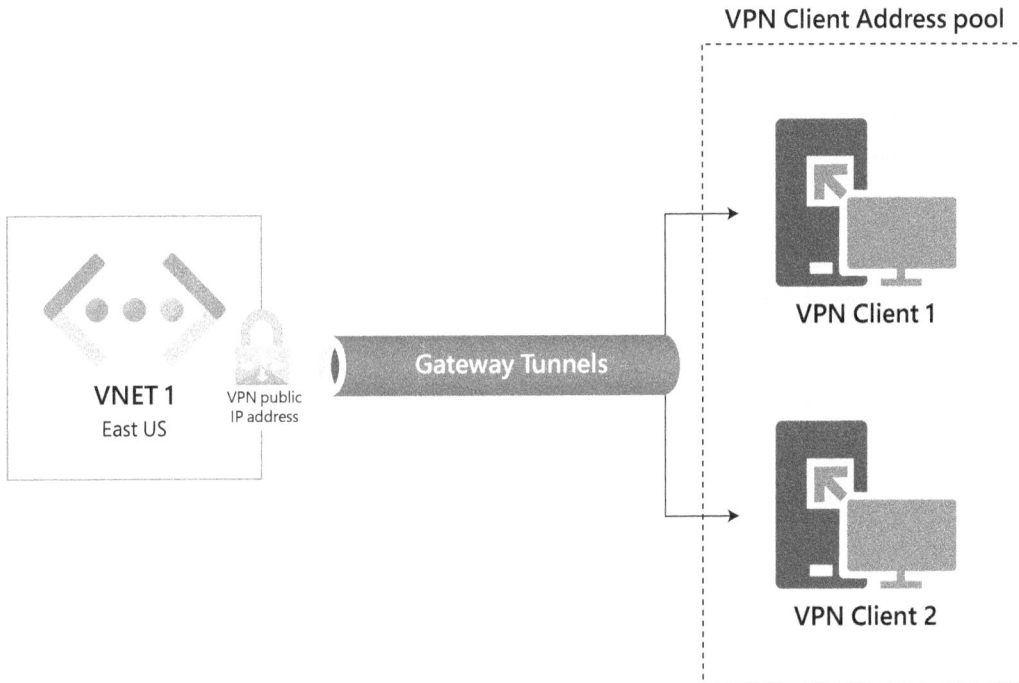

Figure 3.5: P2S VPN architecture

While VPN gateways can solve several headaches with connecting networks and resources, it only solves some of the scenarios. There are situations when you would need to connect remote sites to your Azure VNet but also want the network to be dedicated and non-public internet traffic in between the nodes. For such scenarios, choose the ExpressRoute design model.

ExpressRoute

Both S2S and P2S VPN setups use the public internet for traffic. This model provides a secure data transfer mechanism and is acceptable for many cases. There are times, however, when applications use hybrid technologies, meaning some components are in the Azure cloud and some are at an on-premises data center, and we do not want to use the public internet to facilitate their connection.

Azure offers ExpressRoute as the best solution, offering a secure, high-speed, and reliable connection. It guarantees low-latency connections since the traffic never hits the public internet, but it provides a dedicated private connection through a dedicated Azure network partner.

Ideally, an S2S VPN connection should be provisioned as a failover option for ExpressRoute, but the ExpressRoute circuit is always the primary link. This setup requires two gateways on the same VNet to facilitate each connection.

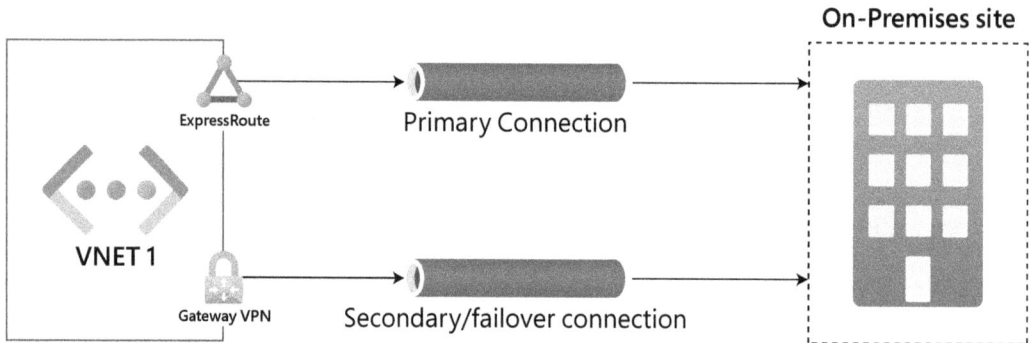

Figure 3.6: ExpressRoute setup with S2S failover

It is important to scope your networking requirements beforehand. A deep and clear understanding of networking and architecture aids you in making the best decisions for your design. It is vital to make decisions for business continuity, so let us explore another cloud service that helps ensure infrastructure stability. This is Azure Application Gateway.

Azure Application Gateway

Azure Application Gateway serves as a web traffic load balancer, facilitating the management of traffic directed toward your web applications. Unlike traditional load balancers, which function at the transport layer (OSI layer 4 – TCP and UDP) and direct traffic based on the source IP address and port to a destination IP address and port, Application Gateway has additional capabilities.

It can make routing determinations based on other aspects of an HTTP request, such as the URI path or host headers. For instance, it can direct traffic based on the incoming URL. If an incoming URL request matches a particular pattern, the traffic can be channeled to a dedicated pool of servers expressly set up for serving that kind of content.

Application Gateway includes the following features:

- **SSL/TLS termination:** This typically leads to unencrypted traffic flowing to the backend servers, thus relieving web servers from the burdensome task of encryption and decryption.

- **Autoscaling**: Application Gateway standard v2 supports autoscaling, enabling it to scale up or down in response to varying traffic load patterns.

- **Zone redundancy**: A standard v2 Application Gateway can span multiple availability zones, enhancing fault resilience and eliminating the need to set up separate application gateways in each zone.

- **Web Application Firewall**: Azure **Web Application Firewall** (**WAF**) provides centralized security for your web applications, protecting them from common exploits and vulnerabilities based on the **Open Web Application Security Project** (**OWASP**) core rule sets.

- **URL-based routing**: URL path-based routing allows traffic routing to specific backend server pools based on the URL paths in the request.

- **Multiple-site hosting**: Application Gateway supports routing based on the hostname or domain name for multiple web applications, enabling you to add over 100 websites to a single Application Gateway.

- **Connection draining**: Connection draining aids in gracefully removing backend pool members during planned service updates or backend health issues.

Now that you understand some networking scenarios and potential solutions, let us explore Azure Storage and patterns.

Azure Storage design

Azure offers secure, highly available, and scalable storage options. These services can provide the following:

- **Blob storage**: Azure Blob Storage can store files for streaming or application content delivery. It can also be used to implement big data analytics solutions. Files can be stored in three different modes:

  - **Hot**: For frequently accessed files. Files are always available and ready to be accessed.

  - **Cool**: For less frequently accessed files. This tier has lower pricing than the hot tier, slower read times, and higher access costs. Data in this tier needs to be stored for at least 30 days.

  - **Cold**: The next level down for less frequently accessed files, after the cool tier. This tier has lower pricing than the cool tier, slower read times, and higher access costs, and data needs to be stored for at least 90 days.

  - **Archive**: The slowest and lowest cost tier for blob storage. Data needs to be stored for 180 days, where files are rarely accessed. This has the slowest read time and the lowest storage costs of all tiers.

- **Files**: A managed file share based on the SMB protocol. It can be used to implement file shares for unstructured data both in the cloud and on-premises.

- **Queues**: A reliable messaging store for implementing messaging between applications.

- **Tables**: A NoSQL and schema-less storage option for semi-structured data. It stores data in key-value pairs.

- **Disks**: Block-level storage for disks (used for virtual machine disks).

Data stored in Azure Storage is encrypted at rest and in transit. Azure Storage gives us the ability to control which users may access blobs and the actions they may perform. Azure Storage can only be accessed via SSL; users must be authenticated and authorized. You can use **shared access signature (SAS)** tokens individually to grant individual access rights to external users. Azure disk encryption is used to secure operating systems and data disks for virtual machines. The following are the two types of encryption used:

- **Client-side encryption**: Used by client applications to encrypt data before it is read/written from Azure Storage. This method requires custom application logic and relies on secrets from Azure Key Vault.

- **Storage service encryption**: Ensures that data is encrypted while being written to storage and decrypted when it is read. No application changes are required to enable SSE.

Several pricing and performance tiers exist to meet your application and implementation needs. The pricing tiers are as follows:

- **Standard**: Allows you to store tables, queues, files, disks, and blobs. This tier is generally suitable for application development and is required when provisioning services such as virtual machines and function apps.

- **Premium**: There are several levels in this tier and it provides all the services of the standard tier with higher performance thresholds. It is required for SSD disk support for virtual machines, Data Lake Storage, and Azure Files.

Recovery is always a major talking point for storage. Azure always maintains multiple copies of storage accounts. The location and number of copies depend on the replication configuration. The options are as follows:

- **Locally redundant storage** (**LRS**): Copies data three times in a single Azure data center in a primary region. This is the most affordable replication option, but you risk losing your data if the single data center suffers from a disaster.

- **Zone-redundant storage** (**ZRS**): Copies data across three Azure data centers in a primary region. This provides more coverage than LRS, but your data is still vulnerable within a single region.

- **Geo-redundant storage** (**GRS**): Copies data three times within a single data center in a primary region and replicates these three copies to a data center in a secondary region.

- **Geo-zone-redundant storage** (**GZRS**): Copies data across three data centers in a primary region and replicates to a secondary region, where it is copied synchronously three times using LRS.

Now that you understand how to use storage services and the different available flavors, let us explore some design patterns that help us best use the offerings.

Storage design patterns

Let us discuss some design patterns that help you build efficient, performant, and scalable solutions to common problems when working with Azure Storage. We'll start by discussing partitioning patterns.

Partitioning is a method of spreading data across multiple partitions. Typically, we use a partition to group records based on a criterion or category across several nodes. This allows for efficient indexing and data retrieval when performing lookups. There are typically four types of partitioning patterns:

- **Range partitioning**: Involves dividing data into partitions based on a range of values in the partition key. This pattern works best with large datasets and distributes the load across multiple storage nodes. In table storage, range partitioning can be implemented by choosing a partition key representing a range, such as a date or time. In this scenario, consider storing invoices and grouping them by year.

- **Hash-based partitioning**: This pattern distributes data across partitions based on the hash value of the partition key. This pattern ensures an even data distribution, helping avoid hotspots and improving scalability. In blob storage, hash-based partitioning can be implemented by using the first few characters of the blob name as the partition key.

- **Cache-Aside pattern**: This pattern relieves the primary data store from often performing expensive operations by using a cache store to store data and improve application performance. Clients first check the cache for data; if it is not present, they retrieve it from the underlying data store and then add it to the cache. Until the data in the cache is invalidated, it becomes a higher-speed lookup for data. Azure Cache for Redis is an excellent choice for implementing this pattern with Azure Storage.

- **Read-through cache pattern**: This pattern retrieves data from the cache as the primary data store. When data is found, or there is a cache hit, then data is returned immediately. When it is not found, or there is a cache miss, the application populates the cache with the missing data after retrieving it from the primary data store, and also returns it to the application.

The previous caching patterns are not unique to Azure storage accounts. Still, they can also be used in standard applications that rely on Azure SQL, Cosmos DB, or any other data store remotely hosted and in a separate location. Beyond standard data record storage, you also have design patterns and considerations surrounding your files and blobs. Some patterns for consideration are as follows:

- **Hierarchical storage management (HSM) pattern**: Involves moving infrequently accessed data to lower-cost storage tiers while keeping frequently accessed data in higher-performance tiers. This pattern implements life cycle management policies to automatically move data between hot, cool, and archive access tiers based on data access frequency.

- **Snapshot-based backup pattern**: Involves taking regular snapshots of your data to enable point-in-time recovery. This can be implemented using the blob snapshot feature, which allows you to create read-only snapshots of blobs.

Understanding and applying these Azure Storage design patterns allows you to create efficient, scalable, and resilient solutions using Azure Storage services. These patterns help you optimize data storage, access, and management, ensuring your application performs well and remains highly available even as your data needs grow.

Let us explore some messaging patterns that lead to high application performance and scalability.

Azure design patterns related to messaging

Performance and scalability are key considerations when designing and deploying applications in the cloud and it is important to understand and apply various strategies and design patterns. Messaging patterns are often used to provide stability in cloud-based solutions, thus facilitating performant and scalable applications.

Ensuring reliable communication between components in a distributed or cloud-based system can be challenging due to network latency, component failures, or data inconsistencies. Implementing messaging patterns such as the Competing Consumers pattern and the Publisher-Subscriber pattern can help ensure reliable communication between components. These patterns use Azure services such as Service Bus queues, Service Bus topics, and Event Grid to manage and distribute messages, ensuring that components can communicate reliably and evolve independently.

Let us explore messaging patterns in more detail and appreciate how they help you to construct durable and scalable systems.

Messaging patterns

Messaging in Azure can be supported using Azure Queue Storage, Service Bus, or Event Grid. Each service has unique characteristics and can be applied to different scenarios. Each service uses message queues, providing a durable and reliable messaging mechanism that can be used to implement performant applications. Message queues are generally used to implement loosely coupled applications where two or more components don't talk directly. Instead, one application will place data, or a message, in a queue, which another application consumes and processes.

This type of implementation is useful when there is a potentially long-running application that the sending application should not perform immediately. This could be as simple as sending an email or processing a payment in an e-commerce application. The receiving application will process this in its own time, allowing the sender to continue to another operation and preserve a good user experience.

Beyond the idea of a single sender and single receiver, we have the idea of **competing consumers**. Each receiver will process a finite number of messages synchronously, but there might be delays in processing times if a single consumer is assigned to a high-volume queue. Here you can have competing consumers listening to messages in the same queue. This can vastly increase the number of messages processed simultaneously and more efficiently.

Each consumer should be independent; this pattern should only be used if each message contains all the information needed to perform the operation. This means that consumers do not know about each other or share dependencies. Each consumer also needs to delete each message that it processes to ensure that they do not get re-processed by another service. Imagine processing a payment several times; this would not be pretty.

The following is a depiction of an application publishing to a queue with competing consumers.

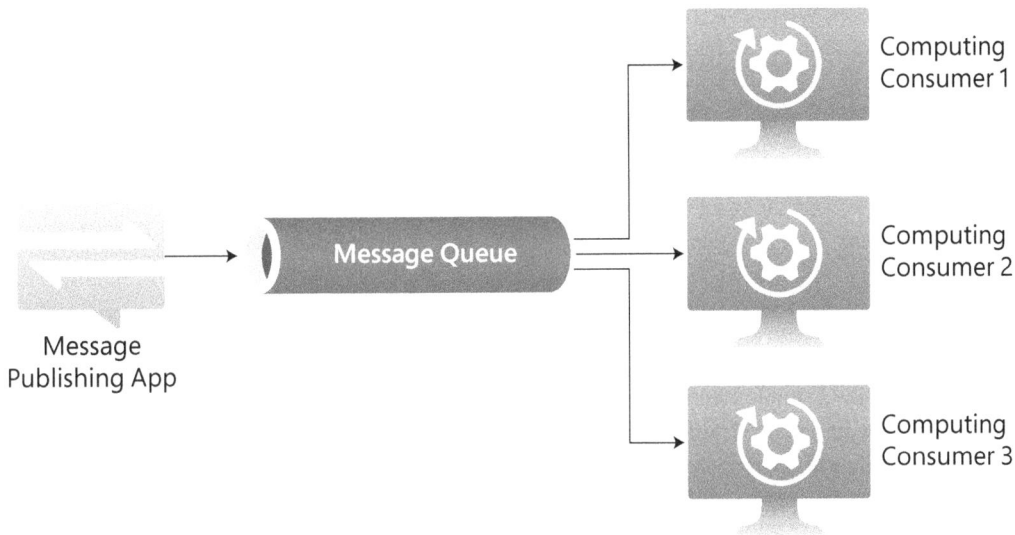

Figure 3.7: Competing consumers for queue messaging

We also have the concept of publisher-subscriber (pub-sub for short) implementations where one application publishes a message to a message exchange distributed to several applications. In this case, they are not competing consumers since each consumer performs their process independently. Azure Service Bus and Event Grid are examples of message exchanges.

Azure Service Bus

This is a powerful service offering that allows subscribers to consume the messages at their own rate. It utilizes message queues but also supports topics and subscribers. A message can be placed on a topic, distributed to each subscriber queue, and consumed by independent applications that will use the information from the message to complete a task. Service Bus queues can be configured to ensure a message is delivered at least once and dropped into a **dead-letter** queue if there are several failures. The following diagram shows how Azure Service Bus can be used to distribute one message from a publisher to many consumers.

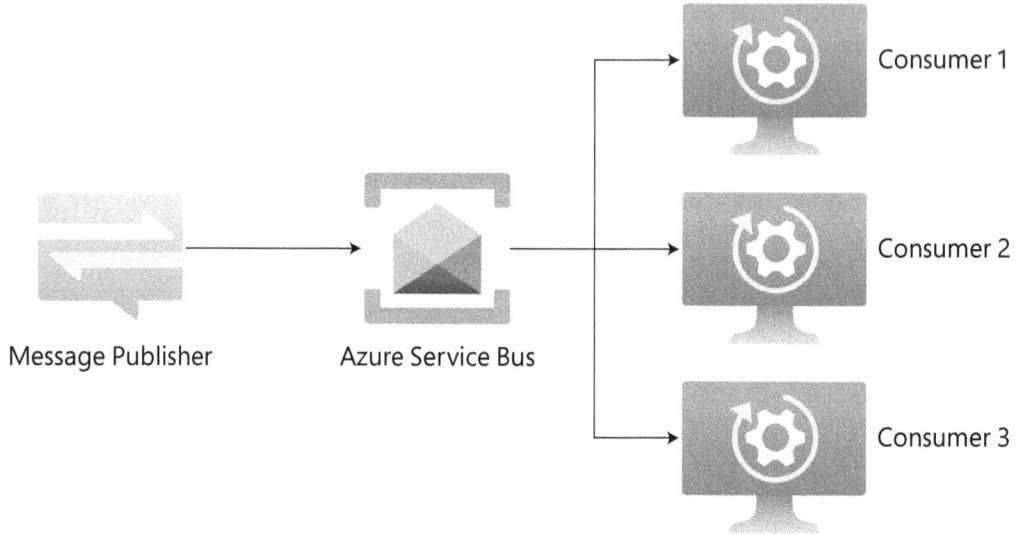

Figure 3.8: Typical pub-sub implementation

Messaging seems like a simple solution to what could be a big problem in distributed systems, but the nuances need to be understood and managed correctly. While any application can publish messages, we must be strategic with the service we use to handle incoming messages. In the realm of IoT devices and telemetry, we may want to use Azure Event Grid. We will explore this next.

Azure Event Grid

This is used to push event-driven applications. Consumers are expected to choose which events they react to, and the grid is not concerned about which events are consumed or how. These events are referred to as telemetry and are usually produced by devices or services that constantly generate log information about changes that occur. It supports topics and subscriptions and is used to simplify event consumption and lower costs associated with constant polling.

It simplifies event consumption and eliminates the need for constant polling. It also supports event consumption from Azure and non-Azure resources while distributing them to registered subscriber endpoints. Event messages have enough information to trigger application reactions to changes in services, devices, and applications.

A significant difference between this and Service Bus is that Service Bus has a default dead-letter queue available. In contrast, Event Grid must be configured using a storage account. Azure resources such as storage accounts, Azure resources, and Azure subscriptions have default integration with Event Grid.

It has the following characteristics:

- Dynamic scalability

- Low cost (pay-as-you-go pricing)

- At-least-once delivery of an event

While we search for a suitable solution to our messaging problem, we must also consider scalable integration solutions for our Azure services. We can implement **functions as a service** (**FaaS**) for these scenarios, where we can have cost-effective, scalable, and performant integration applications. We will discuss this next.

Functions as a service

FaaS is a cloud computing service model that allows developers to build, deploy, and manage serverless functions without worrying about the underlying infrastructure. Microsoft Azure offers Azure Functions, its FaaS offering, to enable developers to create event-driven, scalable, and easily maintainable applications.

One of the key benefits of FaaS is its scalability. Functions can be scaled automatically based on demand, so you only pay for the resources they use. Another advantage is its flexibility. Functions can be developed and deployed independently, so developers can focus on writing and maintaining the function's code without worrying about the underlying infrastructure.

Because FaaS can simplify development and deployment in cloud applications, this is an attractive design pattern option for modern cloud-native applications that require fast development cycles and rapid scalability.

Let us learn more about Azure Functions and how it can help us.

Azure Functions

Azure Functions allows developers to write code in various programming languages, including C#, Java, JavaScript, Python, and PowerShell, and deploy quickly and easily to the cloud. HTTP requests, message queues, or data changes in Azure services such as Cosmos DB or Blob Storage can trigger functions.

Some of the key benefits of Azure Functions are as follows:

- **Serverless architecture**: Azure Functions abstracts away the underlying infrastructure, allowing developers to focus solely on writing code. You don't have to manage servers, networking, or storage, as Azure handles these tasks automatically.

- **Integration**: Functions can be easily integrated with Azure services, such as Service Bus, Event Grid, Cosmos DB, and Azure Storage, and third-party services through bindings and triggers. This enables seamless communication between different parts of your application.

- **Scalability**: Azure Functions automatically scales based on the number of incoming events and the resources needed to process them, allowing your application to handle varying workloads seamlessly.

- **Cost-effective**: With Azure Functions, you pay for the resources you use and the execution time of your functions. It can also be provisioned on an Azure App Service plan for more predictable scaling and costing.

Azure FaaS provides developers with a flexible, scalable, and cost-effective platform for building event-driven applications. Its serverless nature simplifies development and reduces the overhead of managing infrastructure, while its integrations and language support make it a versatile choice for a wide range of projects.

Azure Functions follows a fire-and-forget model where functions do not maintain a state. There are times, however, when we need to facilitate more complex workflows. For this, we use a particular type of function called Durable Functions.

Azure Durable Functions

Azure Durable Functions is an extension of Azure Functions. You can use it to build stateful, long-running, and highly reliable applications in a serverless environment. Durable Functions is designed to simplify complex, stateful patterns in applications by introducing the concept of orchestrator functions and activity functions. Durable Functions lets you define stateful workflows by writing orchestrator functions and stateful entities using entity functions.

Behind the scenes, the extension manages state, checkpoints, and restarts for you, allowing you to focus on your business logic. There are several flavors in which Durable Functions can be implemented:

- **Function chaining**: In this pattern, several entity functions are executed in a specific order. The output of one function is applied to the input of another function, and a queue is used to ensure that the function stays durable and scalable and that the orchestrator can properly track the flow from one function to the next.

- **Fan-out/fan-in**: The orchestrator executes multiple functions in parallel and waits for all functions to finish. This pattern is often used when aggregation work is done on the results returned from the functions. Multiple messages are sent to a queue to fan out, but fanning back in is more challenging. To fan in, custom code tracks when the queue-triggered functions end and then stores function outputs.

- **Async HTTP APIs**: This pattern addresses the problem of coordinating the state of long-running operations with external clients. It uses an HTTP endpoint to trigger the long-running action. Then, it redirects the client to a status endpoint that the client polls to learn when the operation is finished.

- **Monitoring**: Implements a flexible and recurring workflow process that polls until specific conditions are met. This pattern can be implemented using a regular timer trigger to create flexible recurrence intervals, manage task lifetimes, and create multiple monitor processes from a single orchestration.

- **Human interaction**: Many processes require some form of human interaction, which can complicate workflows and compromise our highly available ambitions. This pattern allows the function to wait for human input before moving on to the next step in the workflow. The orchestrator uses a durable timer to request approval. If the timer runs out without the required confirmation, the orchestrator can be made to escalate or abandon the operation.

- **Aggregator (stateful entities)**: This implementation allows you to aggregate event data over a period into a single, addressable entity. In this pattern, the aggregated data may come from multiple sources, be delivered in batches, or be scattered over long periods.

Durable Functions offers a powerful, versatile solution for developing stateful, long-running, and highly reliable serverless applications. It simplifies complex coordination patterns, provides state management and fault tolerance, and allows for seamless integration with other services, all while leveraging the scalability and cost-efficiency of the Azure Functions platform.

Now that we have seen several design patterns and how they can be applied to architect a cloud solution, let us review some best practices that invariably contribute to our application's overall stability and robustness.

Azure solution design best practices

Azure solution design best practices are critical for building robust, scalable, and secure cloud-based applications and infrastructure. Adhering to these best practices ensures optimal performance, reliability, and cost-efficiency while minimizing the risks associated with security breaches and data loss.

By following these principles, you can create resilient solutions less susceptible to failures and protect sensitive data. Moreover, optimizing cost management, application performance, and continuous system monitoring and updating helps organizations stay competitive and agile in a fast-paced technology landscape.

Performance

- Optimize Azure storage implementations by choosing the best storage option and configuration for your needs. Each application is unique, and the best storage option may vary. Be sure to select the correct tiers based on usage and redundancy based on your needs. Azure storage accounts have various options that can be mixed and matched to suit your needs.

- Implementing caching in an Azure architecture can provide significant benefits, including improved performance, reduced latency, increased scalability, and cost savings. Azure Cache for Redis is a fully managed cache service that applications can use to reduce latency and the load on the primary database. Implementing Azure Service Bus or Azure Event Grid in your Azure app architecture can significantly improve application decoupling, scalability, resilience, and flexibility. Both services enable communication between components within your applications through event-driven and message-based patterns.

- Improve the performance of your solution with new features and updates from Azure. These new features can help you optimize your solution for better performance, faster response times, and increased scalability; you improve the reliability of your solution and minimize downtime and ensure that your solution remains relevant and competitive in the long run.

- Use Azure Blob Storage for unstructured data, Azure Files for shared files, and Azure Data Lake Storage for big data scenarios. By using the right storage service for your data and use case, you can ensure that your data is stored in a cost-effective, scalable, and secure manner:

  - **Azure Blob Storage**: A scalable, cost-effective, and secure storage service ideal for storing unstructured data such as text, images, videos, and other multimedia files.

  - **Azure Files**: A fully managed file share service that allows you to create and manage shared file systems in the cloud. It is ideal for enterprise scenarios requiring shared file access across multiple or virtual machines.

  - **Azure Data Lake Storage**: A distributed filesystem optimized for big data analytics.

Security

- Implementing network security best practices in Azure is essential to protect your resources from unauthorized access, data breaches, and other threats. It is also good to get your design right the first time since it is difficult to modify your network infrastructure while it is already in use. **Network security groups** (**NSGs**) and Azure Firewall are key components that can help you achieve a secure network architecture.

- Encrypting sensitive data at rest, in use, and in transit. This practice is crucial for protecting the confidentiality and integrity of the data as it is vulnerable to unauthorized access, interception, and modification, which can result in data breaches, financial loss, and damage to your organization's reputation. The following Azure services can assist with this:

- **Azure Storage Service Encryption**: Automatically encrypts data at rest in Azure Blob Storage and Azure file storage.

- **Azure Disk Encryption**: Encrypts the virtual hard disks of Azure virtual machines using BitLocker encryption.

- **Azure Key Vault**: Provides secure storage of cryptographic keys and allows you to control their use.

- **Azure SSL/TLS certificates**: Provides SSL/TLS certificates for encrypting data in transit over the internet. This ensures that data is encrypted between the user's device and the Azure services.

Resilience

- Using the best disaster recovery option in your Azure design ensures your application's availability, reliability, and resilience. Implementing an effective disaster recovery strategy helps minimize downtime, data loss, and the impact of disasters on your business operations. It is also essential to choose the best option relative to your needs. Implementing a disaster recovery strategy involves some upfront costs. Still, it can save you money in the long run by minimizing the potential financial losses caused by extended downtime or data loss. To choose the best DR option for your design, consider the following factors:

  - **Recovery point objective (RPO)**: The maximum acceptable amount of data loss, measured in time. Determine your RPO to choose a DR option that meets your data protection needs.

  - **Recovery time objective (RTO)**: The maximum acceptable time to restore your applications and data after a disaster. Choose a DR option that meets your RTO requirements.

  - **Cost**: Evaluate the cost of different DR options regarding storage, computing, and network resources, and choose the one that meets your budget constraints.

  - **Complexity**: Consider the complexity of implementing and managing different DR options and choose the one that best aligns with your team's capabilities and expertise.

Scalability/availability

- Using the autoscaling features in Azure can help you optimize your cloud infrastructure by dynamically adjusting resources according to the workload, ensuring efficient resource utilization and cost management. Most, if not all, Azure services and resources allow you to configure autoscaling as a response to load.

- Using PaaS solutions over IaaS whenever possible. PaaS solutions abstract away the underlying infrastructure, allowing developers to focus on designing, developing, and deploying applications without worrying about managing servers, networking, or storage. In contrast, IaaS requires a greater level of involvement in infrastructure management. They also generally follow a pay-as-you-go pricing model, which means you only pay for the resources you use, and allow you to reduce the time to market by reducing provisioning and maintenance overhead. If you have specific infrastructure requirements, need more control over the underlying infrastructure, or have compliance or regulatory requirements that PaaS solutions cannot meet, IaaS might better fit your needs. Consider your specific use case and requirements before deciding between PaaS and IaaS.

Cost management

- Using Azure Cost Management tools to monitor and optimize spending. These tools empower you to effectively track and manage your cloud expenses by providing a comprehensive overview of resource usage. This way, you can make informed decisions on scaling and optimizing their cloud infrastructure. Azure Cost Management tools also facilitate budgeting and forecasting by allowing you to set cost alerts and monitor trends, ensuring you are better equipped to predict and control future expenses.

These best practices provide a solid foundation for building cloud solutions that meet the highest performance, security, and reliability standards, enabling you to focus on your core objectives confidently.

Summary

Cloud architecture design patterns are paramount as they provide a structured, reusable approach to address common challenges while designing modern cloud-based solutions. These design patterns serve as best practices that have been tried and tested in real-world scenarios, offering developers and architects a reliable framework to follow while designing their systems. By implementing proven design patterns, organizations can ensure that their cloud-based solutions can handle increasing workloads and deliver consistent performance as they grow.

This chapter covered the significance of good architectural design in cloud solution development and scoping. We looked at Azure Virtual Network design and Azure Storage design, emphasizing their roles in achieving an efficient and secure cloud infrastructure. We also explored design patterns pertinent to messaging, performance, and scalability, providing insights into how these patterns can be harnessed for optimal cloud solutions.

Lastly, we shed light on effective solution design practices that facilitate the creation of reliable, high-performance, and scalable cloud architectures. While we looked at some aspects of VNets and how they can be designed, there are more aspects that can be uncovered. In the next chapter, we will look in more depth at Azure network infrastructure and design.

4

Azure Network Infrastructure and Design

Planning for and enabling communication between applications, components, and dependent platforms is a key part of architecting any infrastructure, regardless of where it lives. The concept of physical networking components and virtual networking components have been around for decades. It's important to have a well-designed, well-defined, secure, and efficient network environment for your applications. Introducing new networking segments can cause additional latency between application components if proper steps are not taken to anticipate the flow of traffic and keep communications between different components efficient. Not having a well-defined or secure network can open your organization up to liabilities, such as cyberattacks, and compromise proprietary or sensitive data.

Azure provides a wealth of different network services meant to manage, direct, monitor, filter, and handle several types of traffic across many different topologies. Implementing standard design patterns when constructing your Azure networks will help maintain order as well as security, while also providing a solid way to isolate traffic if a segment of the network does happen to get compromised.

This chapter will focus on the various networking services Azure offers, from base networking to advanced traffic control.

In this chapter, you will learn about:

- Core networking patterns
- Networking components
- Common problem spaces

We will first look at standard design patterns that have been established in the industry, along with examples and use cases that correspond to each design.

Core networking patterns

While there is a wide array of networking services offered by Azure, there tends to be a standard set of patterns that can be implemented to address networking concerns. These patterns may vary in component selection or implementation, but the core intent is the same between traditional infrastructure (on-premises servers and datacenters) and virtualized infrastructure (representations of servers and services hosted by a service provider). Let's review some of those core patterns now.

Public facing

Any network that hosts components that can be accessed via the public internet is said to be public facing. That does not mean that virtual machines, Azure App Service, or any other application components should be directly exposed to the internet. This pattern allows for public accessibility of an application, typically in the form of a web user interface. Common implementations can be seen using cloud services such as Azure Front Door or Azure Application Gateway that act as a message broker for communication between the public internet and an application service. In other cases, you may choose to set up a **Demilitarized Zone** (**DMZ**) to handle inbound traffic (sometimes seen with the hub and spoke model) to control what is and what is not available for public internet consumption.

An organization may only have a selected number of public-facing applications or services, while having a wide variety of internal workloads, applications, and services available for consumption. Making proper use of security services such as Azure Defender, along with appropriate network controls such as Azure network security groups, Azure Firewall policies, or Web Application Firewalls, are essential in maintaining the security posture of the organization and only exposing applications that are approved for external consumption.

One example of a non-UI based application that may be publicly available is that of APIs. An organization can choose to expose a single or a set of APIs externally for facilitating integrations with other applications or services it has behind the firewall. The use of Azure services such as Azure Application Gateway and Azure API Management allows you to protect interfaces while also allowing developers to compose APIs, methods, and routes in an organized fashion.

Virtual network isolation

The use of isolated virtual networks can be seen in a few circumstances. The overall pattern dictates that outside traffic is only allowed in through brokered connections, and there may be specific traffic allowed out to another network or cloud service, but it is highly regulated. For example, you may have a need to run a clustered application in isolation for testing or other reasons. To secure entry, you might use a jump server—an RDP connection that is only allowed to connect from internal IP ranges—to interact only with the isolated network. You may even use a web frontend that can only be reached from internally controlled networks.

Another example of isolation is between branch or office locations and a wide area network. You may need to keep different offices' network traffic isolated for business reasons, bandwidth reasons, or even data residency requirements. Being able to control where offices—as well as virtual networks—can connect is crucial in situations where specific traffic isolation is required.

Peering and network protection

Peering refers to the connection of virtual networks to one another, allowing the flow of traffic between them and making them appear as one network. When this is implemented in Azure, any traffic flowing between those networks is sent over the Azure backbone and does not travel across the public internet. Azure supports two types of peering for virtual networks, in-region and across regions. In-region peering connects two virtual networks that live in the same Azure region. For example, if you want to connect a hub network deployed to East US with a spoke network also located in East US, you can do so using an in-region peering connection. Across-region peering allows networks to be connected and appear as one network while being deployed to different Azure regions. This allows traffic to travel between regions using the Azure backbone, keeping it from traversing the public internet.

With either peering, you can adjust the size of IP ranges without incurring any downtime unless you are integrating your network with the Azure Virtual **Wide Area Network** (**WAN**) service. A frequently used pattern involving peering is that of enabling hybrid connectivity between on-premises datacenters and a cloud provider. To use this type of connectivity, you will need to have an ExpressRoute circuit (a dedicated network circuit to a Microsoft partner datacenter) installed in one or more of your existing datacenters, then configure peering between ExpressRoute and the desired virtual networks.

Two types of peering exist in Azure currently: private peering and Microsoft peering. Private peering is designated for connecting two networks together, whether on-premises to Azure in a hybrid model or Azure to Azure for a true cloud model. Microsoft peering is different, where network traffic is routed directly to Microsoft services (i.e., Microsoft 365, public Azure services) and is treated like traffic on your internal network instead of traversing the internet. ExpressRoute circuits provide both private and Microsoft peering options when implemented.

An example from the **Networking Services Overview** page can be seen in *Figure 4.1*, which shows the dual network pipe layout as well as the availability of peering options.

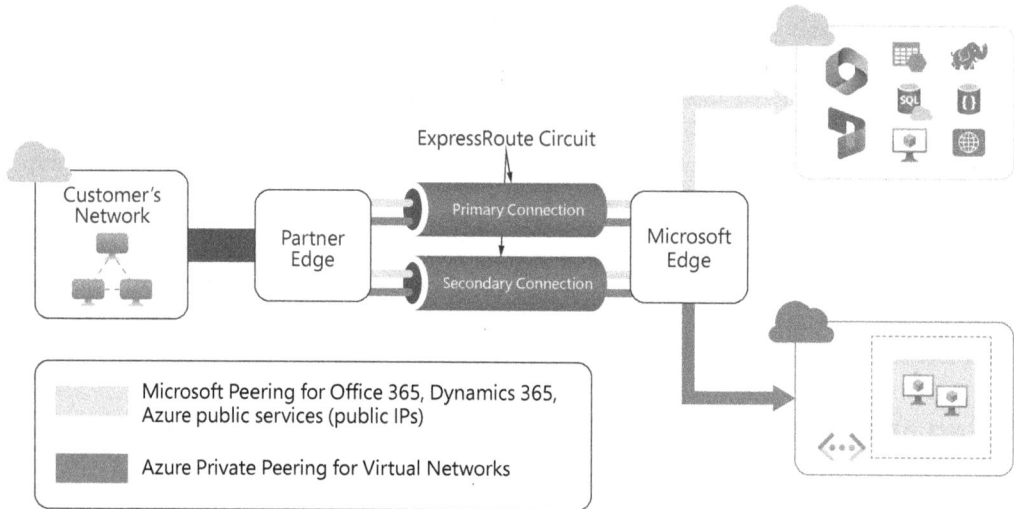

Figure 4.1: Microsoft representation of ExpressRoute with peering options

Hub and spoke

One industry standard for laying out and deploying virtual networks is called the hub and spoke model. This operates with the premise that one virtual network—the hub—contains commonly used components and controls the traffic going into or out of virtual networks connected to various IaaS and PaaS components – the spokes. The **Microsoft Cloud Adoption Framework**, for example, makes heavy use of the hub and spoke model when describing how to appropriately set up your network presence in Azure.

Another example of how the hub and spoke pattern can be utilized is with virtual network appliances, which is covered in more detail in the *Common problem spaces* section, later in this chapter. The network appliances are normally deployed into a hub network and control traffic for both the hub as well as any attached spokes. This makes it easier to isolate specific networks or subnets in the event of a cyberattack.

From a layout perspective, the hub and spoke model helps to logically define traffic for specific regions in Azure and helps further in isolating traffic flow by creating multiple hubs per region if you have applications that serve multiple geographic locations. In some cases, organizations choose to create one production and one non-production hub, then attach networks related to those respective environmental workloads to keep the traffic separated.

An example of a hub and spoke architecture can be found on the `Microsoft Learn website`. *Figure 4.2* gives a high-level overview of the architecture:

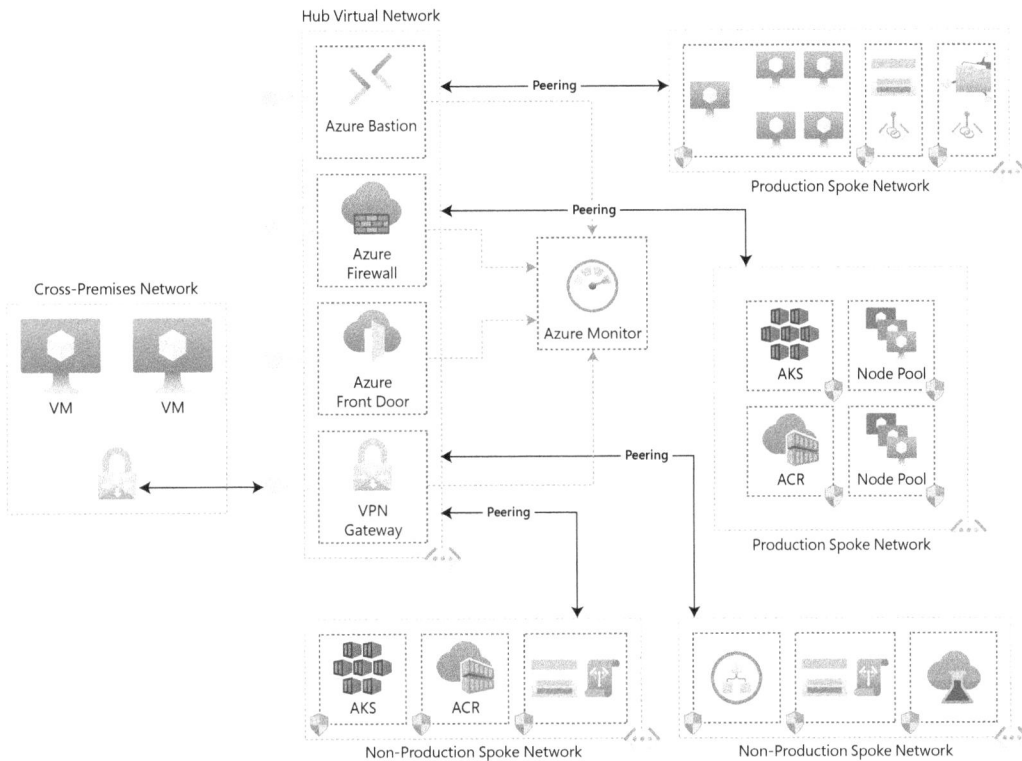

Figure 4.2: Example of hub and spoke architecture

Networking components

Azure offers a wide range of networking components, from the simplistic to the highly specialized. Performing a quick search for network-related services in the Azure portal yields an extensive list.

One way to reference the use cases for the various cloud services provided is to cross-reference them with the **Open Systems Interconnection** (**OSI**) model, which breaks down various levels of communications from the physical network to the application itself and is widely known by many network professionals. *Figure 4.3* illustrates the mapping of Azure network services to the various layers of the OSI model. Keep in mind that this mapping is meant to be illustrative of the general types of communication involved and not necessarily a means of endorsement of specific cloud services for a specific use case.

7 - Application

Application | Traffic | DNS Zones | Firewalls | WAF Policies
Gateways | Manager Profiles

6 - Presentation

5 - Session

4 - Transport

Load | Firewalls | NSGs | WAF Policies | Bastion
Balancers

3 - Network

Public IP | NAT | WAF Policies | Virtual | NSGs | Private Link
Addresses | | | Networks

Load | Firewalls | Virtual | Virtual Networks | Route | Route
Balancers | | WANs | Gateways | Tables | Filters

2 - Data Link

Private / Public
Peering

1 - Physical

ExpressRoute
Circuits

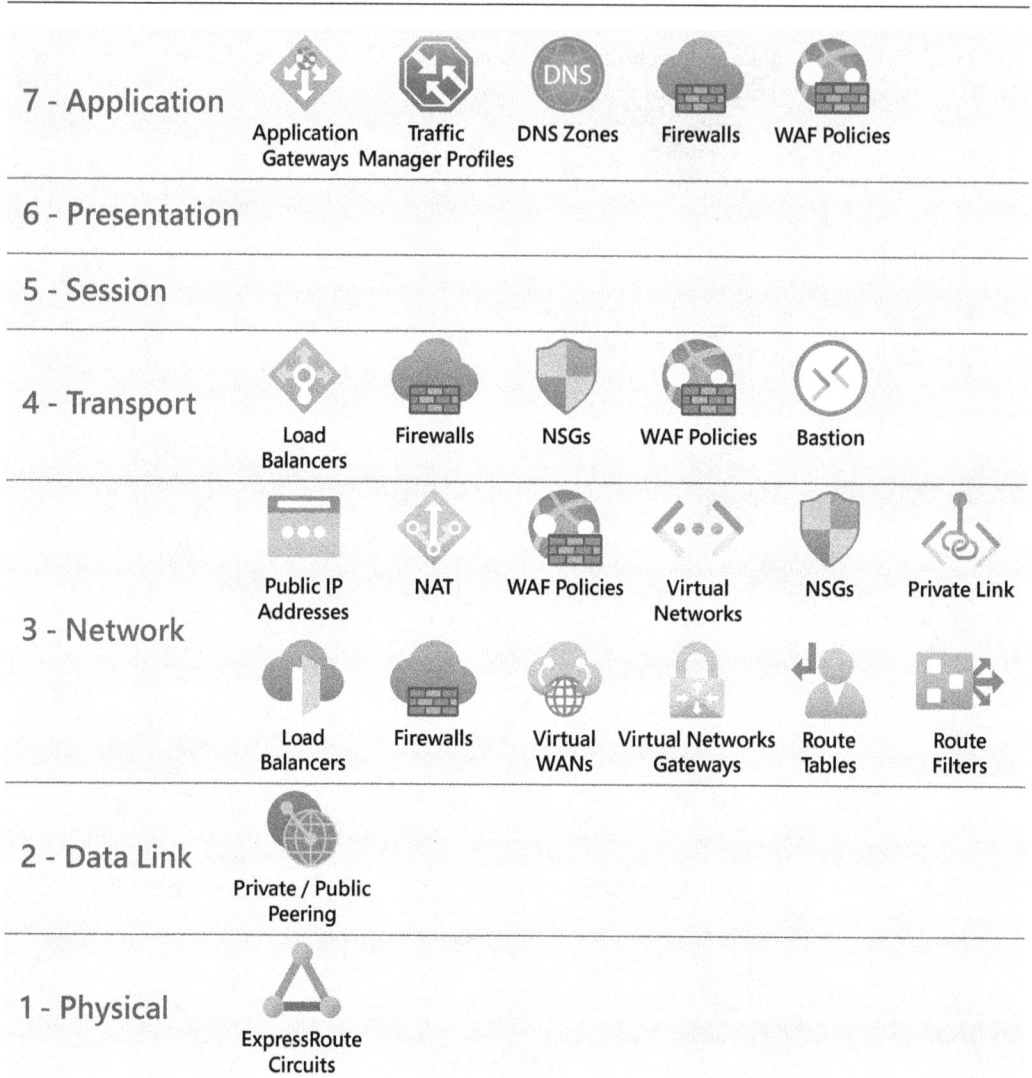

Figure 4.3: OSI model with Azure network components mapped

We will now explore the available Azure networking services along with examples of common uses. It is important to keep the service's limits, quotas, and constraints in mind when deciding on what to use as a part of a solution. Please refer to this detailed article on Azure subscription and service limits, quotas, and constraints on the Microsoft Learn website to get the latest information on all services and their related service limits: https://learn.microsoft.com/azure/azure-resource-manager/management/azure-subscription-service-limits.

Core network connectivity

Much like application development, there are certain foundational blocks you need to start with in order to have a functional and stable design. Using available network services in Azure to design a purpose-built network is no different. We will review several of these core building blocks now.

Virtual networks and subnets

Virtual networks are merely software-defined network circuits. This concept has been a staple of datacenter virtualization platforms for many years. Virtual networks allow for traffic isolation, custom DNS, and custom IP ranges to be configured. Traffic on virtual networks is corralled by the Azure backbone, and components connected to it are not exposed to the public internet unless a public IP is associated with that component. For example, attaching a public IP to a virtual machine that is on a virtual network, then allowing traffic to come in on port 3389 for Remote Desktop, would expose that virtual machine to the internet via the public IP.

VNets support both IPV4 and IPV6 address spaces, along with class A, B, and C addressing. You can use default network blocks or bring your own CIDRs if you need to. By default, Azure provides DNS for each network but allows you to use custom DNS services if you choose. Both public and private DNS services are available in Azure, giving you the flexibility to fine-tune DNS routing based on internally facing or externally facing destinations.

Network peering

Network peering is a resource that allows for two virtual networks to communicate with each other without using the public internet for traffic. In the case of a hub and spoke networking model, the hub is peered with each of the spokes to provide connectivity to shared resources. Spokes are not directly peered with one another, however. Peering is also involved with the use of ExpressRoute as it helps to effectively route traffic using the dedicated circuit and an organization's IP address space. In situations where connectivity is limited or even impossible, the use of services such as Azure Stack HCI or Azure Stack Edge provides the ability to run Azure cloud services on local physical hardware, which can later be connected to a peered network when it is available. This gives customers in verticals such as manufacturing, transportation, oil and gas, and others the ability to have a consistent application stack while still allowing for connectivity back to Azure to be intermittent or non-existent.

Azure Virtual Wide Area Network (WAN)

The Azure Virtual WAN service allows for a central control point to manage and monitor various networks related to a business. Typically, the virtual WAN is used to connect different physical offices to a central network location in Azure. WAN architectures can be very complex, depending on several factors, such as the number of locations, geographic regions, and even network bandwidth. Virtual WAN also supports point-to-site and site-to-site VPN connections, private connectivity using ExpressRoute, inter-cloud connectivity for multi-cloud configurations, ExpressRoute inter-connectivity, and standard features such as routing, Azure Firewall, and encryption to facilitate private connectivity.

For example, you may have a primary office location, six branch offices, and a dozen remote workers who all need to connect to Azure. Virtual WAN enables you to use ExpressRoute for the primary office location if desired, SD-WAN connections for each of the branches, and a VPN gateway to allow remote workers to safely connect to the network. Once connected, you could then add hub and spoke virtual networks as appropriate to facilitate network isolation and consistency in topologies.

Virtual Private Network (VPN) Gateway

The Azure VPN Gateway allows for traffic to flow between secured clients and a defined entry point in Azure. These typically are used to allow for **virtual private networks** (**VPNs**) and offer protected connectivity between either a client and Azure (point-to-site) or an office location and Azure (site-to-site). Controls such as client certificate authentication, IP restrictions for connectivity, and metered connections can be configured out of the box.

Network security groups

Similar to using the Linux-based IPTables utility to govern policies for inbound and outbound traffic, network security groups can be used to allow or restrict traffic between virtual networks, different subnets in different virtual networks, different subnets within the same virtual network, and more. They can be used either as the primary means of traffic control between network resources or in conjunction with other resources or devices, such as virtual network appliances in the case of a security perimeter.

Network security groups have two primary permission structures, namely, allowed traffic and denied traffic. Each directional flow can have a number of allow or deny policies depending on need. By default, when creating a network security group, a deny-all rule is added to both the inbound and outbound directional flows. When creating rules to allow traffic, it's important to order the policies such that the deny-all rule is the last rule in the chain. If it's not, any policies after the deny-all policy will be effectively ignored.

Typically, network security groups are used between subnets of an existing virtual network to help limit and guide traffic between segments. When dealing with many virtual networks or traffic management from the public internet, it's more common to see Azure Firewall or other virtual network appliances guarding the main entry point. This allows for more complex rulesets to be enforced based on traffic patterns and threat vectors, where network security groups provide a simpler means of controlling what is and is not allowed between specific segments.

Application security groups (**ASGs**) are a similar construct for allowing or denying traffic but are created using groups of virtual machines that represent a logical application boundary. Aside from using the grouping to define the traffic boundary, ASGs also do not need explicit IP addresses in the policy configurations, easing the burden of management. NSG policies do require an explicit address or range of addresses using CIDR notation.

Azure Content Delivery Network (CDN)

The Azure CDN service offers a globally distributed cache for static file content, whether that is for websites and web-based applications or for making updates available for device firmware or IoT endpoints. It has an optimized file storage and compression engine allowing for fast downloads of large files, including media files. Due to its global scale, spikes in traffic or regional outages can still be covered seamlessly.

Additionally, Azure CDN offers tight integration with many Azure platforms as a service component and integrates directly with Defender for Cloud, enabling you to configure DDoS protection and other safeguards. The ability to set up custom HTTPS domains to ensure content encryption helps to round out the protection capabilities that Azure CDN has to offer.

Traffic routing

Once the core components are selected for the network design, you will next need to consider how traffic flows from resource to resource, whether it originates from the public internet or from sources considered internal to your network. The following components help guide, filter, and protect network traffic on its journey through your network.

User defined routes (UDRs), route tables, and route filters

These services are configuration-based services that allow for fine-grained control over how network traffic flows between points on the network. With UDRs and route tables, you can completely control the path a network request takes. This can come in handy if you are using a custom DNS server or service and need to ensure traffic routes appropriately to use that service.

Load balancers (internal and external)

Azure load balancers are basic routing services used to control traffic flow between different destinations. They operate solely at the transport layer (Layer 4) and provide baseline functionality for directing traffic to backend targets. Load balancers can be set up to manage internal-only traffic or can be paired with a public IP to expose the load balancer to the internet. This service does not offer built-in functionality such as a web application firewall or DDoS protection. This service also does not allow for co-mingling of traffic, meaning that it can only manage one type of traffic at a time (either internal or external). If using load balancers to manage both types of traffic, you will need to deploy one for each traffic type to be managed.

Azure Front Door

Azure Front Door is a network service that sits at the edge of Microsoft datacenters, dealing primarily with content delivery. It covers communications at both Layer 4 and Layer 7 of the OSI stack. It is a high-performance caching layer that allows for storing static assets and distributing those assets across many regions. Azure Front Door can be used to bring high availability to static content for faster load times and consistent performance. It also facilitates global HTTP load balancing and failover and offers integrations with web application firewalls, DDoS protection, and bot protection.

From a security standpoint, Front Door allows you to use specific ingress points that are at the edge of Azure regions, thus minimizing your footprint with respect to allowed traffic and public IP space.

Azure Application Gateway

The Azure Application Gateway service is a sophisticated network service that allows for both Layer 4 and Layer 7 routing control, SSL offload, URL rewriting, multi-protocol routing, and cookie-based session affinity. App Gateway can handle custom configuration for dozens of custom domain names along with the requisite routing to backend destinations. Its flexibility makes it a commonly implemented service when it comes to controlling ingress traffic, especially from the public internet.

App Gateway also comes with a web application firewall built in, allowing for greater monitoring and prevention of malicious traffic. Alerts can be written using Azure Monitor to capture any potential threats, along with possible auto-remediation steps if your network design allows for it. Application Gateway can also be used to control traffic bound for Azure Kubernetes Service as an ingress controller. This approach could be used instead of using NGINX or a service mesh to control ingress routes.

Azure Traffic Manager

Azure Traffic Manager is a DNS-based managed Azure service that allows for network traffic to be sent to different destinations based on geography, preferred regions, and performance. The main goal of this service is to distribute traffic to components in Azure that may be single or multi-region, while still preserving responsiveness.

Enterprise network security

Some networking services cater to organizations that may have the need to connect or govern large amounts of resources in the cloud and do so with minimal friction. From virtual desktops to resource-specific endpoint configurations, let's look at some of the available networking services that fall into this bucket.

Azure Bastion

Azure Bastion is a fully managed Azure service that allows authorized users to connect to virtual machines without exposing those virtual machines directly to the internet via public IP. The Azure portal is the main ingress point, and users are directed in-browser to a specific virtual machine that is designated for them. Connection points include both Remote Desktop as well as SSH.

Bastion provides additional security controls by utilizing Azure Active Directory, which can be configured with conditional access and/or multi-factor authentication. These authentication conditions are applied before a potential user is even allowed to access the Azure portal, which adds an additional layer of security on top of any network security controls you may implement. Combined with **role-based access control (RBAC)**, it is possible to set fine-grained permissions to specific Azure compute resources to minimize the risk of unauthorized access or usage of cloud services.

If a user does not have Azure AD credentials but rather a username and password, or even a private SSH key, another option is available for granting direct access to a resource hosted in Bastion, which is the Bastion shareable link. This will bypass the Azure portal completely, reducing exposure to other resources in the portal by accident. Any credentials used for authenticating to a virtual machine using Bastion must be provided by the Azure or network administrator.

Private endpoints and service endpoints

Private endpoints are network interfaces that allow connectivity with private or internal networks and platform-as-a-service components. They help route traffic to and from PaaS components on the private network instead of routing traffic to the public endpoints. This allows organizations to treat certain PaaS components as resources that can only truly be reached from behind the firewall. Using private endpoints helps to keep traffic isolated and visible while aligning with a company's security posture. Private DNS zones are used to help route traffic to PaaS components using a private endpoint, using allocated IP blocks to force traffic through private peering connections instead of traversing the public internet. Traffic visibility is attainable through the use of troubleshooting utilities such as Azure Network Watcher or through Log Analytics queries against NSG flow logs.

Service endpoints are special endpoints meant to help isolate inbound and outbound traffic to the public endpoints of certain Azure services. For example, an organization has two applications, one of which works with and stores **personally identifiable information (PII)**. Both applications are domiciled in the same Azure region but have different requirements for accessing and storing data.

ExpressRoute

The ExpressRoute service is a managed physical connection between a connectivity provider and the Azure edge. It can be installed directly with your telecom provider or routed through a partner co-location such as Equinix. The service itself provides two dedicated network pipes that will connect from the provider directly to the Azure network, and the service will specifically route customer traffic through those pipes based on the size of the circuit the customer selects. Aside from facilitating lower latency between on-premises and Azure networks, ExpressRoute also offers peering capabilities, as mentioned earlier in this chapter.

Common cloud networking scenarios

As the industry changes, and along with it, the myriad of cloud services you can work with, so do the patterns available to organizations. Whether companies are looking to create one consolidated network footprint or isolate workloads from existing network segments, there are many potential solutions. Cloud services continue to mature and change, which inevitably makes it challenging to evaluate and implement the right solutions. The common scenarios companies encounter, however, tend to be similar. We'll look at some of those scenarios now.

Enterprise networks

The term "enterprise network" refers to any network estate within a company or organization that is comprised of various segments, security policies, and traffic types. They generally involve traffic flowing between one or more central offices and satellite or branch offices. The most likely use case that tends to arise is that of the hybrid network, where companies have a pre-existing network and wish to integrate an external cloud network with their existing network. While there are different options for integration, a popular option is to use ExpressRoute with private peering to enable a dedicated connection between an on-premises datacenter and a peering location, which then facilitates a direct connection to the Azure edge. *Table 4.1* shows the benefits and drawbacks of extending enterprise networks to the cloud.

Benefits	Drawbacks
Less network friction between on-premises resources and cloud resources	ExpressRoute installations can be costly
Traffic monitoring and visibility across the entire estate	The types of traffic and network load may not necessitate a dedicated circuit
Compatibility with existing monitoring and alerting tools, if desired	Locations of ExpressRoute providers may not be close enough in proximity to on-premises datacenters

Table 4.1: Benefits and drawbacks of extending enterprise networks to the cloud

While the notion of what defines an "enterprise" organization may vary, you will find that enterprises are generally larger organizations that have a mature datacenter presence across different geographic areas and a keen interest in enabling communication between datacenter resources and resources provisioned in the cloud. An example of such communication could be seen with an on-premises Active Directory service that virtual machines in the cloud could register with to ensure they are domain-joined.

Micro-segmentation

It is extremely common to see subnets within a virtual network to manage different workloads or components. An emerging security trend takes that a step further and carves subnets up into much smaller IP ranges that are relegated to specific workloads and use cases. This practice is known as `micro-segmentation`.

Principally, micro-segmentation is comprised of three areas:

- **Visibility**: Network traffic must be visible across all datacenters and cloud environments and be discernable down to the workload level

- **Granular security**: Each segment is governed by network security groups and access control policies to fine-tune how applications and data interact

- **Dynamic adaptation**: In the event of a compromise where a network may be exploited, each segment can be sealed off quickly as needed to protect other segments of the network from further attacks

Micro-segmentation can often be seen in organizations that have pivoted toward a zero-trust security posture, where the baseline premise is that exploits and compromises should be expected, and nothing should be trusted. *Table 4.2* outlines some benefits and drawbacks of adopting micro-segmentation.

Benefits	Drawbacks
Intentional and workload-centric isolation of traffic	Increased complexity in managing dozens, if not hundreds, of separate segments and the flow of traffic between them
Potential for using conventions to help control common types of communications between components and workloads	Compounded complexity of configuration across many regions, should you require multi-region footprints
A greatly reduced blast radius related to changing or isolating a segment on the network in the event it is compromised	Debugging and maintenance of applications can be adversely impacted via the degree of difficulty of troubleshooting as well as the restrictive nature of network controls

Table 4.2: Benefits and drawbacks to adopting network micro-segmentation

Micro-segmentation is useful for organizations that need to have granular control over network traffic flowing to applications as well as between components of those applications. Moreover, organizations that work with sensitive or confidential data may be more likely to implement micro-segmentation to enhance controls around traffic isolation as well as to provide quick measures to shut traffic down to a specific component or application in the event of a suspected or potential breach.

Virtual Network Appliances (VNAs) and security perimeters

It's expected that any company that has an on-premises datacenter also has a network security perimeter, often in the form of physical or virtual firewalls. Implementations may vary, but the core need is the same—protecting core workloads and isolating the exposure of websites and applications to the outside world. Many network appliance vendors, such as Palo Alto Networks, Netscalar, F5, and others, offer virtual network appliances that are virtualized copies of traditional on-premises physical devices. In addition, many of those vendors also offer reference architectures for establishing a security perimeter using those virtual network appliances, with the intent of better managing and monitoring traffic flow.

When looking to set up or understand a security perimeter using VNAs, there are two conceptual patterns to keep in mind, each referring to the flow of network traffic:

- **North/South**: This refers to the traffic that would be seen either entering or exiting the network via the public internet

- **East/West**: This refers to the traffic that would be flowing between resources within the internal network, behind the firewalls

Both concepts are employed when setting up a security perimeter, as ingress and egress need to be monitored just like inter-workload traffic. Ultimately, this gives the security and network teams the ability to further lock down (or allow) traffic between resources regardless of where the traffic is initiated from. *Table 4.3* illustrates some benefits and drawbacks of this approach.

Benefits	Drawbacks
A concentrated and centralized method to ensure traffic is only going where it needs to	The added expense of provisioning and maintaining VNAs as they are virtual machines
Vendor support for VNAs as well as assistance with the implementation of reference architectures	The added complexity of network management (VNA policies and network security groups)
Common control plane for monitoring and configuration	Increased difficulty in troubleshooting application issues, especially if both VNA policies and network security groups are in use
	Third-party VNAs are less integrated into the Azure ecosystem than platform-native tools, such as Azure Firewall or Azure Monitor

Table 4.3: Benefits and drawbacks of using VNA security perimeters

Normally, this type of pattern for securing network traffic can be seen in organizations that have a hybrid model that includes on-premises network appliances as well as cloud-based workloads that need to be governed by the same type of perimeter pattern. Many organizations that utilize network appliances from vendors such as Palo Alto, Kemp, NetScaler, and Barracuda often elect to extend that model into their cloud networking space to provide a single control surface for administration as well as monitoring and troubleshooting.

Capacity planning

As with traditional datacenters, capacity planning is still an exercise that needs to be performed. Current as well as anticipated future needs for workloads and application access will be areas that require additional scrutiny. There are differences in the types of capacity that require planning, however. Common scenarios include the following:

- **IP range planning**: In the case of using a hybrid network and managing a company's purchased IP ranges, it can become difficult to effectively automate and track usage of **classless inter-domain routing (CIDR)** blocks, which provide a range of IP addresses for assignment to virtual networks and subnets. Not properly tracking CIDR ranges could lead to network overlap and misconfigurations, which would invalidate virtual networks or subnets and render certain components impossible to reach. However, virtual networks and subnets do allow for dynamic resizing, and subnets will perform baseline validation of CIDRs when they are being created. This only holds true in cases related to the overall CIDR for a virtual network, however.

- **Capacity for autoscaling**: There will always be a need to plan out network space not only for the core needs of an application or workload but also for scenarios where autoscaling will be enabled. Extra capacity needs to be accounted for when autoscaling is enabled to ensure smooth operations during an event that would trigger a scale-up, such as hitting a limit on CPU or memory resources on a specific PaaS service. It's also important to use the elasticity of autoscaling operations to ensure services are only running for as long as they're needed and not left deployed and active if the scale is not required. Setting lower and upper limits in autoscaling configurations can help automatically manage this for certain services. Having a solid understanding of the traffic patterns and types of workloads being hosted in Azure, along with all relevant non-functional requirements, goes a long way in shaping the capacity needs of your network:

  - **Availability Zones**: When planning for autoscaling and using availability zones, you will need to plan out the range of IP addresses multiplied by the number of availability zones in use. For example, if you are using availability zones in a region that has three zones available, and the resource you are allowing to autoscale has a range of 1 to 5 units, your top end of available IP addresses for that resource's subnet needs to at a minimum be 5 * 3, or 15. This does not include IP addresses that are reserved by Azure for internal management.

  - **IP capacity for VM Scale Sets, AKS node pools, and other elastic services**: This is a slightly less complex planning exercise, but it is important to remember that any IP range being associated with a subnet attached to a scalable resource needs to have room for the upper limit of the scale action and room for one or two more beyond that. In some cases, where image updates or upgrades need to happen, it's possible to have a new resource spinning up while another is spinning down, and this could result in an overallocation of addresses. Leaving a little extra space in the subnet for maintenance operations will help alleviate this issue.

Failover and disaster recovery

Normal operations can be disrupted by any number of things, from individual cloud services being unavailable to entire Azure regions potentially being offline. As with on-premises datacenters, there is usually a backup or secondary location available in the event of a prolonged outage or a disaster. To facilitate planning for these situations, Azure has a few offerings available. In the case of virtual machine workloads, there is Azure Site Recovery, which allows for the replication of machine configurations and disk data between Azure regions. In many cases, regions have what is known as a cross-region replication pairing—a complimentary Azure region that is designed to act as a failover region. For example, East US has a natural pairing with West US.

Azure Site Recovery generally relates to the backup and recovery of virtual machines only. Using a simple example, let's suppose we have an application that has three virtual machines that host an **Internet Information Services (IIS)** application, one virtual machine that hosts several web services, and one virtual machine that hosts a SQL Server database. In this example, you would want to configure not only a backup virtual network for the recovered machines to fail over to but also a Recovery Services vault to store disk information about the virtual machines pertinent to your application. Upon a failover event, you could restore the virtual machines to the backup network using the failover capability of the vault. It's important to note that the vault needs to be provisioned in the region where failover would occur, not where the virtual machines normally live. Additional care needs to be exercised when planning for recovery as data egress charges will come into play when replicating managed disks between Azure regions. Another common scenario is deciding whether to use Azure as a disaster recovery target instead of using Azure to Azure failover and recovery. Some organizations choose to failover from on-premises datacenters to locations in Azure. This option can be useful for organizations that want to limit the cloud exposure they have but also use the potential speed of recovery that Azure can provide. This does not account for application data or secrets that may be stored in mechanisms such as file shares (i.e., distributed file services) or other locations that may not have a correlating service in Azure.

When planning out what to replicate and provision, well-known availability patterns can come into play, such as active-active and active-passive. It's clear that cost and time to recover can be the key factor in choosing these types of patterns and will need to be evaluated by an organization prior to implementation. Another lower-cost option is **just-in-time** (JIT) recovery, where essential information such as application data, configuration, secrets, and key disk resources are replicated to a failover region, and all other infrastructure is provisioned only when needed. For example, accounting for blob data that needs to be available in the event of a disaster would cause you to evaluate the use of storage accounts with geo-replicated data. In other cases, the use of globally available services such as Key Vault for secret, key-value configuration, and certificates ensure that the items you need will be available regardless of region. These types of services also help bolster business continuity plans as they provide seamless access to resources in the event of any disruption to services.

For more information about cross-region network pairings, please consult the following documentation: https://learn.microsoft.com/en-us/azure/reliability/ cross-region-replication-azure#azure-cross-region-replication- pairings-for-all-geographies

Monitoring and troubleshooting

Depending on the networking pattern you elect to implement, there may be tools you can use that are outside the purview of Azure to monitor and identify network traffic as well as network issues. From a platform perspective, Azure comes with a couple of useful services that can help not only monitor but troubleshoot network connections. The primary platform tool available to you is Network Watcher, which is a region-based utility allowing you to capture flow logs from NSGs, view traffic patterns, perform **packet captures** (**PCAPs**) on existing subnets or virtual networks, and even test connections between virtual machines in a subnet.

Network Watcher can be paired with Azure Monitor to enable logging capabilities (discoverable through Log Analytics queries) as well as alerting and auto-remediation policies if you choose to use them. While not completely comprehensive, it can help to identify whether NSGs are configured incorrectly, whether any blockages exist between two machines, or enable capturing traffic flows, which can be sent to either Log Analytics for further analysis or to an enterprise **security information and event management** (**SIEM**) system. Azure does provide a service for SIEM analytics in Azure Sentinel but also supports exporting event information to systems such as Splunk or IBM's QRadar.

Summary

In this chapter, we have examined the world of networking in Azure. We have reviewed several standard design patterns used when configuring and provisioning networking components, a list of many different Azure cloud networking services that are currently available, and a collection of common problem spaces that you may encounter when designing networks in the wild.

You've learned about core components such as virtual networks, subnets, and gateways. You've seen how the OSI model's representation of application communication can be applied to various available network services and when that can help drive decisions on when to use certain services. These decisions on what to use can be combined with those common problem spaces to ultimately provide a solution that will meet the needs of a business or organization.

In *Chapter 5*, we will cover cloud architecture design patterns, including patterns for serverless components, virtual machines, container orchestration, and more. We will explore how to automate the creation and maintenance of the infrastructure required to bring these patterns to life and look into how we can bake scalability and reliability into our design up front.

Automating Architecture on Azure

Introduction

Organizations place great emphasis on efficiency and accuracy, aiming to reduce manual effort and mitigate errors in their operations. Automation is a key enabler in achieving these objectives by bringing about predictability, standardization, and consistency across product development and operations.

As a leader in cloud computing technologies, Azure offers an extensive range of tools and services designed to empower organizations in deploying, operating, and overseeing the infrastructure of their applications and services in the cloud. While it is possible to build an infrastructure by manually creating Azure resources through the Azure portal, this can be time-consuming and tedious when dealing with intricate infrastructures that span multiple environments and regions. In such scenarios, automation emerges as the ideal solution.

Automation is important to business decision-makers and architects. It enables organizations to meet the fluctuating needs of customers by instituting a continuous process of delivering highly available, scalable, and reliable systems. Furthermore, automation offers numerous advantages, such as reducing errors, improving governance, streamlining maintenance processes, and simplifying administrative tasks.

In this chapter, we will explore how automation and **Infrastructure as Code (IaC)** play a crucial role in streamlining the provisioning and management of resources.

The importance of defining infrastructure using code

IaC is an essential tool for managing infrastructure in a cloud computing environment such as Azure. IaC is a methodology for managing and provisioning infrastructure through code. By adopting IaC practices, organizations can define their infrastructure requirements using code, allowing for consistent and repeatable deployments. With IaC, infrastructure configurations become reusable recipes that can be version-controlled, tested, and deployed with ease. This approach eliminates the need for manual configuration and reduces the risk of errors, saving significant time and effort in repetitive deployments. By embracing automation and IaC, organizations can achieve faster provisioning, improved consistency, and increased efficiency in their cloud deployments.

We will begin by looking at IaC and exploring why IaC is essential for automating the provisioning of Azure resources and infrastructure.

Why do we need to consider automating architectures on Azure using IaC?

IaC is a critical component of modern infrastructure management. It enables development teams to automate the process of creating, configuring, and managing infrastructure, making it easier to deploy and manage applications and services. IaC helps organizations manage infrastructure at scale by enabling them to define infrastructure as templates that can be deployed automatically. This enables organizations to manage complex infrastructure more easily and respond to changes in demand.

Here are some additional reasons why organizations need IaC:

- **Consistency**: IaC enables development teams to create and manage infrastructure in a consistent and repeatable way. By defining IaC, the code can be checked into version control systems, tested, and automatically deployed across multiple environments. This ensures consistency and reproducibility across environments, reducing the risk of errors and misconfigurations.

- **Efficiency**: IaC can help reduce the time and effort required to manage infrastructure by automating tasks such as provisioning, configuration, and deployment. This allows for focusing on more strategic work and reduces the risk of human error.

- **Speed**: IaC enables teams to automate the process of creating and configuring infrastructure in a quick and repeatable manner. This reduces the time it takes to provision infrastructure and helps with responding to changes in demand or business requirements faster. This automation also speeds up the development process and enables development teams to deliver new features and fixes to customers more quickly.

- **Scalability**: IaC enables teams to quickly and easily scale infrastructure up or down as needed, based on changing demand. Organizations can define IaC, and then use automation to quickly deploy and manage resources on Azure. This helps organizations to stay agile and responsive to changing customer needs.

- **Collaboration**: IaC promotes collaboration among developers, testers, and operations teams. It simplifies infrastructure management by enabling code sharing and review in version control systems. This improves communication and allows teams to work together more effectively.

- **Security**: IaC can improve security by enabling consistent security policies across environments and ensuring that security updates are applied consistently and in a timely manner.

- **Cost savings**: IaC can help reduce costs by enabling organizations to provision and deprovision infrastructure quickly and automatically, ensuring that they only pay for what they really need.

With IaC, infrastructure configurations are defined and managed through code, allowing for the automated and repeatable provisioning and management of resources. IaC ensures consistent provisioning and reduces errors from manual configuration. Additionally, IaC allows for the thorough testing of infrastructure configurations before they are deployed to production, ensuring that any issues or vulnerabilities are identified and addressed early on. This testing phase provides a higher level of confidence in the deployment process, as well as in the ongoing maintenance and governance of the infrastructure. With IaC, organizations can establish a robust and reliable deployment pipeline, enabling them to deliver infrastructure changes with greater efficiency and reliability.

Why is it important to define infrastructure using code rather than manual processes?

IaC provides significant advantages in reducing human error during deployments. By automating deployments through scripts or templates that have been thoroughly reviewed and tested, the likelihood of errors caused by manual intervention is greatly reduced. For instance, when redeploying a virtual network multiple times, human errors such as misspelling resource names, placing resources in the wrong resource group, or using incorrect naming conventions can be eliminated. This automation also ensures consistency across different environments, as manually deploying and maintaining multiple environments consistently can be challenging for humans. By implementing IaC, organizations can minimize the risk of human error and maintain the desired level of consistency across deployments and environments.

Understanding IaC

IaC is an essential practice within DevOps and a critical component of continuous delivery. It encompasses the management of infrastructure elements, including networks, compute services, databases, storage, and connection topology, through a descriptive model. By adopting IaC, teams can accelerate the development and release of changes across various environments while maintaining a high level of confidence. IaC enables DevOps teams to collaborate seamlessly, providing a unified set of practices and tools to swiftly and reliably deliver applications and their associated infrastructure at scale. This approach promotes agility, scalability, and consistency in the software delivery process, facilitating faster time-to-market and improved overall efficiency.

To get the most out of IaC, development teams should follow these principles:

- **Declarative definition**: IaC uses a declarative definition of infrastructure resources, which describes the desired state of the infrastructure, rather than the steps needed to create it. This approach allows for easier maintenance and repeatability, as changes to the infrastructure can be made by modifying the code rather than making manual changes. We will cover the declarative approach in more detail in the next section.

- **Version control**: IaC treats infrastructure resources as code and manages them using version control systems, such as Git. This allows teams to track changes, collaborate with others, and revert changes if necessary.

- **Idempotent**: IaC code should be idempotent, meaning that it can be run multiple times without changing the state of the infrastructure. This enables teams to easily make changes and roll back if necessary.

- **Testing**: IaC code should be thoroughly tested to ensure that it is working as intended and to catch and fix errors before they reach production environments. This includes testing for performance, security, and functionality.

- **Automation**: IaC emphasizes automation, using tools and scripts to automatically create and manage infrastructure resources. This improves efficiency and reduces errors, as manual intervention is minimized.

- **Reusability**: IaC promotes reusability by allowing teams to define infrastructure resources as modular components that can be used across different projects and environments. This reduces duplication and simplifies maintenance.

- **Consistency**: IaC ensures consistency across infrastructure resources by enforcing a standardized approach to their definition and deployment. This improves reliability and reduces the likelihood of errors caused by differences in configuration.

In the upcoming section, we will explore two distinct approaches to implementing IaC.

Two approaches to implementing IaC

There are two approaches that organizations can take when implementing IaC, namely the imperative approach and the declarative approach:

Imperative IaC	• This approach involves writing scripts in languages such as Azure CLI or PowerShell. • In this approach, we explicitly define the commands and steps needed to achieve the desired outcome. • With imperative deployments, we have control over the sequence of dependencies, error handling, and updates to resources. • While this approach offers flexibility and fine-grained control, it requires more manual management and can be prone to human error.
Declarative IaC	• This approach involves writing a definition that describes the desired state of an environment. • Instead of specifying the steps to achieve the desired outcome, you can focus on defining what the environment should look like. • The underlying tooling is responsible for examining the current state, comparing it with the desired state, and automatically applying the necessary changes to align the environment with the defined configuration. • This approach simplifies the management process by abstracting the implementation details and allows for easier maintenance and scalability.

In this chapter, we will focus on the declarative approach to IaC. Specifically, we will cover the three primary IaC frameworks for Azure:

- **Azure Resource Manager** (**ARM**) templates
- Bicep
- Terraform on Azure

Let's explore each of these IaC frameworks to understand their benefits and capabilities.

Azure Resource Manager templates

Azure Resource Manager (**ARM**) templates provide a native IaC solution specifically designed for Azure. These templates offer a declarative approach to defining and deploying Azure resources using **JavaScript Object Notation** (**JSON**) syntax. It is easy to manage and implement infrastructure changes effectively using ARM templates. The declarative nature of ARM templates allows for a clear representation of resources and their properties, simplifying the process of managing and deploying infrastructure configurations within the Azure environment.

Benefits of ARM templates

The real benefit of using the ARM template system is that it allows having declarative syntax. That means you can deploy any Azure resource and create the necessary infrastructure building blocks that go around it. Templates provide a process that can be run repeatedly in a very consistent manner to manage the desired state of the infrastructure. As a result, the template becomes the source of truth for those infrastructure resources. If you make changes to the infrastructure, it should be done through ARM templates.

In addition to the IaC benefits mentioned earlier, ARM templates offer the following additional benefits:

- **Parallel resource deployment**: The Azure deployment engine sequences resource deployments based on defined dependencies. If dependencies do not exist between two resources, they are deployed at the same time.

- **Modular deployments**: ARM templates can be broken up into multiple template files for reusability and modularization.

- **Day-one resource support**: ARM templates support all Azure resources and resource properties as they are released.

- **Extensibility**: Azure deployments can be extended by using deployment scripts and other automation solutions.

- **Validation**: Azure deployments are evaluated against a validation API to catch configuration mistakes.

- **No state or state files to manage**: Unlike Terraform, which we will cover in the following section, ARM templates do not maintain a state file. All states are stored in Azure. Users can collaborate and have confidence that their updates will be handled as expected.

- **Testing**: The **ARM template test toolkit** provides a static code analysis framework for testing ARM templates: `https://learn.microsoft.com/azure/azure-resource-manager/templates/test-toolkit`.

- **Change preview**: An ARM template **what-if operation** lets you see what will be changed before deploying an ARM template: `https://learn.microsoft.com/azure/azure-resource-manager/templates/deploy-what-if`.

- **Tooling**: Language service extensions are available for both **Visual Studio Code** and **Visual Studio** to help you author ARM templates.

Let's take a look at ARM templates in action with an example.

Automating deployments with ARM templates

The following example demonstrates a simple ARM template for deploying an Azure Storage account. It includes the definition of a parameter to accept a name for the storage account. Within the `resources` section, a storage account is defined, the `storageAccountName` parameter is used to provide a name, and the storage account details are specified:

```
{
    "$schema": "https://schema.management.azure.com/
schemas/2019-04-01/deploymentTemplate.json#",
    "contentVersion": "1.0.0.0",
    "parameters": {
        "storageAccountName": {
            "type": "string",
            "defaultValue": "newStorageAccount"
        }
    },
    "resources": [
        {
            "name": "[parameters('storageAccountName')]",
            "type": "Microsoft.Storage/storageAccounts",
            "apiVersion": "2019-06-01",
            "location": "[resourceGroup().location]",
            "kind": "StorageV2",
            "sku": {
                "name": "Premium_LRS",
                "tier": "Premium"
            }
        }
    ]
}
```

To learn more about ARM templates, use the following resources:

- https://learn.microsoft.com/azure/azure-resource-manager/templates/overview

- https://learn.microsoft.com/training/modules/create-azure-resource-manager-template-vs-code/

- https://learn.microsoft.com/samples/mspnp/samples/azure-well-architected-framework-sample-arm-template/

Bicep

Bicep was created to address the limitations of ARM templates. Bicep is a **Domain-Specific Language (DSL)** and an open-source project from Microsoft that provides a more concise and user-friendly way of defining ARM templates. It uses declarative syntax to deploy Azure resources and provides concise syntax, reliable type safety, and support for code reuse.

With Bicep files, you define the desired infrastructure and its properties for deployment. Notably, Bicep offers a more concise syntax compared to ARM templates, making it more accessible and easier to read and write for non-developers.

Benefits of Bicep

Bicep is designed to be easier to read, write, and maintain than ARM templates, while providing full backward compatibility with them. It is essentially a higher-level abstraction of ARM templates, which allows you to write IaC in a more declarative and readable way.

Bicep provides all the benefits that we stated earlier for ARM templates, with the following addition:

- **Cleaner syntax**: Bicep offers a cleaner syntax than ARM templates, reducing the code and providing a structured, modular approach for easier reading, writing, and maintenance. It allows developers to carry out the same tasks with less code, saving time and effort. Bicep also includes features such as parameter sets and modules for code reuse and consistency.

- **Type safety**: Bicep is a strongly typed language that provides type safety and compile-time checks, which helps to catch errors earlier in the development process.

- **Modularity**: You can break your Bicep code into manageable parts by using modules. The module deploys a set of related resources. Modules enable you to reuse code and simplify development, and it can be easily versioned and managed using source control tools such as Git.

- **Azure integration**: Bicep is designed specifically for Azure and provides a set of tools and features that make it easy to integrate with Azure services and resources.

- **Open source**: Bicep is an open-source project that is actively developed and maintained by Microsoft. This ensures that it will continue to evolve and improve over time.

- **Repeatable results**: Repeatedly deploy an infrastructure throughout the development lifecycle and have confidence that resources are deployed in a consistent manner. Bicep files are idempotent, which means that the same file can be deployed many times and get the same resource types in the same state. It makes it possible to develop one file that represents the desired state, rather than developing lots of separate files to represent updates.

- **Handling dependencies**: With Bicep, developers can define resource dependencies and the deployment order, which can help prevent errors and ensure that resources are deployed in the correct sequence.

- **Validation and linting tools**: Bicep supports validation and linting tools that can help identify potential errors or issues before deployment.

In summary, Bicep is a user-friendly and concise language that simplifies the authoring and maintenance of ARM templates. It provides a variety of benefits over ARM templates, including simplicity, reusability, type safety, Azure integration, and open-source development.

Let's take a look at Bicep in action with an example.

Automating deployments with Bicep

The following example demonstrates a simple Bicep file for deploying an Azure Storage account. It includes the definition of a parameter to accept a name for the storage account. Within the `resources` section, a storage account is defined, the `storageAccountName` parameter is used to provide a name, and the storage account details are specified:

```
param location string = resourceGroup().location
param storageAccountName string =
'stracct${uniqueString(resourceGroup().id)}'

resource storageAccount 'Microsoft.Storage/storageAccounts@2021-06-01'
= {
  name: storageAccountName
  location: location
  sku: {
    name: 'Standard_LRS'
  }
  kind: 'StorageV2'
  properties: {
    accessTier: 'Hot'
  }
}
```

To learn more about Bicep, refer to the following resources:

- https://learn.microsoft.com/azure/azure-resource-manager/bicep/overview

- https://learn.microsoft.com/azure/azure-resource-manager/bicep/frequently-asked-questions

- https://learn.microsoft.com/azure/azure-resource-manager/bicep/file

Terraform

Terraform, developed by HashiCorp, is an open source tool designed to simplify the management of cloud infrastructure using IaC principles. With Terraform configuration files, you can define the desired state of your infrastructure topology and efficiently provision and manage various types of infrastructure, including public clouds, private clouds, and SaaS services. By using Terraform providers, you can seamlessly integrate with different cloud platforms, ensuring a unified and consistent workflow for managing your entire infrastructure. This streamlined approach reduces manual effort, increases efficiency, and enhances the overall management of your cloud infrastructure.

Terraform operates as a declarative framework that empowers the deployment and configuration of infrastructure across multiple cloud platforms, including Azure. One of its key benefits is its cloud-agnostic nature, enabling users to implement the same framework across different cloud providers. While Terraform configurations are specific to each cloud environment, the overall structure and functionality of the framework remain consistent. These configurations are defined using the **HashiCorp Configuration Language** (HCL), a domain-specific language that offers a concise and expressive syntax for describing infrastructure resources and their dependencies. With Terraform, you can achieve efficient and scalable infrastructure management, promoting consistency and ease of use across your cloud deployments.

Benefits of Terraform

In addition to the IaC benefits mentioned earlier, Terraform offers the following additional benefits:

- **Supports multiple cloud providers and hybrid cloud environments**: Terraform is a cloud-agnostic tool, which means it allows you to provision and manage resources not only on Azure but also on other cloud providers and on-premises environments. This flexibility is beneficial for organizations with a multicloud or hybrid cloud strategy, enabling consistent management across different platforms.

- **Cloud resource abstraction**: Terraform abstracts away the complexity of native resource management interfaces in Azure, such as ARM templates. It provides a declarative and simplified syntax that is easier to read, write, and maintain. This abstraction allows you to define infrastructure resources using high-level constructs, making it more accessible to both infrastructure and application teams.

- **Large ecosystem and community**: Terraform benefits from a vast ecosystem and an active community. It has a rich library of community-contributed modules and provider plugins specific to Azure, which can be used to provision various Azure services and configurations. These resources save time and effort by providing reusable and battle-tested configurations. The community also offers extensive support, documentation, and knowledge sharing, making it easier to get started and resolve any issues.

- **State management**: Terraform maintains a state file that captures the current state of your infrastructure. This state file acts as a source of truth and helps Terraform understand the desired state compared to the current state. With Azure, Terraform can use Azure Storage to store the state file, enabling collaboration and synchronization among team members working on the same infrastructure.

- **Continuous integration and delivery (CI/CD) integration**: Terraform integrates well with CI/CD pipelines, allowing you to automate the infrastructure deployment process. By integrating Terraform with tools such as Azure DevOps or Jenkins, you can incorporate infrastructure changes into your existing CI/CD workflows, enabling end-to-end automation and ensuring that infrastructure updates are seamlessly deployed along with your application code.

Overall, Terraform brings the power of IaC, automation, cross-platform support, and a vibrant community to Azure infrastructure management. It enhances productivity, scalability, and reliability. At the same time, it enables the consistent and efficient provisioning of resources in the Azure cloud environment.

Let's take a look at Terraform in action with an example.

Automating deployments with Terraform

The following example demonstrates a simple Terraform configuration that deploys an Azure resource group and an Azure Storage account:

```
resource "azurerm_resource_group" "resgroup" {
  name     = "storageaccountRG"
  location = "eastus"
}

resource "azurerm_storage_account" "stracct" {
  name                     = "storageaccountname"
  resource_group_name      = azurerm_resource_group.resgroup.name
  location                 = azurerm_resource_group.resgroup.location
  account_tier             = "Standard"
  account_replication_type = "GRS"
}
```

It is important to note that the Terraform provider for Azure serves as an abstraction layer over the Azure APIs. This abstraction offers the advantage of hiding the complexities of the APIs, making it easier to interact with Azure resources using Terraform. However, this abstraction may result in some limitations in terms of feature parity with the Azure APIs. While the Terraform provider strives to cover a wide range of Azure capabilities, there may be certain advanced or latest functionalities that are not fully supported. It is recommended to review the documentation and stay updated on the provider's capabilities to ensure that your specific requirements align with the features offered by the Terraform provider for Azure.

To learn more about Terraform on Azure, read the following article: `https://learn.microsoft.com/azure/developer/terraform/overview`

Comparing ARM templates, Bicep, and Terraform

In order to achieve scalability, DevOps teams constantly seek methods for rapidly deploying code using a reliable and repeatable process. For cloud infrastructure, this process is achieved through IaC.

In the preceding sections, we introduced three popular IaC frameworks: ARM templates, Bicep, and Terraform.

The following article aims to compare nine infrastructure and integration features of ARM templates, Bicep, and Terraform: `https://learn.microsoft.com/azure/developer/terraform/comparing-terraform-and-bicep`

By understanding these distinctions, organizations can determine which tool best aligns with their infrastructure and processes, aiding in making informed decisions.

Let's continue, in the next section, to explore reusable IaC modules.

Creating reusable IaC modules

One of the primary objectives of deploying infrastructure using code is to eliminate redundancy and the need for multiple templates serving similar purposes. The key is to create reusable and flexible infrastructure modules that serve a specific and well-defined purpose. This approach ensures efficiency and avoids duplicating work, allowing for the streamlined deployment and management of infrastructure resources.

Modules in IaC are self-contained files that consist of a collection of resources meant to be deployed together. They serve the purpose of breaking down complex templates into smaller, more manageable sets of code. By using modules, we can ensure that each module has a specific task or responsibility and that these modules can be reused across multiple deployments and workloads. This modular approach promotes code reusability, simplifies maintenance, and improves the overall manageability of our infrastructure deployments.

> **Note**
> While it is possible to modularize ARM template files using JSON syntax, Bicep is the preferred solution. Bicep offers an easier and more concise syntax when compared to the equivalent JSON ARM templates.

Bicep modules

With Bicep, you have the ability to create and utilize modules. Once modules are defined, they can be easily consumed from any other Bicep template. A well-structured Bicep module should encapsulate multiple interconnected resources. For instance, when setting up an Azure function, you typically need to deploy the application itself, a hosting plan to support it, and a storage account to store its metadata. While these components can be defined separately, it is advisable to group them together as a module due to their logical relationship. By defining them as a module, you can ensure a cohesive and reusable set of resources for your Azure function deployment.

Bicep modules commonly use the following:

- **Parameters** to accept values from a calling module
- **Output values** to return results to a calling module
- **Resources** to define one or more infrastructure objects for a module to manage

Publishing Bicep modules

You have several options for publishing and sharing Bicep modules based on your preferences:

- **Public registry**: If you prefer to use the public module registry that is hosted in a Microsoft container registry, its source code and the modules it contains are stored in GitHub (`https://github.com/azure/bicep-registry-modules`).
- **Private registry**: If you prefer to create your own modules tailored to your specific organizational requirements, you can use Azure Container Registry to publish modules to a private registry. For information on publishing modules to a registry in a CI/CD pipeline, refer to the following:
  - **Bicep and GitHub Actions**: This Microsoft Learn module shows you how to publish reusable Bicep code by using GitHub Actions (`https://learn.microsoft.com/training/modules/publish-reusable-bicep-code-using-github-actions/`).
  - **Bicep and Azure Pipelines**: This Microsoft Learn module shows you how to publish reusable Bicep code using Azure Pipelines (`https://learn.microsoft.com/training/modules/publish-reusable-bicep-code-using-azure-pipelines/`).
- **Template spec**: Template specs are meant to be complete templates, but Bicep allows you to use template specs to deploy modules. You can use template specs to publish Bicep modules (`https://learn.microsoft.com/azure/azure-resource-manager/bicep/template-specs`).
- **Version control system**: You can load modules directly from version control tools such as GitHub or Azure DevOps.

Terraform modules

Terraform provides the capability to create and call modules. In a Terraform configuration, there is always a root module, which includes the resources defined in `.tf` files located in the main working directory. This root module serves as the entry point for the configuration. Also, modules can be called and utilized within the main configuration file. This allows you to include child modules, organizing your infrastructure into logical components. Additionally, modules can be invoked multiple times within the same configuration or across different configurations, enabling reusability and modularity in your infrastructure provisioning.

Modules are defined with all of the same configuration language concepts. They most commonly use the following:

- **Input variables** to accept values from a calling module
- **Output values** to return results to a calling module
- **Resources** to define one or more infrastructure objects for a module to manage

Publishing Terraform modules

You have several options for publishing and sharing Terraform modules based on your preferences:

- **Public registry**: HashiCorp has its own Terraform module registry that allows users to generate shareable Terraform modules. There are currently several Azure modules published in the Terraform module registry (`https://registry.terraform.io/namespaces/Azure`).
- **Private registry**: You can seamlessly publish Terraform modules to a private repository such as Terraform Cloud Private Registry or Azure Container Registry.
- **Version control system**: You can load private modules directly from version control tools such as GitHub (`https://developer.hashicorp.com/terraform/language/modules/sources`).

One of the best use cases for IaC is for automating the provisioning of **Azure landing zones**. In particular, both Bicep and Terraform are fully supported and widely adopted for provisioning Azure landing zones. In the next section, we will explore the use of IaC with Bicep and Terraform to automate the creation of Azure landing zones.

Automating Azure landing zone provisioning with IaC

For organizations dealing with multiple workloads in the cloud, the need for repeatable and consistent environments is paramount. Azure landing zones serve as a solution to this challenge by offering a standardized approach to configuring environments. These landing zones provide central operations teams, also known as platform teams, with a consistent framework for environmental configuration. By incorporating common design areas, reference architecture, reference implementation, and a flexible deployment process, Azure landing zones enable organizations to achieve consistent and tailored environments that align with their specific design requirements.

The Azure landing zone can be deployed in one of the following ways.

Azure landing zone accelerators

If an organization prefers to not develop its own IaC solutions from scratch, there is an option offered by Azure called the landing zone accelerator. Azure landing zone accelerators provide a portal experience (see *Figure 5.1*) for deploying preprovisioned ARM template code, along with tools and controls to quickly reach a security baseline:

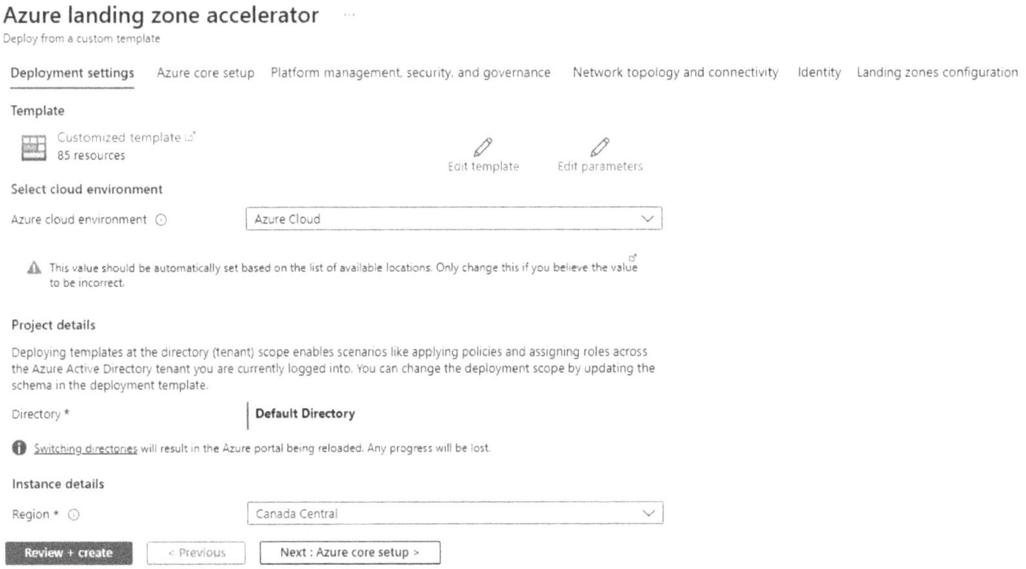

Figure 5.1: Azure landing zone accelerators

To learn more about **Azure landing zone accelerators**, check out the following links:

- `https://learn.microsoft.com/azure/cloud-adoption-framework/
  ready/landing-zone/#azure-landing-zone-accelerator`
- `https://learn.microsoft.com/azure/cloud-adoption-framework/
  ready/landing-zone/design-area/security#security-in-the-azure-
  landing-zone-accelerator`

Azure landing zone – Bicep modules

If your organization is considering IaC deployment options, this is one of the recommended approaches.

The Azure landing zone – Bicep modules allow you to deploy and manage the core platform capabilities of the Azure landing zone conceptual architecture as detailed in the **Cloud Adoption Framework (CAF)**.

To learn more about the Azure landing zone – Bicep modules, check out the following links:

- `https://learn.microsoft.com/azure/architecture/landing-zones/
  bicep/landing-zone-bicep`
- `https://github.com/Azure/ALZ-Bicep`

Azure landing zone – Terraform modules

If your organization is considering IaC deployment options, this is one of the recommended approaches.

The Azure landing zone – Terraform modules provide you with an opinionated approach to deploy and operate an Azure platform based on the Azure landing zone conceptual architecture as detailed in the CAF.

To learn more about the Azure landing zone – Terraform modules, check out the following links:

- `https://learn.microsoft.com/azure/architecture/landing-zones/
  terraform/landing-zone-terraform`
- `https://registry.terraform.io/modules/Azure/caf-enterprise-
  scale/azurerm/latest`

We will learn more about the benefits of using IaC for Azure landing zones in the next section.

Why should we use IaC to build Azure landing zones?

In this section, we will explain why we should use IaC to build Azure landing zones.

Building Azure landing zones using IaC provides the following key benefits:

- Maintaining a complete history of infrastructure changes
- Providing testing environments
- Catching configuration drifts
- Gaining higher confidence
- Managing multiple environments
- Better understanding your cloud resources
- Reducing effort
- Reducing errors

We will explain why each of these benefits is important in the following subsections.

Maintaining a complete history of infrastructure changes

IaC deployments offer the advantage of being backed by a definition file, which enables you to use source control systems to manage the versions of your infrastructure definitions.

Whether you are using Bicep or Terraform, you can store your definition files in a source control repository, allowing you to track changes, collaborate with team members, and roll back to previous versions if needed.

Using source control and the history of deployments, you can maintain a clear record of changes made to your infrastructure definitions over time. This audit trail of modifications enables you to track the evolution of your infrastructure and understand the reasons behind specific configurations or decisions.

Second, source control ensures reproducibility by providing a reliable and versioned source of truth for your infrastructure definitions. You can confidently roll back to previous versions if needed or create new branches for experimentation without impacting the main deployment.

Third, source control facilitates collaboration among team members. Multiple individuals can work concurrently on different branches or collaborate on the same code base by utilizing features such as pull requests, code reviews, and merge approvals. This promotes efficient teamwork and ensures that changes are thoroughly reviewed before being merged into the main code base.

Also, the history of deployments stored in source control helps with traceability. You can easily trace back any issues or incidents to specific changes in the code base, making troubleshooting and debugging more efficient.

Testing environments

The repeatability of IaC deployments allows you to use the same definition to deploy multiple environments based on the desired configuration. This capability is particularly valuable when testing changes before implementing them in a production environment.

Let's consider an example where you want to upgrade your Azure Firewall to the Premium SKU. Instead of directly modifying the production environment, you can use IaC to deploy a separate test environment that mirrors your production setup. By applying the desired changes to the test environment's IaC definition, you can validate the effects and performance of the upgrade without impacting the production environment.

This approach offers several benefits.

- It mitigates the risks associated with making changes directly in a live production environment. By testing the modifications in an isolated environment, you can identify any potential issues or conflicts before applying them to the critical production infrastructure.

- Deploying a test environment using the same IaC definition allows for accurate comparison and validation. You can closely observe the behavior and performance of the upgraded Azure Firewall in the test environment and assess its impact on your applications and network.

- The test environment provides an opportunity for collaboration and gathering feedback from stakeholders, ensuring that all necessary validations and verifications are conducted before implementing the changes in production. This collaborative approach helps to minimize errors and make informed decisions based on real-world testing.

Once the changes have been thoroughly tested and validated in the test environment, you can confidently apply the same IaC definition to update the production environment. This ensures consistency and reduces the chances of misconfigurations or human errors during the deployment process.

Catching configuration drifts

IaC offers a valuable capability to detect and address configuration drift during updates. By comparing the deployed resources with the definition file, IaC deployments can identify instances where the resource configuration deviates from the intended state.

When using IaC to update Azure landing zones, you have the opportunity to catch and rectify configuration drift. If any misconfigurations are detected, you can update the code accordingly to align the deployment with the desired configuration, or address the discrepancies through other means.

In scenarios where changes are made to resources directly through the Azure portal, **command-line interface (CLI)**, or other non-IaC methods, these modifications take effect immediately. However, the next time you perform an IaC deployment, the comparison between the code-defined state and the actual state in the portal can be highlighted using functions such as `what-if` or `plan`. This comparison helps identify whether any changes were made outside of the code file, indicating potential configuration drift.

Once configuration drift is identified, you can use IaC to attempt to realign the deployment with the definition. Depending on the nature of the issues and the specific IaC tool being used, different actions can be taken to remediate the drift. For instance, Terraform aims to restore the baseline configuration for the resources it has deployed. On the other hand, a complete mode deployment in Bicep removes any resources in a resource group that are not part of the definition.

Although IaC tools are designed to detect and repair configuration drift, it is important to note that they may not address all possible issues. Some complex scenarios might require additional manual intervention or specific remediation actions beyond what the IaC tool offers.

Changes that are defined in the portal are cumbersome to implement back into IaC. You must update the code to match the current state, which often involves reviewing each resource change and updating its parameters to match the "as-is" configuration.

If you use IaC to manage your landing zone or other resources, you should only make changes outside of IaC as part of an emergency. Always take the necessary precautions with accounts that have access to make manual changes directly.

Gaining higher confidence

One of the main advantages of IaC is the increased confidence it provides in deployments and your understanding of the infrastructure's configuration:

- **Integrate with your process**: If you implement a peer review system for code changes, you can extend the same process to review infrastructure changes. This approach enables the early identification of problematic configurations that may be overlooked during manual infrastructure modifications, offering proactive detection.

- **Consistency**: By adhering to an IaC process, teams can ensure that a standardized and well-established process is followed. Traditionally, organizations relied on a single or a few individuals to handle infrastructure deployment and configuration. However, with a fully automated process, the responsibility for these tasks shifts from individuals to the automation process and tools. This transition allows a wider range of team members to initiate infrastructure deployments while still maintaining consistency and ensuring high-quality outcomes.

- **Automated scanning**: Automated tooling can scan various types of IaC configurations. One example is linting tools, which identify code errors and inconsistencies. Another type of tool scans proposed changes to Azure infrastructure, verifying adherence to security and performance best practices. Incorporating automated scanning into the workflow is crucial for implementing a continuous security approach.

- **Secret management**: In many cases, managing and safeguarding secrets is a necessary aspect of solution development. This includes maintaining connection strings, API keys, client secrets, and certificates. When adopting an IaC approach, it becomes crucial to implement best practices for secret management. Azure Key Vault, for instance, serves as a secure repository for storing secrets. It seamlessly integrates with various IaC tools and configurations, enabling deployments to be conducted without requiring access to production secrets. By adopting this approach, the principle of least privilege is upheld, enhancing security measures.

- **Access control**: A fully automated IaC deployment pipeline means that an automated process should perform all changes to your infrastructure resources. This approach has many security benefits. By automating your deployments, you can be confident that changes deployed to your environment have followed the correct procedure. You can even consider expanding the number of people who can initiate a deployment since the deployment itself is done in a fully automated way. Ideally, you would remove the ability for humans to manually modify your cloud resources and instead rely completely on automated processes. In emergencies, you can allow for this ability to be overridden, by using a break-glass account or privileged identity management.

- **Avoid configuration drift**: When you use IaC, you can redeploy all of your environment templates on every release of your solution. The beauty of IaC tooling lies in its idempotent nature, ensuring that it can be executed multiple times while consistently producing the same outcome.

Frequently running IaC operations has the following benefits:

- **Avoiding deployment staleness**: Regularly running IaC operations helps prevent unforeseen issues that may arise during redeployment, such as those encountered in a disaster recovery scenario.

- **Reducing complexity**: By consistently practicing a single, well-rehearsed process, the overall complexity of managing the infrastructure is reduced.

- **Preventing configuration drift**: Executing infrastructure changes through the established pipeline helps prevent configuration drift. Any unintentional modifications made outside of the regular pipeline can be swiftly corrected, ensuring that the code remains the authoritative source of truth for the environment's configuration.

Managing multiple environments

Many organizations manage multiple environments, for example, testing, staging, and production. In certain cases, multiple production environments are maintained for multitenant solutions or geographically distributed applications. Ensuring consistency across these environments can pose challenges; using IaC solutions can help:

- **Manage non-production environments**: Organizations often encounter difficulties when their non-production environments differ from their production environments. Manual construction of these environments frequently leads to configuration inconsistencies between them. This discrepancy hampers the testing of changes and undermines confidence in the safety of deploying them to a production system. Fortunately, adopting an IaC approach can alleviate this problem. By using IaC automation, the same set of infrastructure configuration files can be utilized for all environments, resulting in nearly identical setups. When necessary, differentiation can be achieved by employing input parameters specific to each environment. This ensures consistency across environments, streamlines the testing process, and enhances confidence in the deployment of changes.

- **Dynamically provision environments**: After defining your IaC configurations, you can use them to efficiently provision new environments. This agility proves immensely valuable when conducting solution testing. For instance, you can rapidly create a replica of your production environment, which can then be utilized for activities such as security penetration tests, load testing, or assisting developers in bug tracking. This capability empowers you to swiftly set up the necessary environments for various purposes, enhancing the testing and troubleshooting processes.

- **Scale production environments**: IaC configurations allow for the deployment of multiple instances of your solution, ensuring consistency across all environments. This approach proves particularly valuable when following specific deployment patterns or when expanding services to new geographic regions. One such example is the Deployment Stamps pattern, where IaC enables the efficient and consistent deployment of solution instances across various locations.

- **Disaster recovery**: In certain scenarios where the recovery time is not critical, IaC configurations can be employed as a component of a disaster recovery plan. For instance, if there is a need to recreate infrastructure in a secondary region, your IaC configurations can facilitate this process. However, it is essential to carefully consider factors such as deployment time, restoring the state of your infrastructure, and the actual infrastructure components themselves when implementing a disaster recovery strategy. This ensures that the recovery process is efficient and effectively aligns with your specific requirements.

When you plan for disaster and recovery, ensure that your disaster recovery plans are fully tested and that they meet your business metrics: https://learn.microsoft.com/azure/well-architected/resiliency/business-metrics.

Better understanding your cloud resources

IaC can also help you better understand the state of your cloud resources:

- **Audit changes**: By version-controlling your IaC configurations, similar to coding with tools such as Git, you gain the ability to review and track changes, including who made them and when they occurred. This audit trail can be valuable when investigating the reasoning behind specific resource configurations.

- **Metadata**: Many IaC configurations support the inclusion of metadata, such as code comments, which can provide explanations for why certain approaches were chosen. If your organization has a culture of documenting code, apply the same principles to your infrastructure code.

- **Keep everything together**: It is common for a developer to work on features that require both code and infrastructure changes. By keeping infrastructure defined as code, you can group application and infrastructure code to understand the relationship between them better. For example, if you see a change to an IaC configuration on a feature branch or in a pull request, you'll have a clearer understanding of what that change relates to.

- **Better understanding Azure itself**: While the Azure portal is a great way to provision and configure resources, it often simplifies the underlying resource model used. Using IaC means that you gain a deeper understanding of what's happening in Azure and how to troubleshoot it if something isn't working correctly. For example, when creating a set of virtual machines in the Azure portal, some of the underlying resource creation is abstracted for the deployment process. When you use IaC, not only do you have explicit control over resource creation but also little is abstracted from the process, which provides a richer understanding of what's deployed and how it's configured.

Reducing effort

Using IaC to perform updates requires less effort compared to manual changes. IaC deployments provide answers to crucial questions such as the current resource configuration, the planned configuration after the update, and the necessary changes to align with the update. When an IaC toolset is executed, it can generate a comparison or "differential" report showcasing the modifications. Reviewing this report before committing the changes to the environment is essential.

By relying on an IaC toolset, information regarding the changes can be compiled automatically, eliminating the need for an operator or engineer to manually assess and track the modifications. This streamlines the update process and ensures accuracy in capturing the intended changes.

Reducing errors

IaC significantly mitigates the risk of human error during deployments by facilitating programmatic and automated modifications to infrastructure. By relying on IaC, changes are implemented according to the predefined configuration, minimizing the potential for unintended alterations. Additionally, IaC offers preview functionality, allowing users to review and validate changes before applying them. This preview option effectively reduces the probability of service disruptions caused by incomplete or erroneous modifications, enhancing the overall reliability and stability of the deployment process.

In the final section of the chapter, we will learn about automating architectures on Azure using Azure DevOps and GitHub.

Best practices for automating architectures on Azure

Azure DevOps and GitHub are both popular platforms for managing software development projects and collaborating on code.

Azure DevOps is a comprehensive set of tools and services for building, testing, and deploying applications and infrastructure on Azure. It provides a powerful platform for DevOps teams to manage their entire application lifecycle, from planning and coding to testing, deployment, and monitoring. Azure DevOps includes several components, such as Azure Repos, Azure Pipelines, Azure Boards, Azure Test Plans, and Azure Artifacts, which can be used independently or together to automate various aspects of the DevOps process.

GitHub is a web-based hosting service for version control using Git. Similar to Azure DevOps, GitHub provides a platform for collaborative development and allows developers to host and review code, manage projects, and build software.

Here are some common benefits offered by both Azure DevOps and GitHub:

- Azure DevOps and GitHub provide version control for managing IaC files (such as ARM templates, Bicep, and Terraform). This allows organizations to track changes, collaborate with others, and revert changes if necessary. This helps to ensure that infrastructure code is consistent and reliable.

- Azure DevOps and GitHub support CI/CD, which allows organizations to automate the testing and deployment of their IaC files. Not only does this help to ensure that changes are tested and deployed quickly and reliably but also a CI/CD pipeline enforces a standardized and reusable process that guarantees the quality and consistency of deployments in the Azure environment.

- Azure DevOps and GitHub provide collaboration features, such as pull requests and code reviews, which allow team members to work together to improve the quality of their IaC files.

- Azure DevOps and GitHub integrate with a wide range of other tools, such as build systems, testing frameworks, and deployment tools, which allows teams to customize their CI/CD pipeline to meet their specific needs.

- Azure DevOps and GitHub provide security features, such as access controls and secrets management, which help to ensure that the infrastructure code is secure, protected, and only accessible to authorized team members.

To ensure the efficient and reliable provisioning of Azure landing zones using IaC, it is strongly recommended that organizations incorporate GitHub Actions or Azure Pipelines into their automation orchestration.

Both Azure DevOps and GitHub provide extensive functionalities for managing the deployment process, enabling seamless integration with IaC workflows. By using these tools, organizations can streamline the provisioning of Azure landing zones, enhance consistency, and promote best practices in their infrastructure management practices.

To learn more, please read the following articles:

- `https://learn.microsoft.com/training/modules/publish-reusable-bicep-code-using-github-actions/`

- `https://learn.microsoft.com/training/modules/publish-reusable-bicep-code-using-azure-pipelines/`

- `https://learn.microsoft.com/azure/cloud-adoption-framework/ready/considerations/infrastructure-as-code`

- `https://learn.microsoft.com/azure/cloud-adoption-framework/ready/considerations/development-strategy-development-lifecycle`

We will continue to share more best practices and tips for using IaC in the next section.

Best practices for using IaC

To wrap up this chapter, we will share some additional best practices and tips for using IaC:

- Use Git as a version control system to track and manage IaC changes.

- Use private repositories when building Azure landing zones to protect sensitive infrastructure configurations and information, and to ensure that only authorized members are permitted to view or edit the files in the private repositories.

- Use public repositories when sharing non-confidential information, such as open source collaboration material, public documentation, and automation examples.

- Adopt an IaC approach for deploying, managing, governing, and supporting Azure landing zone deployments, as we explained in detail earlier in this chapter.

When considering IaC deployments, it is crucial to take into account the deployment scopes within the Azure management levels and hierarchy (refer to *Figure 5.2*). Understanding the appropriate scope at which Azure resources should be deployed is essential for effective IaC implementations.

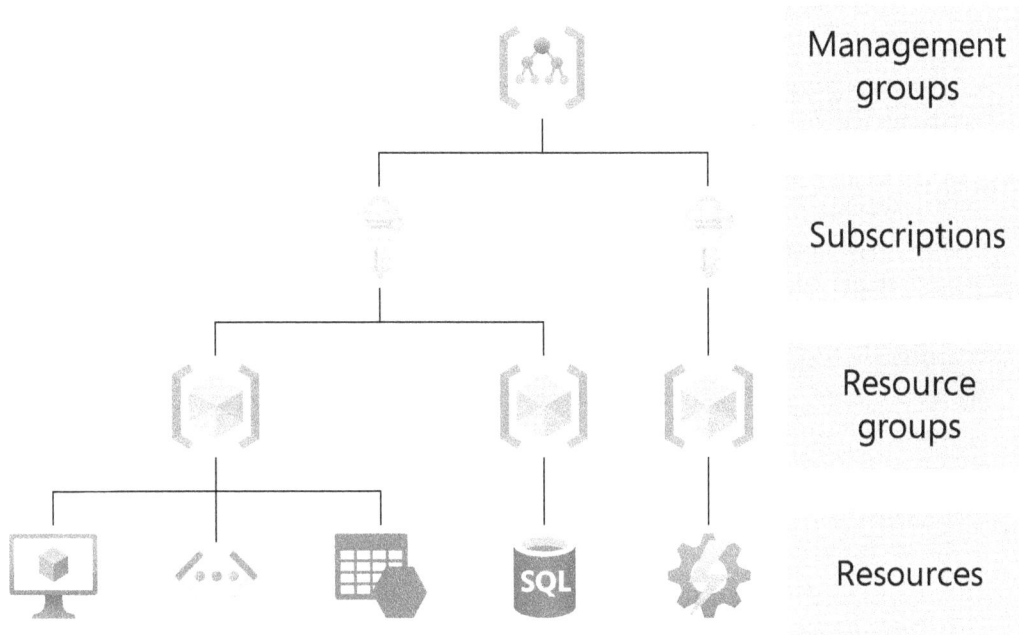

Figure 5.2: Azure management levels and hierarchy

- Evaluate whether to utilize an Azure native or Azure non-native IaC tool, taking into account the following considerations:

  - Use **Azure native tools for IaC** in the following scenarios:

    - You want to use only Azure native tools. Your organization might have previous ARM or Bicep template deployment experience.

    - Your organization wants to have immediate support for all preview and GA versions of Azure services.

    - Azure native tools such as Azure CLI, ARM templates, and Bicep are fully supported by Microsoft, which allows their new features to be integrated faster.

  - Use **non-native tools for IaC** in the following scenarios:

    - Your organization currently uses Terraform to deploy infrastructure to other clouds, such as AWS or GCP.

- Your organization does not need to have immediate support for all preview and GA versions of Azure services.

- Non-native tools such as Terraform allow you to manage IaC across multiple cloud providers, such as AWS or GCP. However, new Azure features can take some time to be included in non-native tools.

- If your organization is multicloud or is already using and well versed in Terraform, consider using Terraform to deploy Azure landing zones.

- Use IaC modules to streamline the deployment of commonly grouped resources. Modules allow you to break down complex templates into smaller, reusable sets of code, focusing on specific tasks. By using modules, you can enhance reusability across multiple deployments and workloads, improving the efficiency and maintainability of your IaC implementations.

- When adopting a publishing strategy for IaC modules, consider selecting between public registries or private registries, or use a version control system such as a Git repository. Assess the specific requirements and constraints of your organization to determine the most suitable approach for sharing and distributing IaC modules effectively.

- Implement a CI/CD pipeline for IaC deployments. By using a pipeline, you can enforce a standardized and reusable process that guarantees the quality and consistency of your deployments in the Azure environment.

- Use reusable IaC modules to avoid repetitive work. By sharing modules across your organization, you can streamline the deployment of multiple projects or workloads, reducing complexity in your code base. This approach promotes code reuse and enhances maintainability.

- Be sure to review the support statement provided by any module provider you consider to ensure that it meets the level of support required by your organization.

- Consider publishing and utilizing IaC modules from **public registries** in the following scenarios:

  - If you intend to use modules for Azure landing zones that have already been published to public registries

  - If you prefer to use modules that are actively maintained, regularly updated, and supported by reputable entities such as Microsoft, Terraform, or other recognized module providers

- Consider publishing and utilizing IaC modules from **private registries** or version control systems in the following scenarios:

  - If you prefer to create your own modules tailored to your specific organizational requirements

  - If you want complete control over all features of the modules and the ability to maintain, update, and publish new versions as needed

By harnessing these best practices, organizations can streamline processes, enhance productivity, and drive innovation in an increasingly competitive landscape.

Summary

In this chapter, we saw how automation on Azure can be achieved using IaC.

We learned about the importance of IaC and how it allows for the consistent and repeatable creation and management of infrastructure. Defining infrastructure using code is important because it facilitates code sharing, review, and version control, which ultimately enhances communication and minimizes the occurrence of errors.

We also explored the various tools available for implementing IaC in Azure, including ARM templates, Bicep, and Terraform.

Implementing IaC with these tools allows for automated deployments and benefits such as reusable modules, maintaining infrastructure history, testing environments, catching configuration drifts, gaining higher confidence, managing multiple environments, and reducing effort and errors.

To wrap up this chapter, we shared some best practices and tips for automating architectures on Azure, emphasizing the use of Azure DevOps, GitHub, and IaC.

In the next chapter, we will look at how to optimize performance with Azure OLTP solutions.

6

Optimize Performance with Azure OLTP Solutions

Data management is at the heart of every application. Whether those applications need real-time updates for business-critical functions or asynchronous updates for longer-running processes, Azure offers a wide variety of services that are up to the task. Azure provides many different options for storing structured and non-structured data, such as Azure Blob Storage, Table Storage, Cosmos DB, Azure SQL Database, and Azure Data Lake. While some of these options are meant for big data storage, analytics, and presentation, there are others that are meant for applications that process transactions.

This chapter will focus on various aspects of using transactional data stores, such as Azure SQL Database and other open source databases that are typically used in **online transaction processing** (**OLTP**) systems, and will cover the following topics:

- OLTP:

  - Properties/traits

  - When this solution should be used

- OLTP in Azure:

  - Azure SQL

  - Azure SQL Managed Instance

  - Cosmos DB

  - Azure Database for PostgreSQL

  - Azure Database for MySQL

  - Choosing the right service

- Scenarios for analytics:

  - Transactional querying

  - Datamarts and data warehouses:

    - Timeboxing transactional versus historical data

    - **Azure Data Lake Generation 2 (ADL Gen2)**

  - Azure Synapse Analytics

  - Azure Databricks

- Pricing and cost optimization

We will begin by exploring common properties and traits of transactional data, scenarios in which OLTP applications are suitable, followed by a comprehensive overview of Azure's OLTP services and their respective use cases.

OLTP applications

OLTP applications help in the processing and management of transactions. Some of the most widely used OLTP implementations can be found in retail sales, financial transaction systems, and order entry. These applications perform data capture, data processing, data retrieval, data modification, and data storage. Let's dive into transactional data a bit further.

Transactional data

The capture and usage of data that encompasses a record of business interaction is generally referred to as a transaction. Information related to creating purchase orders, sales at a cash register, a deposit at a bank, or collection of a bus fare can all be considered transactional. Systems that manage this type of data can vary in size dependent on the volume of transactions handled, as well as regional location requirements, the structure of data being stored, the security requirements for storing and processing the data, or consistency requirements that mandate near-real-time data availability.

Traits and properties

OLTP applications have a few important properties for which they are accountable. These properties are grouped under the acronym **ACID**. Let's discuss these properties in detail:

- **Atomicity**: Atomicity means each transaction is treated as the lowest single unit of execution that either completes successfully or fails. This property states that a transaction must consist of statements and either all statements should complete successfully or no statement should be executed. If multiple statements are grouped together, these statements form a transaction.

- **Consistency**: This property focuses on the state of data in a database. It dictates that any change in state should be complete and based on the rules and constraints of the database, and that partial updates should not be allowed.

- **Isolation**: This property states that there can be multiple concurrent transactions executed on a system and each transaction should be treated in isolation. One transaction should not know about or interfere with any other transaction. If the transactions were to be executed in sequence, by the end, the state of data should be the same as before.

- **Durability**: This property states that the data should be persisted and available, even after failure once it is committed to the database. A committed transaction becomes a fact.

The four properties that comprise the ACID acronym are seen as guarantees, and for an application to be considered ACID-compliant, it must adhere to each of the properties strictly. A deficiency in one property would mean the application is not considered ACID compliant. Along with ACID compliance, there are other characteristics of transactional data and OLTP systems that are considered:

- **High integrity**: The quality and integrity of the data being maintained by the system is of paramount importance. Missing information related to a bank deposit or withdrawal could impact a customer's account by misrepresenting the available balance. This could undermine the customer's trust in the bank, and if the discrepancy is large, it could lead to unintended fees if the customer's balance drops below zero.

- **Data normalization**: Data used by OLTP systems is normalized, meaning it is broken up into logical groupings (such as tables), and it only stores information that is immediately relevant to the transaction or table. For example, a sale record may contain information such as the register number, the store number, and the total amount of the sale. Additional information, such as the items purchased, may be stored in another table. Keeping data in smaller chunks speeds up write operations to that table, making it easier to write higher volumes of transactions.

Now that we've delved into the common traits and properties of transactional data and OLTP systems, we can focus on when it makes sense to use OLTP principles in your application.

Use cases for OLTP

As mentioned earlier in this section, OLTP applications are often seen in retail and finance, but could also be seen in government services, manufacturing, and travel verticals. You should consider using OLTP as a solution for your application in the following scenarios:

- The data being managed represents key interactions that take place during the course of business operations

- There is a need to guarantee the integrity of the data being managed

- The system is considered a system of record—an authoritative source of truth for the business

- There is a need to guarantee that data is captured regardless of the outcome of the operation (success or failure)

Relational databases

OLTP applications have generally relied on relational databases for their transaction management and processing. Relational databases typically come in a tabular format consisting of rows and columns. The data model is converted into multiple tables where each table is connected to another table (based on rules) using relationships. This process is also known as normalization.

There are multiple services in Azure that support OLTP applications and the deployment of relational databases along with support for non-relational database services such as Cosmos DB. In the next section, we will look at the services in Azure that are related to OLTP applications.

OLTP in Azure

There are several Azure services that support OLTP applications, covering relational as well as non-relational data:

- Azure SQL Database

- Azure SQL Managed Instance

- Azure Cosmos DB

- Azure Database for PostgreSQL

- Azure Database for MySQL

Azure SQL Database

Azure SQL Database provides a relational database engine hosted as PaaS. Customers can provision this service, bring their own database schema and data, and connect their applications to it. Azure SQL Database provides many of the features of SQL Server when deployed on a virtual machine. These services do not provide a user interface to create tables and schemas, nor do they provide any querying capabilities directly via the portal. SQL Server Management Studio, Azure Data Studio, or the SQL CLI and command-line tools should be used to connect to these services and directly work with them.

Azure SQL Database comes with three distinct deployment models:

- **Single instance**: In this deployment model, a single database is deployed on a logical server. This involves the creation of two resources on Azure: a SQL logical server and a SQL database.

- **Elastic pool**: In this deployment mode, multiple databases are deployed on a logical server. This involves the creation of two resources on Azure: a SQL logical server and a SQL elastic database pool, which holds all the databases.

- **Managed instance**: This deployment reflects a collection of databases on a logical server, providing complete control over the resources in terms of system databases. Generally, system databases are not visible in other deployment models, but they are available in this model. The managed instance model comes very close to the deployment of SQL Server on-premises:

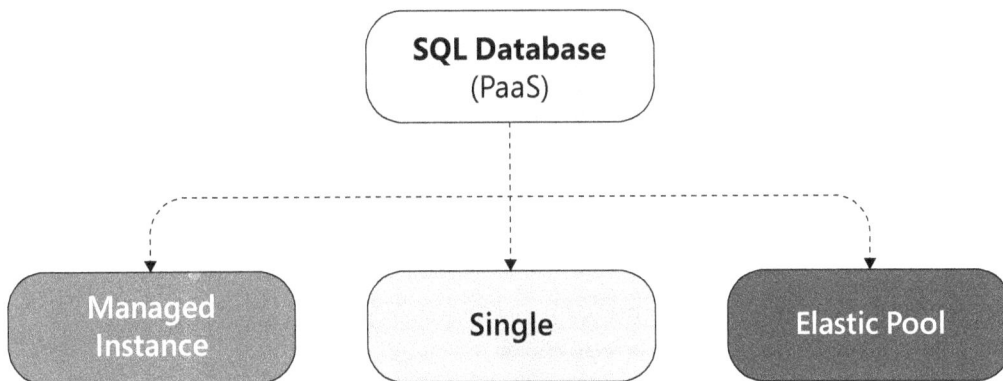

Figure 6.1: Azure SQL Database

To understand when to use which deployment model, you should look at a feature comparison between Azure SQL Database and Azure SQL Managed Instance. Key decision points for choosing either Azure SQL or Azure SQL Managed Instance are shown in *Table 6.1*. Please note that both **database transaction units** (**DTUs**) and **virtual cores** (**vCores**) are supported for Azure SQL.

Key Point	Azure SQL	Azure SQL Managed Instance
Automatic index tuning	Yes	No
Azure Resource Health	Yes	No
Backup storage options	LRS, GRS, ZRS	LRS, GRS, ZRS, GZRS
Compute limits	Up to 128 vCores	Up to 80 vCores
Cross-database queries	No	Yes, within the instance only
Database size	Up to 100 TB	Up to 16 TB
Distributed Transaction Coordinator (DTC) support	No	Yes
Files and file groups	Primary file group only	Yes, paths are auto-assigned
High availability	99.99%, 99.995% with availability zone configuration	99.99%
Hyperscale architecture	Yes	No
Private connectivity	Yes, with private endpoint	Yes, with Vnet
Query Performance Insight	Yes	No
Read-only replicas	1-4 highly available replicas or 0-30 named replicas 0-4 geo replicas	1 highly available replica 0-4 geo replicas
Virtual network support	Partial (VNet endpoints)	Yes
Windows Authentication	No	Yes, with AD sync

Table 6.1: Key factors in selecting Azure SQL or Managed Instance

Many of the platform capabilities, supported toolsets, and overall features between the two services are the same or have similarities that support many different use cases. One feature, hyperscale support, is relevant to OLTP applications as support for in-memory OLTP is only supported under a hyperscale architecture. In-memory OLTP puts all data in memory and there is no latency in reading the storage for data. Storing in-memory OLTP data on SSD provides the best possible performance for Azure SQL.

Serverless versus provisioned compute

Another decision factor that can weigh heavily on your overall design is whether or not to leverage serverless or provisioned compute when it comes to Azure SQL. Serverless compute is measured by vCores, with a fixed amount of memory and IOPS associated with each vCore. Provisioned compute is measured in DTUs, which are calculated using a blended model of CPU, memory, and IOPS. DTUs have lower resource limits associated with them than vCores, and switching between DTU configurations will incur a minimal disruption in services, whereas changing vCore counts will not as the underlying infrastructure is designed to ensure resources are available to the workload. Serverless compute will scale or shrink depending on the boundaries you set and the resources required to support the workload. DTUs are considered an upper limit and will not scale automatically if more resources are required.

For a complete feature and capability comparison between Azure SQL and Azure SQL Managed Instance, please visit https://docs.microsoft.com/azure/azure-sql/database/features-comparison. Next, let's explore each deployment model in a little more detail.

Single instance

Single-instance databases are hosted as a single database on a single logical server. These databases do not have access to the complete features provided by SQL Server. Each database is isolated and portable. Single instances support the vCore-based and DTU-based purchasing models.

Another added advantage of a single database is cost efficiency. If you are in a vCore-based model, you can opt for lower compute and storage resources to optimize costs. Dynamic scalability is a prominent feature of single instances that helps to scale resources dynamically based on business requirements. If you need more compute or storage power, you can always scale up. Single instances allow existing SQL Server customers to lift and shift their on-premises applications to the cloud. For more information about the differences between Azure SQL and SQL Server, please refer to https://learn.microsoft.com/en-us/azure/azure-sql/database/transact-sql-tsql-differences-sql-server?view=azuresql.

Other features include availability, monitoring, and security. For more information about key differences in T-SQL execution between Azure SQL and SQL Server, please visit https://learn.microsoft.com/en-us/azure/azure-sql/database/transact-sql-tsql-differences-sql-server?view=azuresql.

At the start of the *Azure SQL Database* section, we mentioned elastic pools as well. You can also transition a single database to an elastic pool for resource sharing.

Elastic pools

An elastic pool is a logical container that can host multiple databases on a single logical server. Using elastic pools is very useful if the databases in question can experience spikes or fluctuations in resource consumption and transaction processing, often at seemingly random or non-linear times. Elastic pools are available in the vCore-based and DTU-based purchasing models. The vCore-based purchasing model is the default and recommended method of deployment, where you'll get the freedom to choose your compute and storage resources based on your business workloads, as well as autoscaling based on configuration settings. In the DTU model, scaling is manual and requires updating the total number of DTUs and/or the SKU of the product. As shown in *Figure 6.2*, you can select how many cores and how much storage is required for your database:

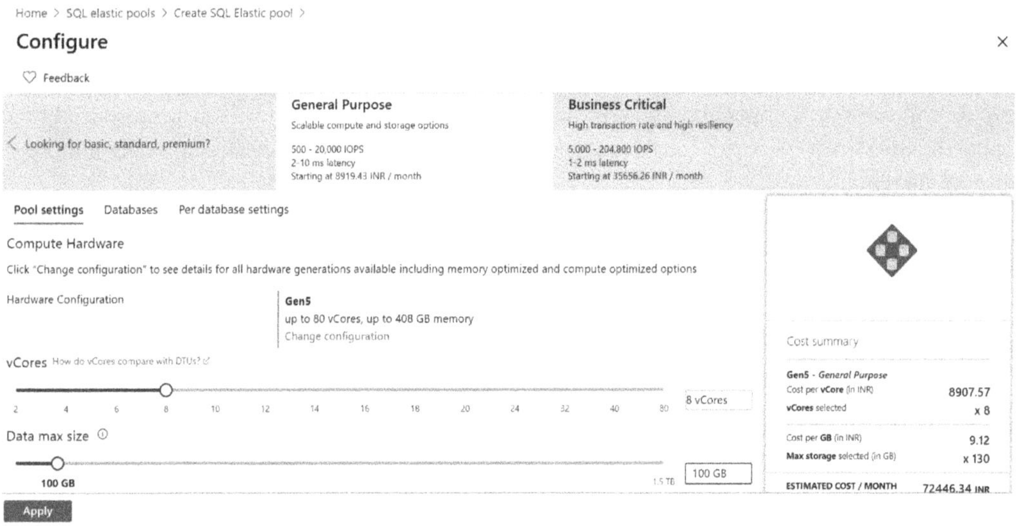

Figure 6.2: Setting up elastic pools in the vCore-based model

At the top of the preceding figure, you can see there is an option that says **Looking for basic, standard, premium?**. If you select this, the model will switch to the DTU model.

The SKUs available for elastic pools in the DTU-based model are as follows:

- Basic
- Standard
- Premium

Figure 6.3 shows the maximum amounts of DTUs that can be provisioned for each SKU:

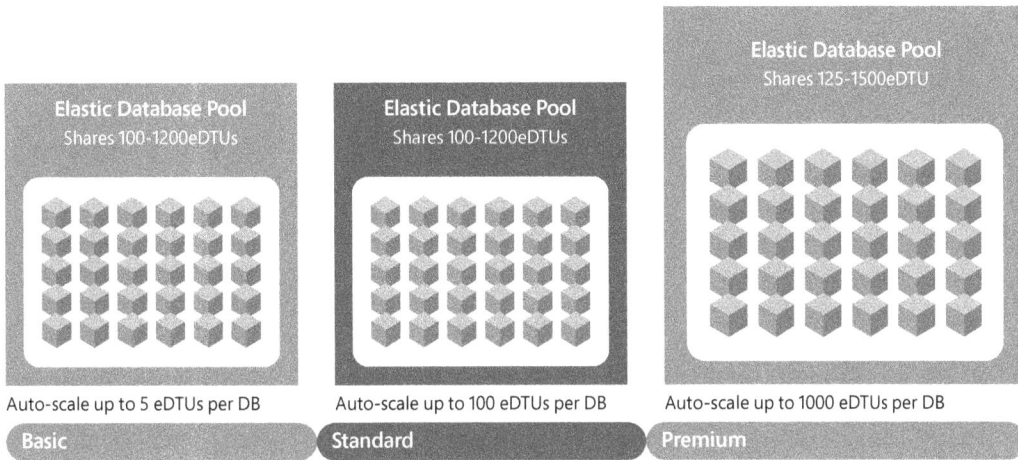

Figure 6.3: Amount of DTUs per SKU in an elastic pool

All the features discussed for Azure SQL single instances are available for elastic pools as well. However, horizontal scalability is an additional feature that enables sharding. Sharding refers to the vertical or horizontal partitioning of data and the storage of that data in separate databases. This allows larger datasets to be stored in smaller chunks across many data nodes. Doing so helps the performance in the case of reads and also provides a greater storage volume. It is also possible to have autoscaling of individual databases in an elastic pool by consuming more DTUs than are actually allocated to that database.

Elastic pools also provide another advantage in terms of cost. You will see in a later section that Azure SQL Database can be priced using DTUs or vCores, and DTUs are provisioned as soon as the SQL Server service is provisioned. DTUs are charged irrespective of whether those DTUs are consumed. If there are multiple databases, then it is possible to put these databases into elastic pools and for them to share the DTUs among them. Using vCores provides you with more autoscaling capabilities as well as the ability to scale units down when they are not needed. This can lead to more efficient operations as well as the more cost-effective management of resources.

All information for implementing sharding with Azure SQL elastic pools is provided at `https://docs.microsoft.com/azure/sql-database/sql-database-elastic-scale-introduction`.

Next, we will discuss the managed instance deployment option, which is a scalable, intelligent, cloud-based, fully managed database.

Azure SQL Managed Instance

Azure SQL Managed Instance is a unique service that provides a managed SQL server like what's available on on-premises servers. Users have access to master, model, and other system databases. Managed Instance is ideal for customers who are migrating their instances to Azure but need support for SQL Server features such as DDL/DML triggers, cross-database query support, or **Distributed Transaction Coordinator** (**DTC**) for specific components of the application. This provides greater compatibility while reducing the number of application changes needed to use the new database service.

Azure SQL Database Managed Instance provides almost 100% compatibility with the SQL Server Enterprise Edition Database Engine. This model provides a native virtual network implementation that addresses the usual security issues and is a highly recommended business model for on-premises SQL Server customers. This native network support enables you to configure Managed Instance as if it were another SQL Server on your network, without needing any service endpoints enabled. The defaults cater to network isolation, whereas Azure SQL requires more configuration in order to achieve a similar network topology. Managed Instance allows existing SQL Server customers to lift and shift their on-premises applications to the cloud with minimal application and database changes while supporting SQL Server functionality that is not present in Azure SQL and preserving all PaaS capabilities at the same time. These PaaS capabilities drastically reduce the management overhead and total cost of ownership, as shown in *Figure 6.4*:

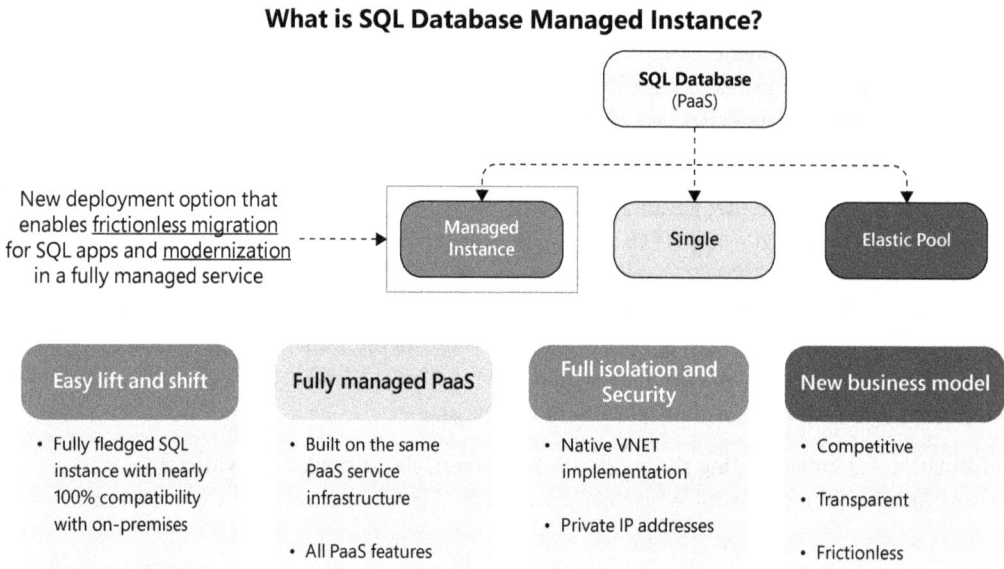

Figure 6.4: SQL Database Managed Instance

Some key capabilities to consider between Azure SQL, Azure SQL Managed Instance, and SQL Server are shown in *Table 6.2*.

Capability	Azure SQL	Azure SQL Managed Instance	SQL Server
Infrastructure management	Fully managed by Azure	Shared management	Fully managed by you
Backups	Automatic backups	Automatic backups	Backups must be configured
Compatibility with SQL Server features	Most features are compatible	Nearly all features are compatible	All features are compatible
Security automation	Built-in advanced intelligence and security	Built-in advanced intelligence and security	Not available
High availability	99.95% available	99.99% available	You are required to set up your own high-availability solution
Supported individual database size	Up to 100 TB	Up to 16 TB	Up to 256 TB

Table 6.2: Key capabilities between Azure SQL, Managed Instance, and SQL Server

The complete comparison between Azure SQL Database, Azure SQL Managed Instance, and SQL Server on an Azure virtual machine is available here: https://docs.microsoft.com/azure/azure-sql/azure-sql-iaas-vs-paas-what-is-overview#comparison-table.

The key features of Managed Instance are shown in the following figure:

The key features of Managed Instance are shown in the following table:

Feature	Description
SQL Server version / build	SQL Server Database Engine (latest stable)
Managed automated backups	Yes
Built-in instance and database monitoring and metrics	Yes
Automatic software patching	Yes
The latest Database Engine features	Yes
Number of data files (ROWS) per the database	Multiple
Number of log files (LOG) per database	1
VNet - Azure Resource Manager deployment	Yes
VNet - Classic deployment model	No
Portal support	Yes
Built-in Integration Service (SSIS)	No - SSIS is a part of Azure Data Factory PaaS
Built-in Analysis Service (SSAS)	No - SSAS is separate PaaS
Built-in Reporting Service (SSRS)	No - use PowerBI or SSRS IaaS

Figure 6.5: SQL Database Managed Instance features

Azure Cosmos DB

Cosmos DB is Azure's cross-region, highly available, distributed, multi-model database service. Cosmos DB is for you if you would like your solution to be highly responsive and always available. As this is a cross-region multi-model database, we can deploy applications closer to the user's location and achieve low latency and high availability. Throughput and storage can be scaled across any number of Azure regions by using the Azure portal, the Azure CLI, PowerShell, or **infrastructure as code (IaC)**. There are a few different database models to cover almost all non-relational database requirements, including the following:

- SQL (documents)
- MongoDB
- Cassandra
- Table
- Gremlin graph
- PostgreSQL

The hierarchy of objects within Cosmos DB starts with the Cosmos DB account. An account can have multiple databases, and each database can have multiple containers. Depending on the type of database, the container might consist of documents, as in the case of SQL—semi-structured key-value data within Table Storage; or entities and relationships among those entities, if using Gremlin and Cassandra to store NoSQL data.

Cosmos DB can be used to store OLTP data. It accounts for ACID regarding transaction data, with a few caveats. For example, ACID-compliant transactions are managed for data grouped by a logical partition key. Using partition keys allows you to group your data objects by a common property, preferably with a high degree of cardinality. For multi-item ACID transactions, you will need to implement stored procedures or triggers in Cosmos DB. This can be achieved by writing the code for those stored procedures or triggers in JavaScript, which provides a performance gain since Cosmos DB is optimized to use JSON objects.

Cosmos DB provides ACID requirements at the single document level. This means data within a document, when updated, deleted, or inserted, will have its atomicity, consistency, isolation, and durability maintained. However, beyond documents, consistency and atomicity have to be managed by the developer themself.

Pricing information for Cosmos DB can be found here: `https://azure.microsoft.com/pricing/details/cosmos-db/`.

The following figure shows some features of Azure Cosmos DB:

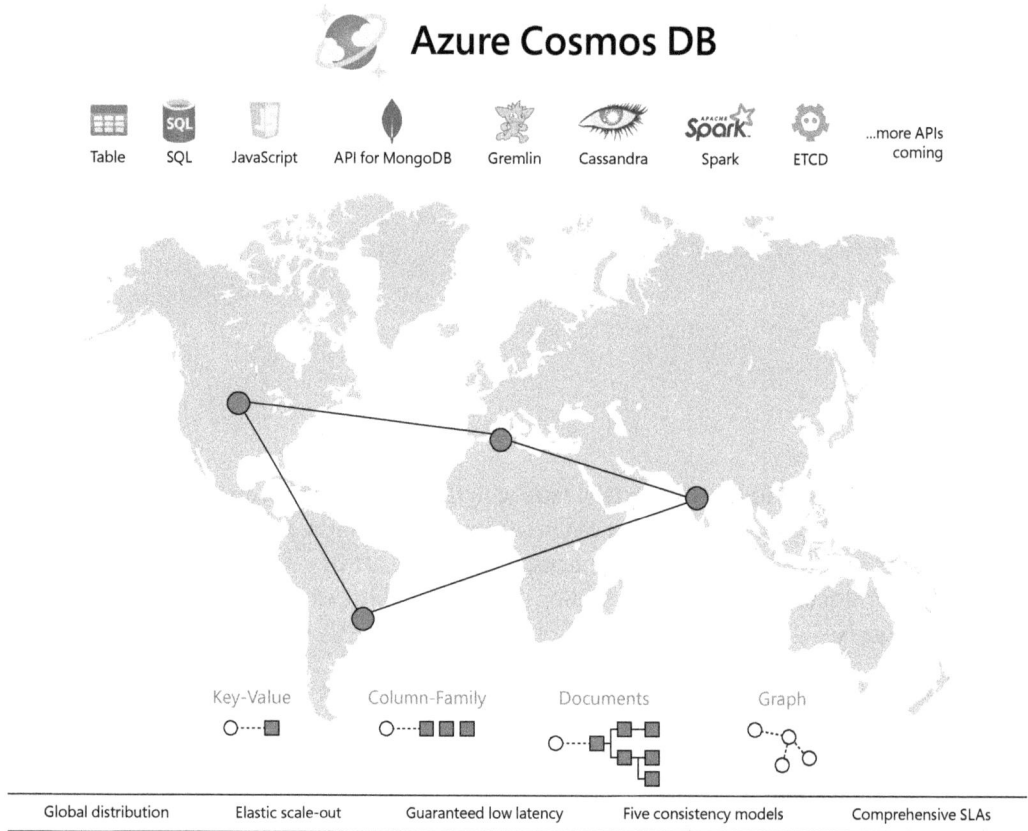

Figure 6.6: An overview of Azure Cosmos DB

In the next section, we will cover some key features of Azure Cosmos DB.

Key features

Some of the key features of Azure Cosmos DB are as follows:

- **Global distribution**: Highly responsive and highly available applications can be built worldwide using Azure Cosmos DB. With the help of replication, replicas of data can be stored in Azure regions that are close to users, hence providing less latency and global distribution. The high degree of data consistency is also important when looking at Cosmos for OLTP applications, as one of the main characteristics of an OLTP system is high consistency, and Cosmos DB provides high consistency out of the box.

- **Ease of replication**: You can opt into or out of replication to a region at any time you like. Let's say you have a replica of your data available in the East US region, and your organization is planning to shut down its processes in East US and migrate to UK South. With a configuration change, East US can be removed, and UK South can be added to the account for replication. This can also be achieved using the Azure CLI, or through your IaC provider of choice.

- **Always on**: Cosmos DB provides 99.999% of high availability for both read and write operations. The regional failover of a Cosmos DB account to another region can be invoked via the Azure portal or programmatically. This ensures business continuity and disaster recovery planning for your application during a region failure.

- **Scalability**: Cosmos DB offers unmatched elastic scalability for writes and reads all around the globe. The scalability response is massive, meaning that you can scale from thousands to hundreds of millions of requests/second with a single API call. The interesting thing is that this is done around the globe, but you need to pay only for throughput and storage. This level of scalability is ideal for handling unexpected spikes.

- **Low latency**: As mentioned earlier, replicating copies of data to locations nearer to users drastically reduces latency; it means that users can access their data in milliseconds. Cosmos DB guarantees less than 10 ms of latency for both reads and writes all around the world.

- **TCO savings**: As Cosmos DB is a fully managed service, the level of management required by the customer is low. The customer also doesn't have to set up datacenters across the globe to accommodate users from other regions.

- **SLA**: It offers an SLA of 99.999% high availability.

- **Support for Open-Source Software (OSS) APIs**: Cosmos DB supports OSS APIs, in which it implements APIs for Cassandra, MongoDB, Gremlin, PostgreSQL, and Azure Table storage.

All Azure database service offerings can configure data redundancy, backups, security, restoration points, and custom networking, as well as choosing scaling and compute models that match the needs of your application. With Azure Database for PostgreSQL and MySQL, there is an added benefit of using open-source-backed database engines, which can result in a reduction in the total cost of ownership and maintenance. Let's take a closer look at those services next.

Azure Database for PostgreSQL

In the open source world, one of the more popular database engines is PostgreSQL. Azure has enhanced this offering by providing options to leverage AI-driven performance optimization, as well as providing a low-friction configuration called **Flexible Server**. Flexible Server allows for the easy deployment of zone-redundant instances and automates maintenance, patching, and updates. You are still able to fine-tune the database engine configuration as well, giving you complete control over the operationalization of the database.

You can also protect your database with not only Azure Security Center but also services such as Azure IP advantage and Microsoft Defender for open-source relational databases. Check the following links to learn more:

- Azure IP advantage: `https://azure.microsoft.com/solutions/iot/ip-advantage-program/`

- Microsoft Defender for open-source relational databases: `https://learn.microsoft.com/azure/defender-for-cloud/defender-for-databases-usage`

Azure Database for MySQL

Another popular open source database engine is MySQL, which tends to cater more toward application developers with its range of supported languages and frictionless development integration. Having a fully managed and highly available MySQL instance in Azure also helps to lower the total cost of ownership, from not only a licensing perspective but also a maintenance perspective. Azure Database for MySQL also has intelligent optimizations built into the service, providing predictive insights into database performance and recommendations on changes to the service to further bolster performance. It is also tightly integrated with both Azure App Service and Azure Kubernetes Service, allowing for an even more frictionless development experience when building applications using those compute models.

With all the available options, it can be a daunting task to pick the right database service for your needs. This is why we will look at using your requirements and a set of questions to help narrow down your choices in the next section.

Choosing the right service

As with any service available in the cloud, it is important to weigh the benefits and drawbacks of choosing one type of service over another, and this is applicable to database services as well. There are a few aspects that should help drive the decision toward the service you choose, along with some related questions you should ask regarding the use case you're trying to address when planning for OLTP applications. There is also an informational page on OLTP data stores in the `Azure Architecture Center` that gives some side-by-side comparisons of key database services and features:

- **Non-functional requirements**:

  - **Availability**: What is the guaranteed uptime of the database service? Does it meet the uptime requirements of your application?

  - **Maintainability**: Is the database service mostly, if not fully, managed by the platform? Are there any aspects of the service that require additional configuration? If so, how complicated is that configuration?

- **Observability**: How easy or difficult is it to know when the database service is operating at its peak versus operating at a deficit? Are there common patterns available to aid in identifying issues?

- **Reliability**: Does the service provide mechanisms to promote ACID compliance and guaranteed data capture?

- **Scalability**: Can the service perform without noticeable degradation when traffic spikes or normalized high-throughput interactions occur?

- **Geographic distribution**: Does the service exist in the Azure regions you need to target for your application? Is the service geo-redundant or zone-redundant? Can the service handle multiple write operations in different regions at the same time?

- **Data structure**: When looking at the data being captured per transaction, is there a requirement for it to be stored in specifically formatted ways, or can the information be captured at a point in time and processed by application components later?

- **Storage requirements**: Does the application have a need to store large volumes of data, or does it operate on large amounts of enriched data gleaned from individual application components? Does the backing storage associated with the service have IOPS thresholds that meet the needs of your application?

- **Pricing models**: Does the application require services to always be available at a constant rate, or are workloads more interrupt-driven or sporadic? Is there a way to capture the steady state transactional throughput the application experiences, and is it low enough to possibly warrant a smaller set amount of compute?

Each database service covered in the last section has its own service limitations page, detailing what can (and can't) be done using each service. In some cases, limits are not only based on the database service but also on the SKU selected, so weighing the required SKU against other factors, such as cost, can take diligence.

Just as decisions need to be made on how to appropriately store transactions in your OLTP application, it is also important to examine the different options available for using that data, whether for snapshot-style reports or for analyzing trends over time. In the next section, we'll walk through several scenarios where analytics services can be particularly useful.

Scenarios for analytics

Being able to glean insights from your data is just as important as choosing the right type of data store. Many options exist for harvesting and reporting on that data. **Online Analytics Processing (OLAP)** is one method that can be used to capture and transform transactional data into a structure more suited for reporting and analytics. There are several options available for compiling and reporting on OLTP data, which we will look at now.

Transactional querying

While this may be the least efficient way to compile analytics from an OLTP data store, it is possible to directly query your OLTP database. There will be performance implications, however, as you will be querying the database while also allowing writes as a natural occurrence from application or platform usage. You may wish to address the performance issues by processing transactional writes through the database infrastructure and processing reads and aggregations through in-memory temporal tables. This would effectively split the reads and writes up but could result in memory bottlenecks if a resource-intensive query is executing using the same allocated CPU and memory for the database.

In lower-volume scenarios, where applications may not process thousands or millions of transactions per hour or even per day, gathering insights from same-day transactional data may be less taxing on the system. That's not to say that query performance implications could not severely limit the transactional operations that are managed by the application. Proper diligence should be exercised when determining resource allocation for data stores that are expected to handle both read and write operations with consistent volume.

Normally, running queries or reports against transactional data is more efficiently managed if you are using a separate **operational data store** (**ODS**), where transactional information is curated after a certain duration. A popular implementation of an ODS can be seen in the form of a datamart or data warehouse.

Datamarts and data warehouses

A common scenario for people looking to get reporting information from applications or platforms is to use an ODS—something that affords users the opportunity to write queries and reports against data with a known time boundary that is not considered near real time. Typically, data is loaded into a data warehouse via **extract-transform-load** (**ETL**) operations using utilities such as **Azure Data Factory**. Depending on the volume of data being stored, it may be more cost effective to define boundaries on data stored using datamarts or data warehouses based on the age of the data. These boundaries generally manifest in the form of date dimensions, where older data may be segmented to increase efficiencies in querying the ODS.

Timeboxing transactional versus historical data

Creating time boundaries on transactional data stored in an ODS is an important undertaking as it can lead to more cost-effective storage mediums and facilitate more meaningful analysis of historical data based on that timeboxing. For example, you may only need to keep 90 days of transactional data available in an ODS for direct reporting, and then move data that has aged out into a separate storage alternative. This allows users to query trend data using both transactional and historical data sources, while keeping the transactional data volume at a manageable level. Keeping datasets lean will ultimately keep indexes smaller and allow for faster query execution.

ADL Gen2

Another way to improve data access speed, especially when dealing with structured and non-structured data, is to leverage the ADL Gen2 capabilities through Azure Storage. Setting up a storage account and enabling the Gen2 capabilities gives you the following:

- Hierarchical data storage, allowing your data to be stored akin to a file system and queried using optimized search techniques

- A storage option built to support the Hadoop Distributed File System, which itself is optimized for querying and analyzing large amounts of data from disparate sources

- Optimized performance and cost implications through the use of automated lifecycle policy management and object-level tiering, as well as removing the need to perform transformations on data prior to executing queries

- Fine-grained control using POSIX-compliant **access control lists** (**ACLs**) as well as Azure **role-based access control** (**RBAC**)

- No limitations on the amount of data stored, individual file size, or account size

For more information on the features of ADL Gen2, please visit `https://learn.microsoft.com/en-us/azure/storage/blobs/data-lake-storage-introduction`.

Having examined the use cases for querying transactional as well as enriched reporting data, we will next look into additional Azure services that can provide near real-time analytics that ingest disparate data sources.

Azure Synapse Analytics

Azure Synapse Analytics is a managed cloud service that allows users to gain insights into their data across a variety of sources, including big data sources. Azure Synapse combines the enterprise-class SQL Server toolsets with Apache Spark for big data processing, and using Azure Data Explorer or Power BI reports allows for in-depth reporting and data exploration. Azure Synapse is useful when looking to gain insights from many disparate sources in a short period of time. It also cuts down the execution time of ETL operations by directly importing data using Azure Synapse Link. For more in-depth information related to Azure Synapse, please visit `https://learn.microsoft.com/en-us/azure/synapse-analytics/`.

Azure Databricks

Azure Databricks offers users the ability to create intuitive query objects and models while keeping things grouped into manageable chunks or bricks. The intended use for Databricks is normally with a data lake, ADL Gen2, for example. It is referred to as a **data lakehouse** for its ability to stand as a central point for consolidating views on analytics and AI workloads. In some cases, Databricks can be used in conjunction with Azure Synapse to help provide data insights over vast territories of information.

We have mentioned many different OLTP service and storage options, as well as consumption plans such as the vCore-based pricing model and DTU-based pricing model. Now, let's take a closer look at these pricing models. For more information about Azure Databricks and its capabilities, please visit https://learn.microsoft.com/en-us/azure/databricks/.

Cost optimization

Azure SQL previously had just one pricing model (a model based on DTUs) but an alternative pricing model based on vCores has also been launched. The pricing model is selected based on the customer's requirements. The DTU-based model is selected when the customer wants simple and preconfigured resource options. On the other hand, the vCore-based model offers the flexibility to choose compute and storage resources. It also provides control and transparency. There is also a cost model unique to Cosmos DB called **request units** (**RUs**), which are similar to the other two models in terms of blending CPU, memory, and IOPS but differ with respect to factors such as the API model being used, regional deployments, object size, data consistency, and the property count of the object(s).

Let's take a closer look at each of these models.

DTU-based pricing

The DTU is the smallest unit of performance measure for Azure SQL Database. Each DTU corresponds to a certain number of resources. These resources include storage, CPU cycles, IOPS, and network bandwidth. For example, a single DTU under the Basic Azure SQL SKU would provide 3 IOPS, a few CPU cycles, and IO latencies of 5 ms for read operations and 10 ms for write operations.

Azure SQL Database provides multiple SKUs for creating databases, and each of these SKUs has defined constraints for the maximum amount of DTUs. For example, the Basic SKU provides just 5 DTUs with a maximum of **2 GB** of data, as shown in the following screenshot:

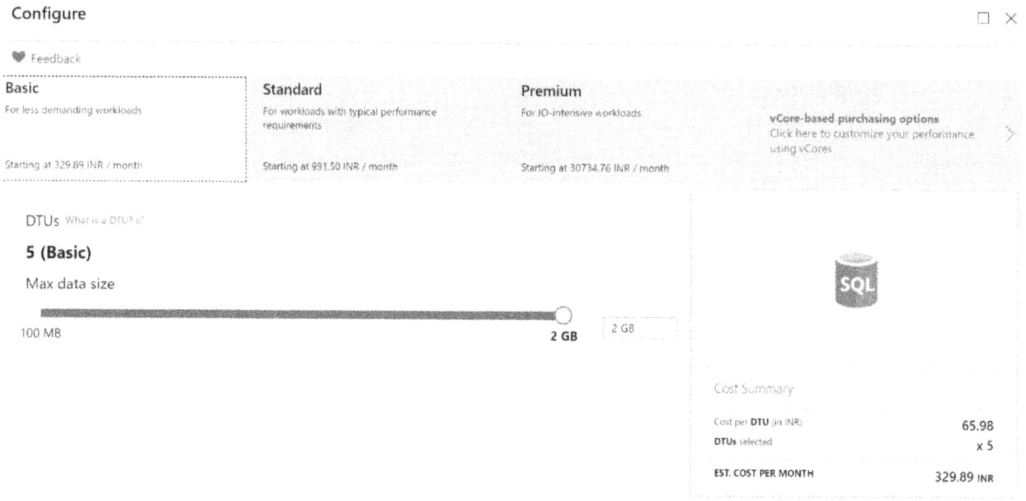

Figure 6.7: DTUs for different SKUs

On the other hand, the Standard SKU provides anything between 10 DTUs and 300 DTUs with a maximum of **250 GB** of data. As you can see here, each DTU costs around 991 rupees, or around $1.40:

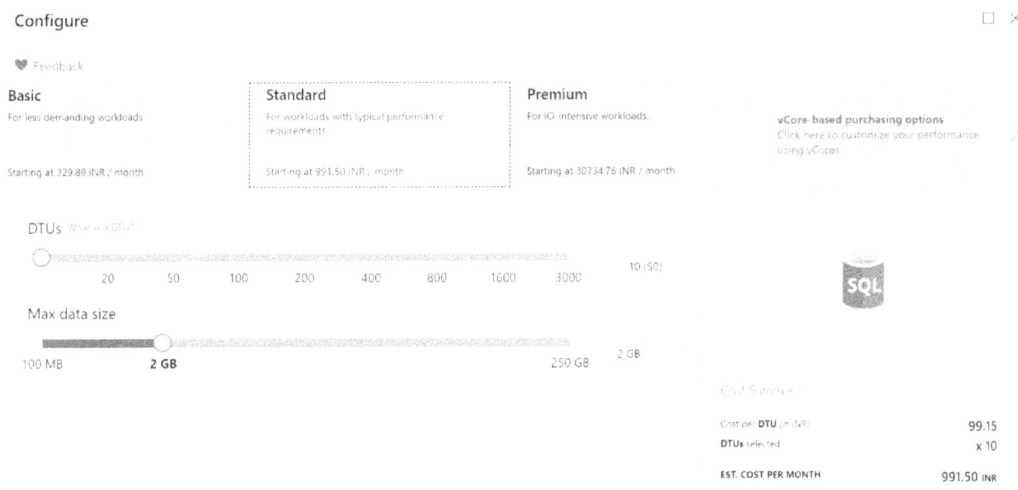

Figure 6.8: Cost summary for the selected number of DTUs in the Standard SKU

A comparison of these SKUs in terms of performance and resources is provided by Microsoft and is shown in the following screenshot:

	Basic	Standard	Premium
Target workload	Development and production	Development and production	Development and production
Uptime SLA	99.99%	99.99%	99.99%
Backup retention	7 days	35 days	35 days
CPU	Low	Low, Medium, High	Medium, High
IO throughput (approximate)	2.5 IOPS per DTU	2.5 IOPS per DTU	48 IOPS per DTU
IO latency (approximate)	5 ms (read), 10 ms (write)	5 ms (read), 10 ms (write)	2 ms (read/write)
Columnstore indexing	N/A	S3 and above	Supported
In-memory OLTP	N/A	N/A	Supported

Figure 6.9: SKU comparison in Azure

Once you provision a certain number of DTUs, the backend resources (CPU, IOPS, and memory) are allocated and are charged for whether they are consumed or not. If more DTUs are procured than are needed, it'll lead to wastage. On the other hand, there would be performance bottlenecks if insufficient DTUs were provisioned.

Azure provides elastic pools for this reason as well. As you know, there are multiple databases in an elastic pool and DTUs are assigned to elastic pools instead of individual databases. It is possible for all databases within a pool to share DTUs. This means that if a database has low utilization and is consuming only 5 DTUs, there will be another database consuming 25 DTUs to compensate.

It is important to note that collectively, DTU consumption cannot exceed the amount of DTUs provisioned for the elastic pool. Moreover, there is a minimum amount of DTUs that should be assigned to each database within the elastic pool, and this minimum DTU count is pre-allocated for the database.

An elastic pool comes with its own SKUs:

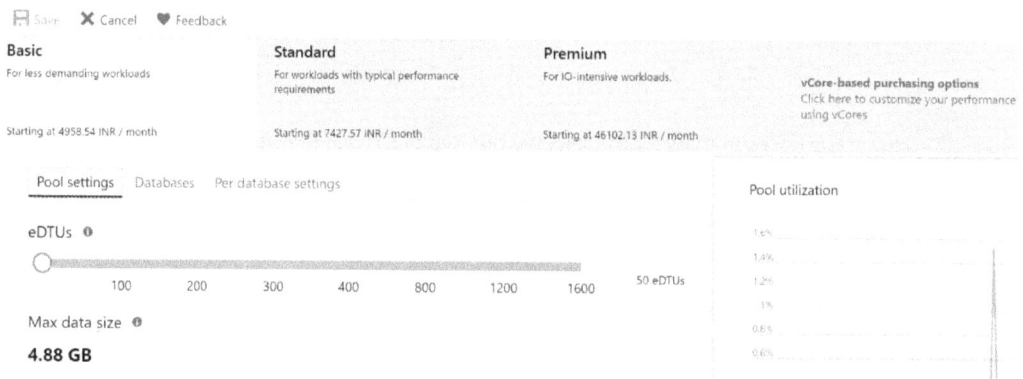

Figure 6.10: SKUs in an elastic pool

Also, there is a limit on the maximum number of databases that can be created within a single elastic pool. The complete limits can be reviewed here: https://docs.microsoft.com/azure/azure-sql/database/resource-limits-dtu-elastic-pools.

vCore-based pricing

This is an alternative pricing model for Azure SQL. This pricing model provides options to procure the number of **virtual CPUs (vCores)** allocated to the server instead of setting the number of DTUs required for an application. A vCore is a logical CPU with attached hardware, such as storage, memory, and CPU cores. In addition, there are several more benefits to using a vCore model:

- **Clearer resource allocation**: While it is possible to determine how much CPU, memory, and IOPS are included in a specific number of DTUs, the vCore model provides clearer communication and configuration when setting up or reconfiguring the database.

- **Transparent scaling options**: Autoscaling with the vCore model is transparent to the users of the system as the additional units can be added with no downtime and minimal latency. Scaling in the DTU model requires reconfiguration and typically involves some downtime while the service adjusts.

- **Performance impacts**: With vCores, you may see better performance out of your database service with fewer resources. For example, because the resource limits per vCore are higher than those of the DTU model, applications that are particularly IOPS heavy can see better performance using fewer vCores as a baseline.

In this model, there are three SKUs: **General Purpose**, **Hyperscale**, and **Business Critical**, with a varied number of vCores and resources available. The General Purpose SKU is great for all-around usage but shines in areas where heavy transactional load or querying are not required. For Hyperscale, the main use case is for applications that need to support transactional processing and also have the ability to scale rapidly to meet demands. The in-memory OLTP feature with Azure SQL is available at this tier. Business Critical offers the benefits of Hyperscale along with guarantees for high resiliency and high transaction throughput. This pricing is available for all SQL deployment models:

Figure 6.11: vCore pricing for the General Purpose SKU

Request units (RUs)

RUs are a specific measure of consumption related to Cosmos DB instances. Any time you request an operation from a Cosmos DB account or container, that operation consumes one or more request units.

Reserved capacity

Reserved capacity is a cost modifier that can be applied to situations where resource consumption is well known and there is a need for the data store to be in use for a long duration. This allows you to purchase a set amount of capacity upfront for either a one- or three-year term. While not recommended for highly variable load applications or even burstable workloads, it can be very beneficial for applications where a standard amount of capacity is required, and there is a constant usage model across time. Architects need to weigh the cost benefits of using reserved capacity against the needs of the application as well as the capacity being purchased. More information regarding reserved capacity can be found at `https://learn.microsoft.com/en-us/azure/cost-management-billing/reservations/save-compute-costs-reservations`.

How to choose the appropriate pricing model

Architects should be able to choose an appropriate pricing model for Azure SQL Database. DTUs are a great mechanism for pricing where there is a usage pattern applicable and available for the database. Since resource availability in the DTU scheme of things is linear, as shown in the next diagram, it is quite possible for usage to be more memory-intensive than CPU-intensive. In such cases, it is possible to choose different levels of CPU, memory, and storage for a database.

In DTUs, resources come packaged, and it is not possible to configure these resources at a granular level. With a vCore model, it is possible to choose different levels of memory and CPU for different databases. If the usage pattern for an application is known, using the vCore pricing model could be a better option compared to the DTU model. In fact, the vCore model also provides the benefit of hybrid licenses if an organization already has on-premises SQL Server licenses. The hybrid use benefit is available to anyone who has SQL Server Standard Core or Enterprise Core licenses through the Software Assurance program, and they can be applied to those SKUs running on Azure VMs, or leveraged in Azure SQL single instance and elastic pools. There is a discount of up to 30% provided to these SQL Server instances.

In *Figure 6.21*, you can see from the left-hand graph that as the number of DTUs increases, resource availability also grows linearly; however, with vCore pricing (in the right-hand graph), it is possible to choose independent configurations for each database:

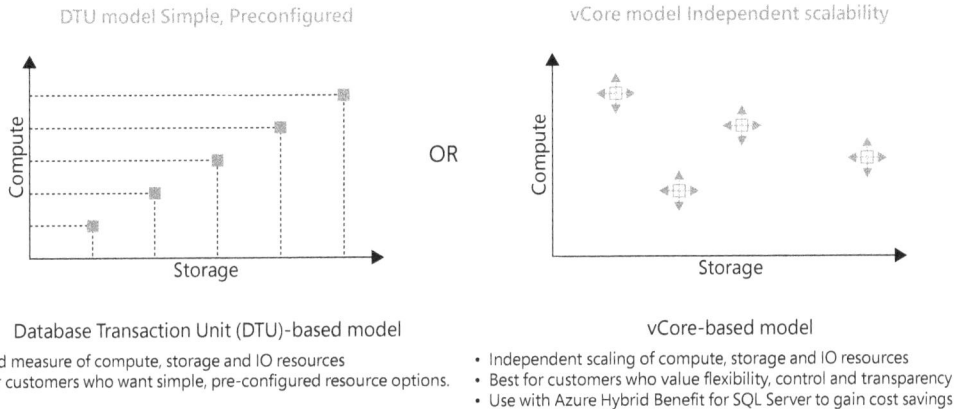

Figure 6.12: Storage-compute graph for the DTU and vCore models

With that, we can conclude our coverage of Azure SQL Database. We discussed different deployment methods, features, pricing, and plans related to Azure SQL Database.

Summary

In this chapter, we have discussed what OLTP systems are, including what constitutes transactional data along with some properties and traits that all OLTP systems share. We've explored several different Azure offerings that support OLTP applications, including Azure SQL Database, Azure SQL Managed Instance, Azure Database for PostgreSQL, Azure Cosmos DB, and Azure Database for MySQL. We have inspected the different deployment types for Azure SQL Database, such as single instance, managed instance, and elastic pools. We walked through the different features of Cosmos DB, which is a globally available data store for non-structured data that is OLTP compatible. We've looked at the different hardware tiers available to all database services in Azure, including General Purpose, Hyperscale, and Business Critical.

Architects should perform a complete assessment of their requirements and choose the appropriate deployment model. After choosing a deployment model, they should choose a pricing strategy between DTUs and vCores, or RUs in the case of Cosmos DB. We walked through several examples of analytics toolsets available in Azure, including transactional querying, data warehouses and datamarts, timeboxed data, historical data, and near real-time analytics using highly scalable components such as Azure Synapse and Azure Databricks.

In the next chapter, we will be discussing how to build secure applications in Azure. We will cover the security practices and features of most services.

7

Designing Serverless Architecture Solutions in Azure

In the previous chapter, we explored the wide array of data services offered by Azure, including both IaaS and PaaS options. Now, let's shift our focus to the buzzword that has been captivating the tech world for several years – serverless computing. For businesses seeking flexibility, agility, and cost-efficiency, serverless is an excellent choice.

Imagine the possibilities with serverless, where developers can effortlessly create applications that automatically scale based on events, saving on costs by paying only for actual usage. This event-driven approach ensures optimal resource utilization, especially in microservices architecture.

Organizations can efficiently manage batch processing and real-time data streams in big data analytics scenarios without the complexities of maintaining infrastructure. For e-commerce businesses, holiday sales don't pose as much of a challenge anymore, even when facing the traffic surges sales and promotions invite.

Serverless technology offers a lot of benefits that help businesses streamline their operations and save on costs so they can focus on delivering value to their customers. That's why, in this chapter, we will provide an overview of the serverless platform within the landscape of Microsoft Azure. We'll cover essential serverless offerings such as Azure Functions, Durable Functions, Logic Apps, and Event Grid.

We'll explore use cases, language runtimes, hosting plans, triggers and bindings, performance considerations, and scalability to equip you with the knowledge needed to implement serverless architecture effectively.

By the conclusion of this chapter, you'll have gained a comprehensive understanding of developing serverless applications utilizing Azure Functions, as well as implementing event-driven architectural solutions through the effective utilization of various Azure services on the Azure serverless platform.

Understanding the serverless platform in Microsoft Azure

Serverless computing is a deployment model that allows organizations to focus solely on their application code and configuration, without the need to manage the underlying platform and infrastructure. While servers are still required to run the code and handle compute, storage, and networking resources, the customer is shielded from the intricacies of these components. This arrangement allows customers to utilize the benefits of serverless computing while offloading the complexities of managing underlying resources to the cloud provider.

By adopting a serverless approach, customers benefit from an environment that can dynamically scale resources up and down, both vertically and horizontally, without intervention. This scalability is automatically handled behind the scenes by the cloud provider, allowing customers to focus solely on their business problems and deliver value to their organizations.

Functions as a Service (**FaaS**) is a subcategory of serverless computing. It enables organizations to break down complex functionalities into smaller, self-contained functions. Those functions can be triggered and executed automatically through scheduled jobs and automated triggers.

Several prominent serverless computing platforms are available, offering a range of capabilities. Azure Functions, for example, is a widely used serverless compute platform offered by Microsoft Azure. These platforms empower organizations to leverage the benefits of serverless computing and select the solution that best aligns with their requirements and preferences. Check out an overview of the Microsoft serverless platform on the following page: `https://azure.microsoft.com/en-us/solutions/serverless#overview`.

Now let's take a closer look at Azure Functions in the next section.

Building serverless apps with Azure Functions

Azure Functions is a serverless solution designed to streamline the development process, minimize infrastructure maintenance, and optimize cost efficiency. By eliminating the need to manage servers, the cloud infrastructure seamlessly provides the necessary resources to ensure continuous application operation.

With Azure Functions, organizations can prioritize their core code, focusing on what matters most to them, while the platform takes care of the remaining operational aspects. This empowers organizations to work in the language that aligns best with their productivity, enabling a seamless development experience.

Use cases and scenarios

Azure Functions offers a versatile range of event-driven triggers and bindings that facilitate seamless integration with various services, eliminating the need for writing additional code. The platform presents a diverse array of use cases and scenarios:

- **Processing file uploads**: With Azure Functions, you can effortlessly execute code whenever a file is uploaded or modified in Blob Storage. This enables you to automate processes associated with file handling, such as data extraction, transformation, and analysis.

- **Real-time data processing**: By capturing and transforming data from events and IoT source streams on its way to storage, Azure Functions enables real-time data processing. This functionality facilitates immediate data analysis, ensuring organizations take action in a timely manner.

- **Inferencing on data models**: Azure Functions can seamlessly integrate with AI services, enabling the extraction of text from a queue and presenting it for analysis and classification. This empowers organizations to derive insights from textual data and apply AI capabilities without additional complexity.

- **Scheduled tasks**: You can utilize Azure Functions to run scheduled tasks, executing specific code at predefined intervals. This feature is particularly useful for performing regular data cleanup, maintenance activities, or generating periodic reports.

- **Building scalable web APIs**: Azure Functions provides HTTP triggers, allowing you to create a set of REST endpoints for web applications. This enables you to build scalable, serverless web APIs, empowering seamless integration with frontend applications or external systems.

- **Creating serverless workflows**: Azure Functions supports the creation of event-driven workflows using Durable Functions. This feature allows you to design complex, serverless workflows by orchestrating a series of functions, achieving efficient and reliable automation of business processes.

- **Responding to database changes**: Azure Functions can be triggered to execute custom logic, for instance, when creating or updating a document in Azure Cosmos DB. This functionality enables real-time responsiveness to database changes, facilitating the execution of tailored actions based on specific events.

- **Reliable message systems**: Azure Functions supports the processing of message queues, utilizing various storage options such as Queue Storage, Service Bus, or Event Hubs. This capability enables the creation of reliable and scalable message-driven systems, facilitating seamless communication and event processing.

To read more details about those scenarios, check out this documentation: `https://learn.microsoft.com/en-us/azure/azure-functions/functions-scenarios?pivots=programming-language-csharp`.

With Azure Functions, organizations can build event-driven systems using modern architectural patterns. Azure Functions provides flexibility and an extensive range of use cases to help developers streamline their processes, automate tasks, and create efficient and scalable cloud-native applications.

Language runtime

The language runtime of Azure Functions plays a vital role since it determines the programming languages that can be used to write functions and provides the necessary execution environment for running the code.

The language runtime of Azure Functions is of utmost importance as it supports a wide range of programming languages, including C#, F#, Java, JavaScript, PowerShell, Python, and TypeScript. This broad language support ensures that developers can leverage their existing skills and choose the language that best suits their project requirements and preferences. Check out this documentation to get the most up-to-date information about supported language runtimes for Azure Functions: `https://learn.microsoft.com/en-us/azure/azure-functions/supported-languages`.

Additionally, Azure Functions provides extensibility options, allowing developers to use a feature called custom handlers to extend language support beyond the built-in offerings. This means developers can incorporate additional languages and frameworks, catering to specific requirements for those businesses whose choice of language is outside of the mainstream language support while utilizing the same capabilities that are supported already by Azure Functions.

Triggers and bindings

Triggers and bindings are fundamental components of Azure Functions, playing a pivotal role in its functionality and versatility. Triggers are responsible for invoking the execution of functions, causing them to run based on specific events or conditions. It is important to note that each function must have exactly one trigger. Bindings facilitate seamless integration with various external services and various data sources. They are bi-directional, which means they work in "in" and "out," in both directions.

By leveraging triggers and bindings, Azure Functions abstracts away the complexities of integrating with other services. Functions receive data from triggers as function parameters, simplifying the consumption of external data sources. Conversely, functions can also send data to external systems by utilizing the return value, enabling a seamless and intuitive approach to interacting with connected resources.

Through the utilization of triggers and bindings, Azure Functions facilitates businesses integrating with diverse services. This functionality simplifies the consumption and interaction of external data sources, reducing the required coding time. This streamlined process enhances operational efficiency and enables developers to concentrate on their core functions while delivering value to their organizations.

Hosting plans

Azure Functions offers multiple hosting plans to cater to the different requirements of developers and organizations.

Consumption plan

The Consumption plan offers the convenience of automatic scaling and cost optimization. Under this plan, the Functions host instances dynamically adjust their capacity according to the incoming events. Consequently, you are billed solely for the compute resources utilized while your functions are active. This default choice guarantees efficient resource allocation, particularly during periods of high demand. However, the *on-demand* nature of the Consumption plan can lead to even greater flexibility and cost-effectiveness for your applications.

Elastic Premium plan

The Premium plan is designed for specific use cases that demand continuous or near-continuous function execution. This plan offers advanced features such as pre-warmed workers, which eliminate any delay when running applications after being idle.

Behind the scenes, it also utilizes more powerful instances and supports integration with virtual networks. The Premium plan is ideal when you have a high number of small executions, require more CPU or memory options, need longer execution times, or seek features that are not available in the Consumption plan. Additionally, if you want to run your functions on a custom Linux image, the Premium plan allows you to do so.

Dedicated plan

The Dedicated plan enables you to run functions within an App Service plan at regular App Service plan rates. An App Service Regular plan is a hosting option provided by Microsoft Azure for running web applications, APIs, and mobile backends. It is one of the pricing plans offered under Azure App Service, a fully managed platform that enables developers to build, deploy, and scale web applications without worrying about the underlying infrastructure. This plan is best suited for long-running scenarios where Durable Functions cannot be utilized. If you already have underutilized **virtual machines** (**VMs**) running other App Service instances, the Dedicated plan allows you to leverage those existing resources. It also provides predictive scaling and cost management capabilities for optimal resource allocation and budget planning.

App Service Environment

Azure Functions also supports additional hosting options for specific scenarios. One such option is the App Service Environment, which provides a fully isolated and dedicated environment for running App Service and Azure Functions at a high scale. App Service Environments are suitable for workloads that require very high scale, full compute isolation, secure network access, and high memory usage. With App Service Environment, you can ensure robust and secure execution of your Azure Functions. To know more about App Service Environment, check out this documentation: `https://learn.microsoft.com/en-us/azure/app-service/environment/overview`.

Azure Container Apps

Another hosting option is Azure Container Apps, which offers a serverless platform for running microservices and containerized applications. Azure Container Apps utilizes the power of **Azure Kubernetes Service** (**AKS**) while abstracting the complexity of working with Kubernetes APIs. This environment is well-suited for running functions within containers, enabling you to take advantage of the scalability and orchestration capabilities provided by AKS.

Kubernetes directly or through Azure Arc

Additionally, you have the flexibility to host your functions directly on Kubernetes, either in a direct Kubernetes cluster or using Azure Arc. This option allows you to implement a fully isolated and dedicated environment on top of the Kubernetes platform. Kubernetes hosting is beneficial for workloads that require custom hardware requirements, isolation, secure network access, the ability to run in hybrid or multicloud environments, and the capability to coexist with existing Kubernetes applications and services.

By offering these hosting options, Azure Functions allows choosing the most suitable environment for specific application requirements. Whether it's the fully isolated App Service Environment, the power of Azure Kubernetes Service through Azure Container Apps, or hosting directly on Kubernetes with Azure Arc, organizations can ensure optimal performance, scalability, and security for their Azure Functions deployments.

You can get further details about the pricing on the following page: `https://azure.microsoft.com/en-us/pricing/details/functions/`.

Performance and scale

Azure Functions provides excellent performance and scalability capabilities, allowing applications to handle varying workloads with ease. With its serverless architecture, Azure Functions automatically scales to accommodate increased demand.

Horizontal scaling

By default, Azure Functions continuously monitors the load on applications and dynamically provisions additional host instances as required. For instance, when using QueueTrigger, Azure Functions uses predefined thresholds, such as message age and queue size, to intelligently determine the appropriate time to add instances. This intelligent scaling mechanism is called **horizontal scaling**. It ensures optimal resource allocation and efficient scaling, empowering your applications to handle workload fluctuations effectively.

Event-driven scaling

Event-driven scaling in Azure Functions, available in both the Consumption and Premium plans, utilizes the addition of more instances of the Functions host to scale CPU and memory resources. The scaling is directly tied to the number of events that trigger a function. In the Consumption plan, each instance of the Functions host is typically limited to 1.5 GB of memory and one CPU. It's important to note that an instance of the host encompasses the totality of the function app, meaning all functions hosted on the same function app share resources within that instance and scale simultaneously. However, function apps that share the same Consumption plan scale independently and provide isolation and scalability on a **per-function-app basis**.

In the Premium plan, the available memory and CPU for all apps within the plan on a given instance are determined by the plan size. This allows for more flexibility in resource allocation and performance tuning across multiple function apps. It's worth mentioning that function code files are stored on Azure file shares within the function's main storage account. It's essential to exercise caution as deleting the main storage account of a function app will result in the permanent deletion of the function code files, making them irrecoverable. This underscores the importance of maintaining proper backups and version control to safeguard code and ensure its availability.

Target-based scaling

Azure Functions employs target-based scaling to efficiently allocate resources based on the rate of events. The **scale controller**, a crucial component within Azure Functions, continuously monitors event rates and determines whether scaling out or scaling in is necessary. Each trigger type, such as Azure Queue Storage triggers, is associated with specific heuristics used by the scale controller. *Figure 7.1* shows the Azure Functions scaling mechanism:

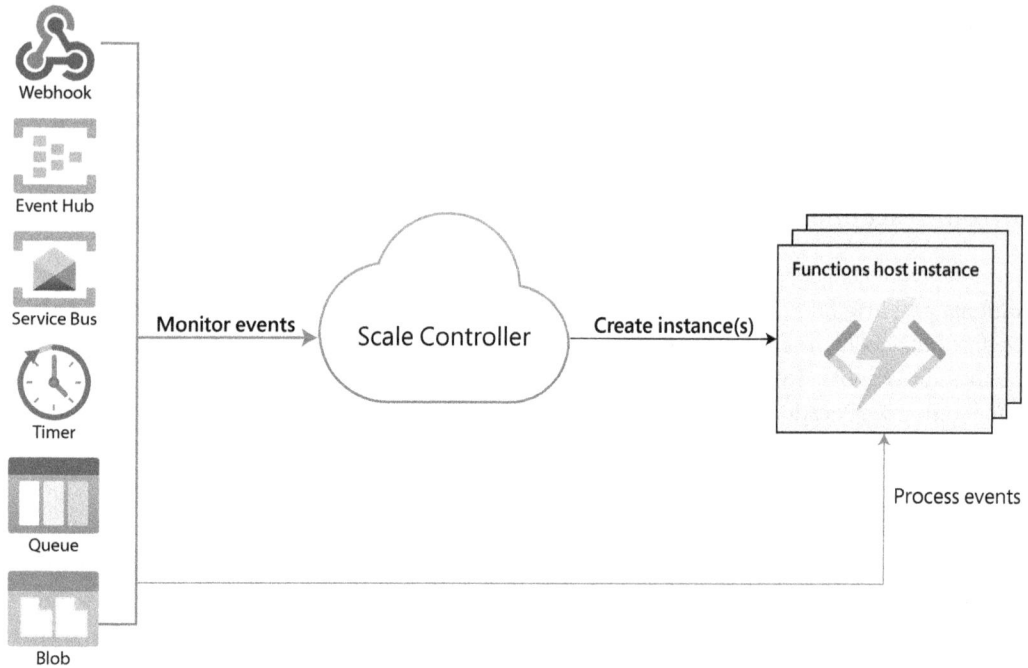

Figure 7.1: Azure Functions scaling mechanism

In target-based scaling, the function app serves as the unit of scale. Scaling out involves allocating additional resources to run multiple instances of the Azure Functions host, while scaling in reduces the number of function host instances when compute demand decreases. Scaling in occurs when there are no running functions within a function app.

Target-based scaling provides an agile and intuitive scaling model for customers and the best part is it currently supports various extensions, including Service Bus queues and topics, Storage Queues, Event Hubs, and Azure Cosmos DB. It replaces the previous incremental scaling model, which had more complex scaling decisions. With target-based scaling, up to four instances can be scaled up simultaneously, and the scaling decision is based on a simple target-based equation that takes into account the event source length and target executions per instance.

The default target executions per instance values are derived from the SDKs utilized by the Azure Functions extensions, requiring no manual adjustments for target-based scaling to function properly.

In cases where multiple functions within the same function app vote to scale out, the desired instances change is determined by summing the votes. Scale-out requests take precedence over scale-in requests. If there are no scale-out requests but scale-in requests exist, the maximum scale-in value is used. To achieve the most accurate scaling based on metrics, it is recommended to have one target-based triggered function per function app.

By using target-based scaling, Azure Functions efficiently allocates resources based on event rates, ensuring optimal performance and resource utilization for your applications. To learn more about target-based scaling, check out the documentation here: `https://learn.microsoft.com/en-us/azure/azure-functions/functions-target-based-scaling?tabs=v5%2Ccsharp`.

Cold start

When an Azure function app remains idle for a certain duration, the platform may scale down the number of instances, running the app to zero. This behavior is what we call **Cold Start**. As a result, the subsequent request incurs additional latency due to the need to scale from zero to one instance. This latency is commonly known as a cold start. The cold start time can be influenced by the number of dependencies required by the function app. Cold starts tend to have a more noticeable impact on synchronous operations, particularly HTTP triggers that necessitate a prompt response. If cold starts significantly affect the performance of your functions, it is advisable to consider running them in a Premium plan or in a Dedicated plan with the Always On setting enabled. These options can help mitigate the effects of cold starts by keeping instances warm and ready to handle incoming requests.

Business continuity

Business continuity is the ability of an organization to continue essential operations during and after disruptions such as natural disasters or other unfavorable scenarios with the goal of ensuring resilience and minimal downtime. Ensuring business continuity for Azure Functions in the face of region-wide downtime is crucial for maintaining the processing of mission-critical code. To address this, you can employ strategies for deploying functions that enable effective disaster recovery. In Azure Functions, functions run within a function app in a specific Azure region without built-in redundancy.

To minimize execution loss during outages, redundant deployment of functions to function apps in multiple regions is advised. You can adopt two patterns when using the same function code across regions: active/active and active/passive. In the active/active pattern, functions in both regions process events concurrently or in rotation. For critical HTTP-triggered functions, it's recommended to combine this pattern with Azure Front Door. Azure Front Door acts as a global load balancer, routing incoming HTTP requests to the nearest available region, ensuring lower latency and improved performance for end users. This combination enhances fault tolerance and optimizes response times for essential functions, making it ideal for critical scenarios.

On the other hand, in an active/passive pattern, functions actively run in the region where events are received, while identical functions in a second region remain idle. When failover becomes necessary, the second region is activated to take over the event processing. This pattern is suitable for event-driven functions triggered by services such as Service Bus and Event Hubs.

HTTP trigger geo-redundancy

For achieving redundancy in HTTP trigger functions, the recommended deployment model is the active/active pattern. To facilitate this pattern, Azure Front Door is instrumental in coordinating requests between multiple regions. By using Azure Front Door, HTTP requests can be intelligently routed and load-balanced across functions running in different regions. Additionally, Azure Front Door performs regular health checks on each endpoint. If a function in one region becomes unresponsive during health checks, Azure Front Door automatically removes it from the rotation and directs traffic exclusively to the remaining healthy functions. This ensures seamless request handling and enhances the overall reliability and availability of your HTTP trigger functions, as shown in *Figure 7.2*, depicting Azure Functions HTTP trigger geo-redundancy:

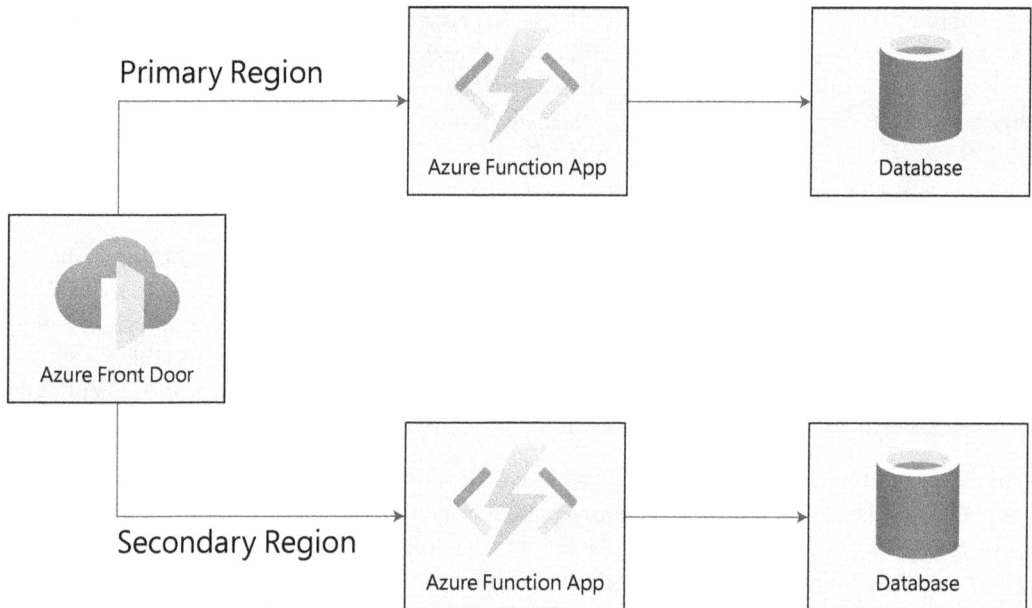

Figure 7.2: Azure Functions HTTP trigger geo-redundancy

Non-HTTP trigger geo-redundancy

To achieve redundancy for non-HTTP trigger functions, a different pattern is employed, taking into account the failover behaviors of related services.

Active/passive redundancy is a suitable approach for non-HTTP trigger functions, providing a mechanism for a single function to process each message while enabling failover to a secondary region (or failover region) in the event of failure. This pattern aligns with the failover capabilities of partner services such as Azure Service Bus geo-recovery and Azure Event Hubs geo-recovery. In an example scenario using an Azure Event Hubs trigger, the active/passive pattern entails the following components:

- Deployment of Azure Event Hubs in both a primary and secondary region
- Enabling geo-disaster recovery to pair the primary and secondary event hubs, creating an alias that simplifies connection switching between the primary and secondary without modifying the connection information
- Deploying function apps in both the primary and secondary (failover) regions, where the secondary function app remains idle as messages are not being sent to it
- Each function app triggers on the direct connection string of its respective event hub (non-alias)
- Publishers sending messages to the event hub should publish to the alias connection string

Figure 7.3 shows how Azure Functions non-HTTP trigger geo-redundancy works:

Primary Region

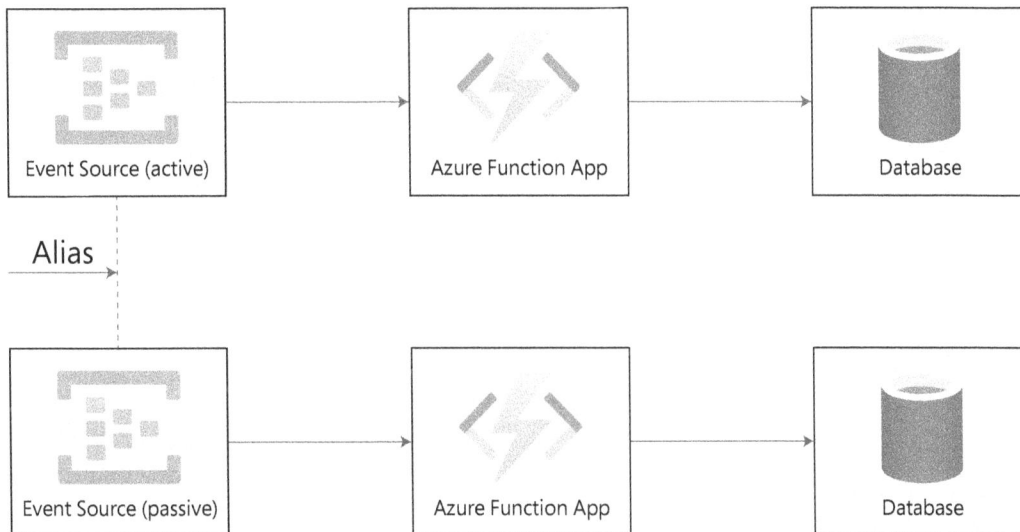

Secondary Region

Figure 7.3: Azure Functions HTTP trigger geo-redundancy

The preceding diagram can be described as the following process:

1. Prior to failover, publishers direct messages to the shared alias.
2. The shared alias routes messages to the primary event hub.
3. The primary function app exclusively listens to the primary event hub.
4. The secondary function app remains passive and idle.

Once failover is initiated, the following occurs:

1. Publishers send messages to the shared alias.

2. The shared alias routes messages to the secondary event hub.

3. As a result, the secondary function app becomes active. The secondary function app triggers automatically.

4. Failover to the secondary region is driven by the event hub.

For non-HTTP triggered functions, their activation relies on the event hub's availability. While active/active redundancy is possible, it requires careful coordination between regions. One approach involves deploying the same function app to two regions, competing as consumers on a shared Service Bus queue. However, this introduces a potential single point of failure. Alternatively, deploying separate Service Bus queues in primary and secondary regions, with each region having its own function app, simplifies redundancy. Yet, challenges such as message duplication and data consolidation arise. To ensure a straightforward and reliable redundancy strategy, it is advisable to use the active/passive pattern for non-HTTP trigger functions.

Building stateful workloads with Durable Functions

Durable Functions, as an extension of Azure Functions, offers a powerful solution for stateful workloads in a serverless computing environment. With Durable Functions, you can develop stateful workflows by creating orchestrator functions and stateful entities through the familiar Azure Functions programming model. The extension takes care of managing the underlying state, checkpoints, and restarts, allowing you to focus on implementing your core business logic.

By abstracting away the complexities of state management, Durable Functions enables you to build robust and reliable applications that maintain their state across multiple function invocations. This makes it particularly well-suited for scenarios that require long-running processes, coordination between multiple functions, and reliable state management, all while leveraging the scalability and cost-efficiency benefits of serverless computing.

To know more about Durable Functions, check out the official GitHub repository: `https://github.com/Azure/durabletask`.

Understanding stateful workloads in the serverless world

Understanding stateful workloads in the serverless world is crucial for designing efficient and scalable applications. In traditional computing models, managing state across function invocations can be complex and resource-intensive, hence the concept of stateful workloads comes into play. In this section, we'll dive into Durable Functions and see how it helps address the pain points in the serverless environment.

Key scenarios and use cases

In a serverless environment, stateful workloads refer to applications that require the preservation and management of data or context between function executions. This could involve maintaining user sessions, processing sequential workflows, or managing long-running processes. Here are a few example scenarios where Durable Functions comes into play:

- **Order Processing**: A durable workflow can be designed to handle end-to-end order processing, involving multiple steps such as order validation, inventory management, payment processing, and shipping coordination. Durable Functions ensures the reliability and consistency of the entire process, even if it spans multiple function executions or external systems.

- **Approval Workflows**: Durable Functions can orchestrate approval workflows, where multiple stakeholders need to review and approve a request. The workflow can be designed to handle tasks such as sending approval requests, tracking responses, and triggering subsequent actions based on the approvals received. Durable Functions provides built-in support for human interactions through external events or timers.

- **Data Processing Pipelines**: Complex data processing tasks, such as **Extract, Transform, Load** (**ETL**) processes or batch processing, can be efficiently handled using Durable Functions. The workflow can orchestrate the steps involved, such as data extraction, transformation, and loading into target systems. Durable Functions enables fault tolerance, allowing the workflow to automatically recover from failures and resume processing.

- **IoT Device Management**: Durable Functions can manage the lifecycle of IoT devices by orchestrating tasks such as device provisioning, configuration updates, and firmware upgrades. The workflow can handle device registration, scheduling tasks, and monitoring the status of devices. Durable Functions provides a reliable and scalable approach to managing large numbers of IoT devices.

- **Chatbots and Conversational Flows**: Durable Functions can be used to build conversational flows for chatbots or virtual assistants. The workflow can manage the dialog state, handle user inputs, make API calls, and provide dynamic responses. Durable Functions ensures that the conversation state is maintained across multiple interactions and can be easily extended to support complex conversational scenarios.

These are just a few examples of how Durable Functions can be utilized to streamline and manage various workflows and processes in a reliable and scalable manner. The flexibility and durability provided by Durable Functions makes it a powerful tool for building long-running applications.

Why does Durable Functions matter?

Durable Functions is an excellent fit for stateful workloads in the serverless world. It addresses the need to maintain and manage state across function invocations, which is not natively supported in traditional serverless architectures. With Durable Functions, orchestrator functions serve as the central control flow for stateful workflows, enabling the preservation of variables, coordination of function execution, and tracking of workflow state. The complexity of state management, including checkpointing and recovery, is abstracted away, allowing developers to focus on implementing business logic rather than handling state transitions and failures.

By leveraging tools such as Durable Functions in Azure, developers can build stateful applications with ease, as the underlying infrastructure handles state management, checkpoints, and restarts. This allows developers to focus on implementing business logic while ensuring data integrity and consistency. Understanding the nuances of stateful workloads in the serverless world is essential for unlocking the full potential of serverless computing and designing resilient and scalable applications.

Language support

Durable Functions offers language support for all Azure Functions programming languages, although the minimum requirements may vary depending on the specific language. The minimum supported app configurations are determined based on the language stack and Azure Functions runtime versions, ensuring compatibility and optimal performance for each supported language.

To simplify the development of Durable Functions and enable developers to get started quickly, templates are available within popular development tools such as Visual Studio, Visual Studio Code, and the Azure portal. These templates serve as a starting point and expedite the creation of functions and applications using Durable Functions. By leveraging these templates, developers can enjoy a seamless and efficient development experience, saving time and effort in setting up and configuring Durable Functions projects.

For more comprehensive information regarding the language support provided by Durable Functions, including the minimum requirements for each language, you can refer to the following official documentation: https://learn.microsoft.com/en-us/azure/azure-functions/durable/durable-functions-overview?tabs=csharp-inproc#language-support.

Function types

In Durable Functions, there are four primary function types: activity, orchestrator, entity, and client. These functions work together to enable complex orchestration scenarios. Let's explore each function type in more detail:

- **Activity Functions**: Activity functions represent the individual units of work within a durable function app. They perform specific tasks or operations and can be invoked independently. Activity functions encapsulate discrete actions and can be reused across multiple orchestrations.

- **Orchestrator Functions**: Orchestrator functions serve as the central coordination mechanism within a Durable Functions app. They define the flow and sequence of activities, making decisions, handling timeouts, and managing the state of the orchestration. Orchestrator functions enable the composition and coordination of activity functions, providing a higher-level view of the overall workflow.

- **Entity Functions**: Entity functions introduce stateful entities within a Durable Functions app. They allow for shared state and stateful operations to be maintained across multiple function invocations. Entity functions provide an abstraction to manage and interact with stateful data, enabling scenarios such as counters, distributed locking, and collaborative workflows.

- **Client Functions**: Client functions serve as the entry point for initiating and interacting with a Durable Functions app. They can start an orchestration, query the status of an ongoing orchestration, or send external events to running orchestrations. Client functions enable external systems to interact with and trigger the execution of Durable Functions workflows.

By leveraging these function types, developers can design and implement complex orchestration logic, define stateful entities, and interact with Durable Functions apps from external systems. This rich set of function types empowers developers to create scalable and reliable solutions by combining the power of serverless computing with stateful coordination and execution capabilities provided by Durable Functions.

Application patterns

Durable Functions offers several application patterns that simplify complex, stateful coordination requirements in serverless applications. These patterns enable developers to address various scenarios efficiently. Let's explore each of these application patterns:

- **Function chaining**: This pattern, as shown in *Figure 7.4*, involves invoking multiple functions in a sequential manner, where the output of one function serves as the input for the next function. Durable Functions simplifies function chaining by allowing developers to define orchestrator functions that coordinate the execution of individual functions in a specified order.

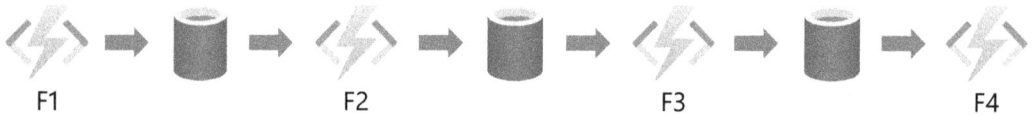

Figure 7.4: Function chaining pattern

- **Fan-out/fan-in**: The fan-out/fan-in pattern, as shown in *Figure 7.5*, is used when multiple parallel operations need to be performed simultaneously and then aggregated into a single result. Durable Functions enables developers to spawn multiple functions concurrently (fan-out) and later aggregate the results (fan-in) using the built-in capabilities of the framework.

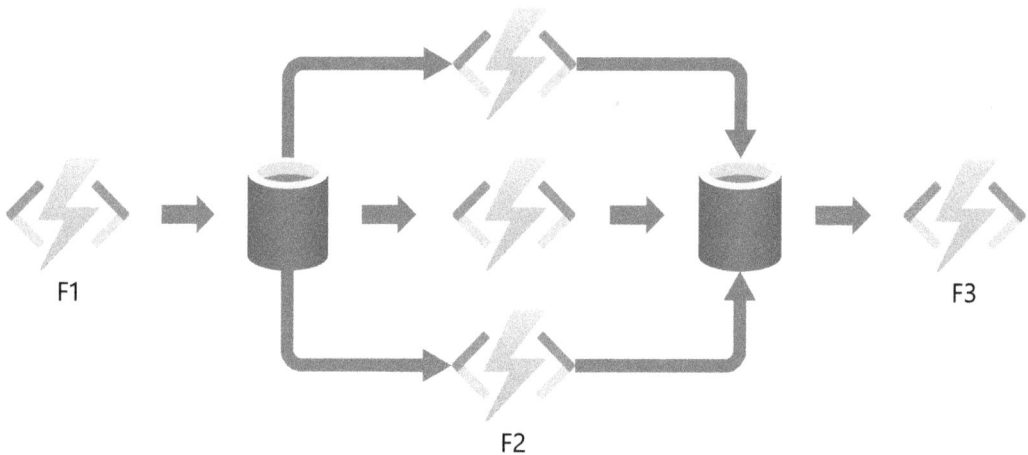

Figure 7.5: The fan-out/fan-in pattern

- **Async HTTP APIs**: Durable Functions can be used to create asynchronous HTTP APIs that can handle long-running operations. This pattern is shown in *Figure 7.6*, By leveraging the durable nature of Durable Functions, developers can initiate an operation, receive an HTTP response with a correlation ID, and later query the status or retrieve the result using the same correlation ID.

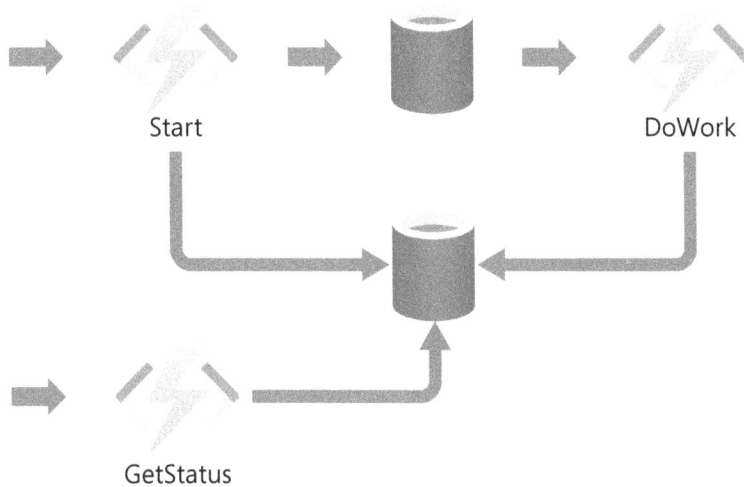

Figure 7.6: Async HTTP APIs pattern

- **Monitoring**: Durable Functions can play a crucial role in monitoring scenarios, where periodic checks or notifications need to be triggered based on certain conditions. As shown in *Figure 7.7*, with this pattern, developers can use Durable Functions to orchestrate the monitoring process, ensuring timely checks, and triggering appropriate actions when specific conditions are met.

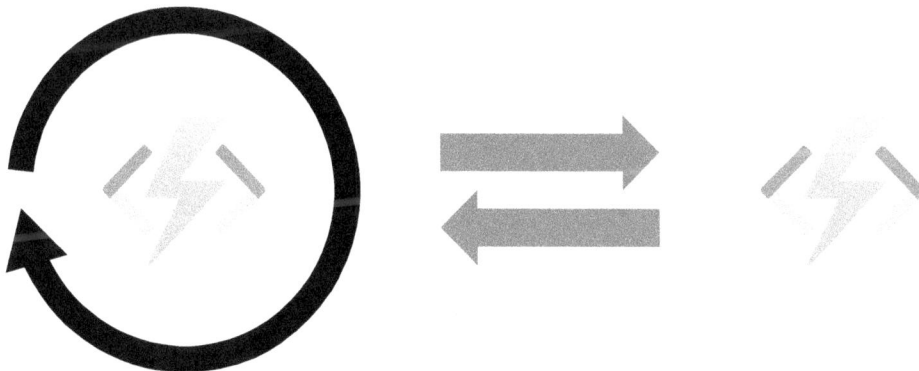

Figure 7.7: Monitoring pattern

- **Human interaction**: Durable Functions can facilitate human interaction scenarios where manual approval, intervention, or decision-making is required, as shown in *Figure 7.8*. Developers can design workflows that involve human interaction, where Durable Functions pause the workflow, wait for human input, and resume processing based on the received input.

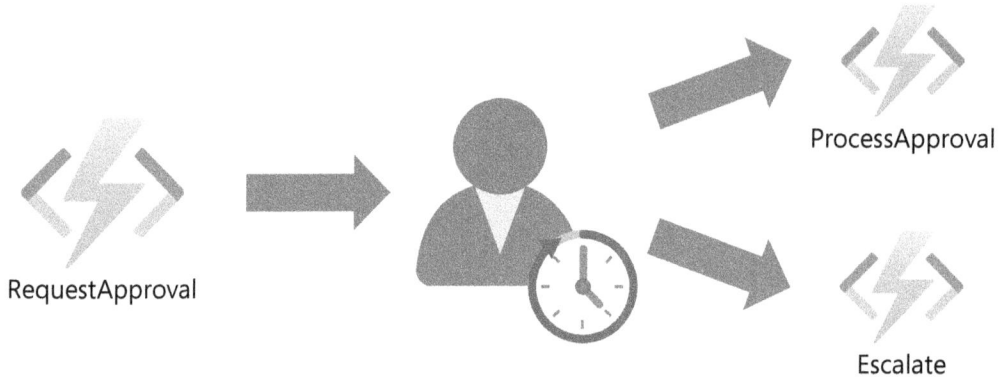

Figure 7.8: Human interaction

- **Aggregator (stateful entities)**: Durable Functions supports the concept of stateful entities that can maintain and aggregate state across multiple function invocations. Developers can use stateful entities to implement aggregators that collect data from various sources, apply aggregation logic, and maintain the aggregated state over time. This pattern is shown in *Figure 7.9*.

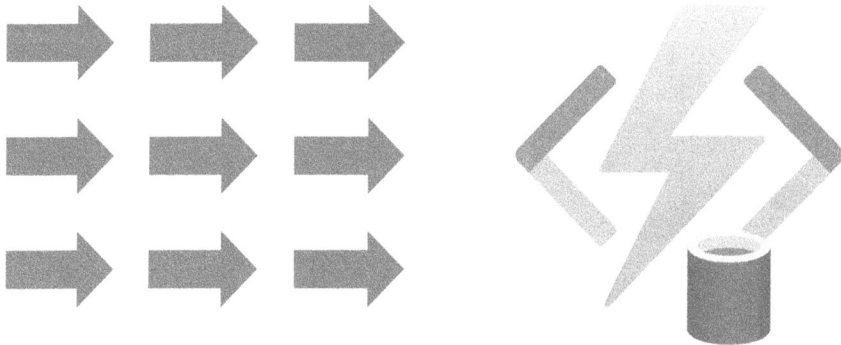

Figure 7.9: Aggregator

By leveraging these application patterns, developers can harness the power of Durable Functions to address complex coordination requirements, implement stateful workflows, and simplify the development of serverless applications. These patterns enable the efficient orchestration of functions, seamless handling of parallel operations, integration of human interaction, and management of stateful entities. Check out further details here: https://learn.microsoft.com/en-us/azure/azure-functions/durable/durable-functions-overview?tabs=csharp-inproc.

Storage providers

Durable Functions supports multiple storage providers to handle the persistence of orchestration and entity state:

- **Azure Storage**: The default storage provider is Azure Storage, which uses queues, tables, and blobs to store data. It requires no additional setup and offers a consumption-based pricing model. Azure Storage provides robust tooling support, integrates with popular development environments, and is considered the most mature and battle-tested storage backend.

- **Netherite**: Another storage provider is Netherite, developed by Microsoft Research. It offers significantly higher throughput at a lower cost compared to other providers. Netherite utilizes Azure Event Hubs and FASTER database technology on top of Azure page blobs. It is designed to handle high-throughput workloads and allows for price-performance optimization. The Netherite storage provider has extensive technical documentation and source code available on GitHub.

- **Microsoft SQL Server (MSSQL)**: The third option is the MSSQL storage provider, which persists state in a SQL Server database. It is compatible with both on-premises and cloud-hosted SQL Server deployments, including Azure SQL Database. MSSQL storage provider supports disconnected environments, offers strong data consistency, and integrates seamlessly with existing database applications through built-in stored procedures. Technical documentation and source code for the MSSQL storage provider are available on GitHub.

To know more about those storage providers, check out this documentation: `https://learn.microsoft.com/en-us/azure/azure-functions/durable/durable-functions-storage-providers`.

The availability of multiple storage providers gives developers flexibility in choosing the most suitable option based on cost, performance, scalability, and specific requirements for their Durable Functions applications. Each provider offers distinct benefits, allowing developers to seamlessly handle state persistence and optimize their applications accordingly.

Versioning

As functions are continuously added, removed, and modified throughout the lifecycle of an application, it is essential to consider how these changes impact versioning. Durable Functions introduces the ability to chain functions together in unprecedented ways, transforming the possibilities for handling versioning scenarios.

With Durable Functions, the intricate chaining of functions opens up new avenues for managing versioning effectively. This powerful capability allows for seamless transitions between different versions of functions within an application. By orchestrating the flow of function execution, Durable Functions enables graceful handling of version updates, ensuring smooth transitions and minimal disruption to the overall application workflow.

You can refer to the official documentation available at the following link for guidance on different scenarios as well as best practices to ensure a smooth transition: `https://learn.microsoft.com/en-us/azure/azure-functions/durable/durable-functions-versioning?tabs=csharp`.

Data persistence and serialization

Durable Functions offer seamless data persistence and serialization capabilities, ensuring reliable execution by automatically storing function parameters, return values, and other critical state information in the task hub. This built-in persistence mechanism guarantees the integrity of data throughout the execution process. However, it's important to note that the volume and frequency of data persisted to durable storage can impact both application performance and storage transaction costs.

To optimize performance and minimize storage costs, it's crucial to carefully evaluate the data being stored and consider the specific requirements of your application. By fine-tuning the data persistence strategy, you can strike a balance between retaining essential information for reliable execution and avoiding unnecessary storage overhead.

In addition, based on the nature of the data your application handles, you must also take into account data retention and privacy policies. Compliance with regulations and privacy standards may require implementing appropriate data retention practices and ensuring the protection of sensitive information. All factors considered, you can ensure your application aligns with the necessary data governance and privacy guidelines.

Durable Functions provides the flexibility to adapt the data persistence and serialization approach based on your specific application requirements. By striking the right balance between data persistence, performance, and compliance considerations, you can leverage the full power of Durable Functions while maintaining optimal application performance and adhering to data management policies.

You can refer to the official documentation available at the following link to learn more about data persistence and serialization in Durable Functions: `https://learn.microsoft.com/en-us/azure/azure-functions/durable/durable-functions-serialization-and-persistence?tabs=csharp-inproc`.

Automating workflows with Azure Logic Apps

Azure Logic Apps is a powerful cloud platform that enables users to create and automate workflows with ease, requiring little to no code. It offers a visual designer and a wide selection of prebuilt operations, allowing users to quickly build workflows that integrate and manage their apps, data, services, and systems.

With Azure Logic Apps, organizations can streamline their operations and enhance productivity across various scenarios. Here are a few key examples of tasks, business processes, and workloads that can be automated using Azure Logic Apps:

- **Email Notifications**: Schedule and send email notifications using Office 365 when specific events occur. For instance, you can automate the process of sending email notifications once a new file is uploaded to a targeted destination.

- **Order Processing**: Efficiently route and process customer orders across a mix of on-premises systems and cloud services. Logic Apps can help automate the workflow, ensuring seamless order management and reducing manual effort.

- **File Management**: Move uploaded files from an SFTP or FTP server to Azure Storage. This automation eliminates the need for manual file transfers, improving efficiency and data management.

- **Social Media Monitoring**: Monitor tweets, analyze sentiment, and create alerts or tasks based on specific criteria. This capability allows organizations to stay updated on social media trends, identify customer sentiment, and proactively address any concerns or opportunities.

Figure 7.10 shows how Azure Logic Apps look when an event is triggered and in reaction to it, an SMS and email notification is sent using Azure Functions through Logic Apps:

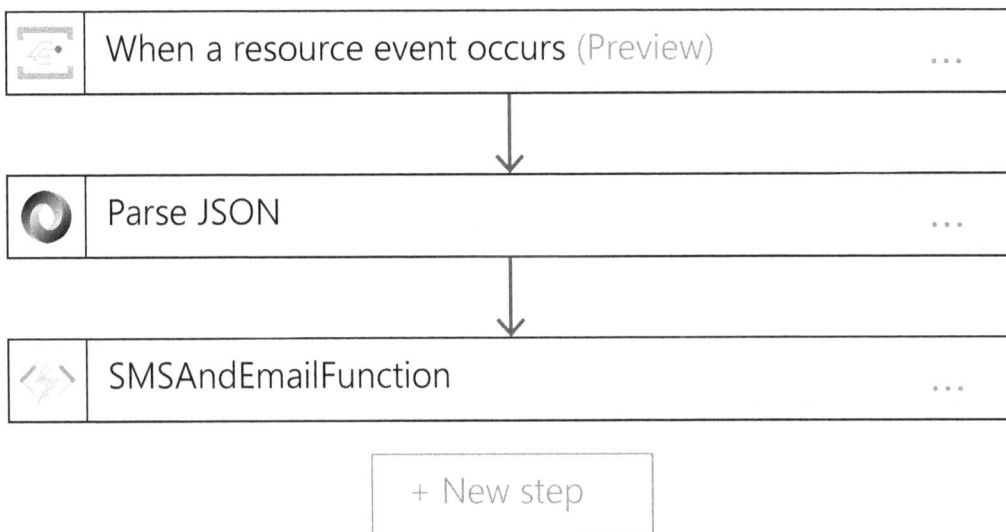

Figure 7.10: Azure Logic Apps

Azure Logic Apps simplifies the integration of legacy, modern, and cutting-edge systems across different environments, including cloud, on-premises, and hybrid setups. Its low-code and no-code approach empowers users to develop scalable integration solutions for enterprise and business-to-business scenarios. By leveraging the capabilities of Azure Logic Apps, organizations can automate processes, streamline operations, and unlock new levels of efficiency and productivity.

Integrating apps with Azure Event Grid

Azure Event Grid is a highly scalable and fully managed message distribution service that allows for seamless integration of applications. With Azure Event Grid, you can easily build data pipelines, integrate applications, and create event-driven serverless architectures. This service enables publishers to announce system state changes (events) to subscriber applications through HTTP, facilitating event-driven solutions. Event Grid supports both push and pull delivery, allowing subscribers to connect and read events or receive events directly, as shown in *Figure 7.11*:

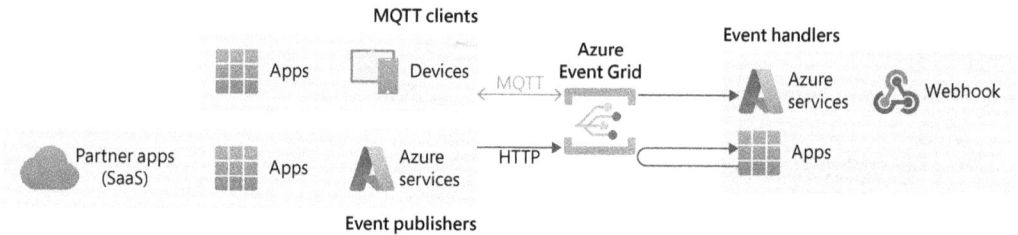

Figure 7.11: Azure Event Grid messaging

With its support for the CloudEvents 1.0 specification, Event Grid ensures interoperability across systems. Whether it's data ingestion from IoT devices or data distribution using push and pull delivery modes, Azure Event Grid serves as a crucial component of data pipelines and integration scenarios. It can seamlessly integrate with various data sources, including Azure services, custom applications, and external partner systems, enabling efficient data distribution and integration throughout your ecosystem.

Building event-driven architecture

Event-driven architecture is a design approach that focuses on the exchange and processing of events. This allows systems to react and communicate in a decoupled manner based on the occurrence of specific events or triggers. Building an event-driven architecture involves designing systems that respond to events, enabling real-time communication and flexibility. Components communicate through events triggered by various sources, allowing for loose coupling, scalability, and extensibility. This approach fosters modular systems that can evolve independently, making it ideal for microservices, event sourcing, and real-time analytics. By embracing event-driven architecture, organizations can create resilient, responsive systems that efficiently handle complex interactions and adapt to changing business needs.

Building an event-driven serverless solution

Let's create an event-based, serverless solution using Azure Functions and Logic Apps, optimizing efficiency with Azure Event Grid. This integration enables seamless communication and coordination between the different serverless services. In this architecture, Azure Functions Apps publish events to Event Grid using HTTP. Event Grid acts as a highly scalable message distribution service, receiving these events and forwarding them to Azure Logic Apps for further processing and automation.

By using serverless services as shown in *Figure 7.12*, Azure Functions with Event Grid and Azure Logic Apps, developers can enjoy increased productivity and reduced effort compared to traditional computing models. The serverless approach eliminates the need to manage and maintain infrastructure, allowing developers to focus solely on building and deploying their application logic. This results in improved time-to-market and resource efficiency.

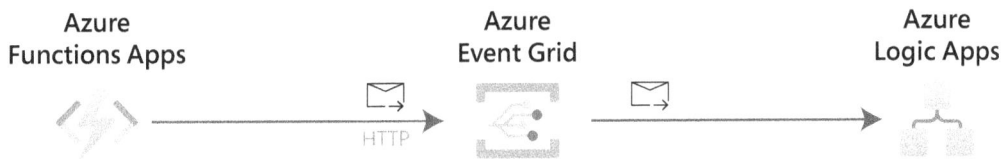

Azure Functions Apps   **Azure Event Grid**   **Azure Logic Apps**

HTTP

Figure 7.12: Event-driven serverless solutions

Event-driven serverless solutions offer a range of benefits, including automatic scalability, pay-per-use pricing, and event-based triggers. With Event Grid as the central event routing service, developers can easily orchestrate complex workflows, integrate with external systems, and react to events in real time. The seamless integration between Azure Functions, Logic Apps, and Event Grid provides a powerful foundation for building robust and scalable serverless applications.

Understanding lambda architecture

For most big data analytic solutions, lambda architecture is widely used. It is a design pattern that aims to provide efficient and scalable processing of large-scale data by combining batch and real-time data processing techniques. It addresses the challenges posed by the velocity, volume, and variety of data in big data systems.

In lambda architecture, incoming data is processed in parallel through two separate paths: the batch layer and the speed layer as shown in *Figure 7.13*:

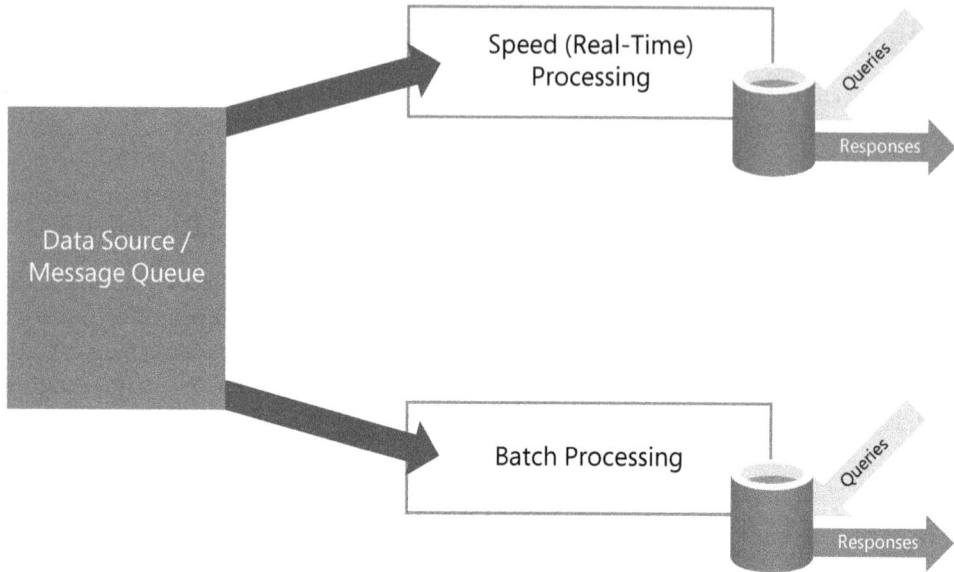

Figure 7.13: Lambda architecture

The batch layer handles large volumes of data. The outputs from both layers are then combined in a serving layer to provide a unified and holistic view of the data. This approach ensures that the system can handle both historical and real-time data, providing timely insights and analytics.

By utilizing the strengths of both batch and real-time processing, lambda architecture enables organizations to build robust and scalable data processing systems capable of meeting the demands of modern big data applications.

Building an event-driven big data analytics solution

In the preceding sections, we explored the mechanics of an event-driven serverless solution and leaped into the concept of lambda architecture. Now, let's delve into a real-life scenario that showcases an event-driven big data analytics solution for ContosoPackt where we seamlessly integrated the principles of event-driven architecture with the spirit of lambda architecture.

Scenario

Contoso is a fictional company that is working on building an event-driven big data analytics solution.

They aim to solve the problem of users and organizations not receiving notifications when their Azure Key Vault secrets expire. This issue leads to applications failing while causing inconvenience and disruptions. The challenge is the lack of infrastructure provided by Azure to monitor Key Vault secrets, keys, and certificates.

Challenges

To overcome this challenge, Contoso proposes a solution that combines multiple Azure services to proactively notify users about the expiration of secrets. The solution utilizes Azure Key Vault, **Azure Active Directory** (**Azure AD**), Azure Event Grid, Azure Automation, Logic Apps, Azure Functions, SendGrid, and Twilio SMS.

Solution

The architecture of the solution involves integrating these services in a coordinated manner. Azure Key Vault serves as the central repository for storing secrets, keys, and certificates. Azure Event Grid facilitates the detection of expiration events in Key Vault. Azure Automation, Logic Apps, and Azure Functions play essential roles in orchestrating workflows and executing actions based on the detected events. SendGrid and Twilio SMS are used to send notifications to users via email and SMS, respectively.

The workflow begins with Azure Event Grid monitoring Key Vault for expiration events. Once an expiration event is detected, it triggers Logic Apps, Azure Functions, and Azure Automation to orchestrate the workflow. Logic Apps is responsible for sending email notifications using SendGrid, while Azure Functions integrates with Twilio SMS to send SMS notifications to users. Azure Automation can be employed to perform additional actions if required.

The architecture of the solution comprises multiple services, as shown in *Figure 7.14*:

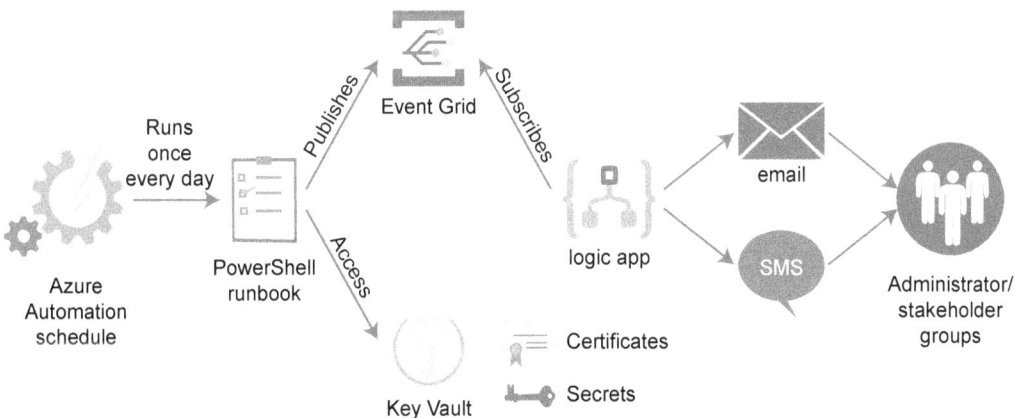

Figure 7.14: ContosoPackt solution architecture

Benefits and advantages

By implementing this architecture, Contoso creates an end-to-end solution that automates the notification process for secret expiration. The solution ensures that users and organizations are promptly informed, allowing them to take necessary actions to prevent application failures due to expired secrets.

This architecture enables Contoso to build an event-driven big data analytics solution that seamlessly integrates various Azure services to address the problem of secret expiration notifications. It eliminates the manual effort of monitoring and ensures that users and organizations stay informed, enhancing the overall reliability as well as the performance of their cloud-native applications.

Summary

In this chapter, we talked about Azure Functions and its Durable Functions extension, and we explored the development of serverless applications using Azure Functions and the implementation of event-driven architectural solutions by leveraging various Azure services such as Azure Event Grid, Logic Apps, and others. In the upcoming chapter, our focus will shift toward discussing security policies and governance models that can be effectively implemented to safeguard Azure resources.

8

Deploying, Managing, and Scaling Containers with Azure Kubernetes Service

Kubernetes is by far one of the fastest-growing technologies ever, thanks to the increasing popularity of containerization in the tech industry. Organizations use Kubernetes to take advantage of the portability of containerization technology with efficient resource utilization. The richness of the Kubernetes ecosystem also makes it easy to enable agile DevOps practices and reduce operational costs. In this chapter, we will provide you with a comprehensive understanding of containers and Kubernetes, covering their history and the role of container orchestrators such as Kubernetes.

We will delve into various aspects, including the upstream Kubernetes and **Azure Kubernetes Service** (**AKS**) cluster architecture and the use of add-ons, extensions, and third-party integrations with AKS. We will explore application development by looking at Kubernetes primitives and application life cycle management.

Additionally, we will discuss Kubernetes networking by covering the kubenet and **Container Network Interface** (**CNI**) models, Ingress controllers, and network policies. Lastly, we will touch upon AKS cluster security and introduce managed AKS through Azure Container Apps.

By the end of this chapter, you'll have the knowledge and skills required to build and scale applications on AKS clusters and Azure Container Apps.

In this chapter, we'll cover the following topics:

- Containers and Kubernetes concepts
- Understanding Kubernetes architecture
- Deplying applications on AKS
- AKS networking concepts

- Understanding AKS security
- Demystifying managed AKS – Azure Container Apps

Let us start by exploring the basic concepts of containers and Kubernetes.

Understanding containers and Kubernetes

Containerization is an application management approach that involves encapsulating all the necessary dependencies, libraries, and configurations within a lightweight, standalone, and executable software package called a container image. Let's take a look at containers in more detail.

Container concepts

Containers are self-contained units that can run consistently across different computing environments. Containerized applications can run on any platform, such as Linux, Windows, or macOS, uniformly without any changes being needed, which makes them highly portable.

Containers provide a way to encapsulate applications, their dependencies, and configurations into a single, portable unit that can be easily deployed and scaled. This helps organizations to be free from getting tied to a single cloud provider and to easily lift and shift their workloads from on-premises to the cloud, or even to move between multiple clouds. This approach offers numerous benefits, including improved efficiency, faster deployment times, increased scalability, and simplified management.

Managing a few containers for development and testing is relatively straightforward. However, the true challenge arises when dealing with hundreds or even thousands of containers, particularly for enterprise-grade product workloads. The management of networking, deployment, configuration, and more becomes complex. This is where a container orchestrator plays a vital role.

Kubernetes concepts

Many organizations still ask, "Do we need Kubernetes, or indeed any container orchestrator?" When we think about container management on a large scale, we need to think about several points, such as scaling, load balancing, life cycle management, continuous delivery, logging and monitoring, and more.

Kubernetes supports different workloads, including stateless, stateful, and data-processing applications. This enables the containerization and smooth deployment of virtually any application, irrespective of complexity or requirements.

Kubernetes equips developers and organizations with the necessary tools and resources to harness the power of containerization and efficiently manage complex environments. By leveraging Kubernetes, organizations can confidently navigate the path to scalable, reliable, and highly available applications, optimizing efficiency and embracing technological excellence.

However, the complexity associated with managing this tool remains a significant hurdle for enterprises to fully leverage its potential. By acquiring knowledge about Kubernetes and its ecosystem, organizations can become effective in deploying, managing, and operating Kubernetes clusters. Kubernetes benefits from a thriving and rapidly expanding open source community. With over 60 known platforms and distributions in the market, there is a wealth of options to choose from. Let's take a look at vanilla Kubernetes in the community and managed Kubernetes from public cloud providers.

Upstream vanilla Kubernetes

Upstream vanilla Kubernetes is a widely adopted choice for organizations seeking to manage their own Kubernetes clusters within their on-premises infrastructure or cloud-based virtual machines. This distribution derives its source code from the upstream Kubernetes community project, which encourages contributions and welcomes individuals to join **Special Interest Groups** (**SIGs**) to have a meaningful impact on the community. Feel free to explore opportunities for collaboration and contribution at `https://kubernetes.io/docs/contribute/generate-ref-docs/contribute-upstream/`.

Managed Kubernetes

Managed Kubernetes distributions fall under the purview of cloud vendors. These distributions are typically built upon the vanilla Kubernetes cluster, with each vendor adding their own features and capabilities to suit their infrastructure.

With a managed Kubernetes offering, the vendor takes care of the control plane management, allowing users to focus on managing worker nodes and delivering value based on their core expertise. With the vendor managing the control plane infrastructure, teams can save time and resources, as they no longer need to handle routine maintenance or upgrades. Managed Kubernetes offerings often come with built-in scaling, monitoring, and security features, while integrating seamlessly with other cloud services. This arrangement empowers users to leverage Kubernetes efficiently, enhance development processes, and deliver valuable solutions with a robust managed infrastructure.

Major cloud providers, such as Microsoft Azure (via Azure Kubernetes Service), Amazon Web Services (via Elastic Kubernetes Service), and Google Cloud Platform (via Google Kubernetes Engine), offer their own managed Kubernetes solutions. Other notable Kubernetes distributions include VMware's Tanzu, Red Hat OpenShift, Canonical Charmed Kubernetes, and Kubernetes from Rancher Labs.

Whether opting for upstream vanilla Kubernetes or exploring managed Kubernetes solutions provided by reputable cloud vendors, the broad ecosystem ensures flexibility and caters to a wide range of deployment scenarios.

So far, we have covered the basics of Kubernetes. You may ask how Kubernetes achieves all this. In the next section, we will be looking at the components of Kubernetes and how they work hand in hand.

Understanding Kubernetes cluster architecture

To start, let's dive into the different Kubernetes architectures and have a look at each one of them in detail.

Upstream vanilla Kubernetes architecture

A Kubernetes cluster has a set of worker nodes that are responsible for running the actual containerized applications or workloads. A Kubernetes cluster can have as few as 1 or as many as 5,000 worker nodes, with the latest version being Kubernetes 1.27 at the time of writing this chapter.

For quick testing purposes, it is common to spin up a single node. However, in production environments, a Kubernetes cluster typically consists of multiple worker nodes to ensure high availability and fault tolerance.

Kubernetes follows a master/slave architecture, where one device or process acts as the master to control one or more slave nodes. This architecture facilitates efficient communication and coordination within the cluster.

In a general Kubernetes cluster architecture, you will find the components shown in *Figure 8.1*, working together in harmony:

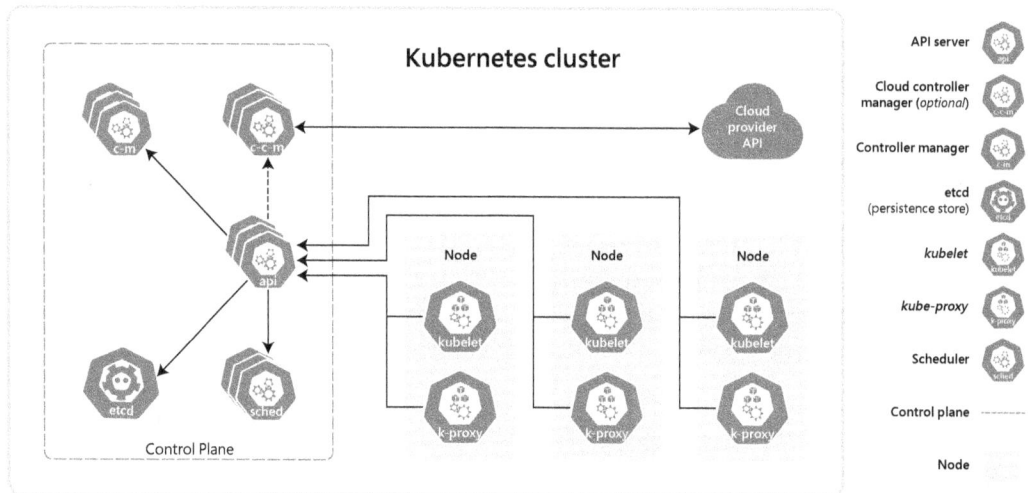

Figure 8.1: Kubernetes cluster architecture overview

The Kubernetes master node, also known as the control plane, plays a vital role in responding to cluster events. It encompasses several key components:

- **API server**: The API server serves as the central communication hub within the Kubernetes control plane. It exposes the Kubernetes REST API and facilitates seamless interaction between various components across the entire cluster.

- **etcd**: etcd serves as a distributed key-value store, storing essential information about the cluster's state and its elements. It maintains data related to Kubernetes cluster Nodes, Pods, ConfigMaps, Secrets, service accounts, roles, bindings, and more.

- **Kubernetes scheduler**: The Kubernetes scheduler, a crucial part of the control plane, handles the task of scheduling Pods onto available nodes. kube-scheduler, the default scheduler in Kubernetes, can be likened to a diligent postal officer. It dispatches Pod information to the targeted Nodes, and once the Pod arrives at its designated node, the kubelet agent provisions the actual containerized workloads based on the received specifications.

- **Controllers**: Controllers form the backbone of Kubernetes, ensuring that the cluster operates in the desired state. Several built-in controllers, housed within kube-controller-manager, serve various purposes. Examples include replication controllers, endpoint controllers, and namespace controllers.

Apart from the control plane, each worker node in a Kubernetes cluster is responsible for executing the actual workloads. It comprises the following components:

- **kubelet**: The kubelet acts as an agent running on each worker node. It accepts Pod specifications sent from the API server or locally (for static Pods) and provisions the containerized workloads, such as Pods, StatefulSets, and ReplicaSets, on the respective node.

- **Container runtime**: The container runtime serves as the software virtualization layer responsible for executing containers within Pods on each node. Common container runtimes, such as Docker, CRI-O, and Containerd, seamlessly integrate with Kubernetes.

- **kube-proxy**: kube-proxy operates on each worker node and handles network rules and traffic forwarding when a Service object is deployed within the Kubernetes cluster.

These components collectively form the intricate architecture of a Kubernetes cluster, enabling the efficient management and execution of containerized workloads.

The discussed components apply to both unmanaged and managed AKS clusters. In the case of AKS, Azure manages the control plane by shielding end users from them.

In the upcoming section, we'll explore the AKS architecture to help you understand the difference between the managed Kubernetes clusters and vanilla Kubernetes clusters.

AKS cluster architecture

In the previous section, we examined the architecture of an unmanaged cluster. Now, let's take a look at the architecture of AKS. By the end of this section, you will be able to discern the key distinctions between the architecture of unmanaged clusters and managed clusters such as AKS.

When an AKS instance is created, only the worker nodes are provisioned, while Azure takes charge of managing the control plane. The control plane includes the API server, scheduler, etcd, and controller manager, as we discussed earlier. On the other hand, the kubelets and kube-proxy are deployed exclusively on the worker nodes. Communication between the worker nodes and the control plane occurs through the kubelets, acting as agents for the Kubernetes clusters on each node. To get a clear picture, see *Figure 8.2*:

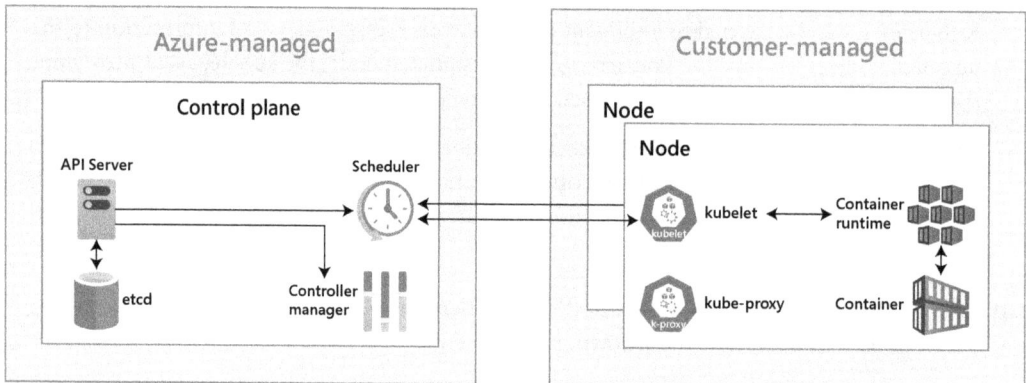

Figure 8.2: AKS architecture

Kubernetes follows a structured workflow where its components collaborate seamlessly to achieve the desired outcome.

Let's explore a typical workflow to gain a better understanding of how Kubernetes operates. When interacting with the Kubernetes cluster, the workflow involves several steps:

1. **API server**: Interactions with the cluster, whether through kubectl commands, YAML specifications, or API calls, start with the API server. It creates a Pod definition for the desired application.

2. **Scheduler**: The scheduler is responsible for efficient resource allocation. It identifies available nodes suitable for the new Pod through two steps: filtering and scoring. Filtering selects a set of candidate nodes, while scoring ranks them based on compatibility with the Pod's requirements.

3. **kubelet**: The API server transfers information to the kubelet agent on the targeted worker node. The kubelet creates the Pod on the node and instructs the container runtime engine to deploy the application image.

4. **Status update**: Once deployment is complete, the kubelet communicates the status back to the API server. The API server updates the data in the etcd store, ensuring consistent information.

5. **User notification**: The user is promptly notified of the successful Pod creation, completing the workflow.

This streamlined workflow highlights the interaction between different components, ensuring the successful creation and deployment of Pods within the Kubernetes cluster.

This workflow is repeated each time a task is performed, be it executing kubectl commands, deploying a YAML definition, or triggering a REST API call via the API server. The underlying mechanism ensures seamless coordination and consistent operations within the Kubernetes cluster.

Add-ons, extensions, and third-party integrations

Managed Kubernetes clusters such as AKS provide valuable benefits through add-ons and third-party integrations. These features enhance functionality and simplify the deployment of modern application workloads. AKS offers additional supported functionality in the form of pre-packaged add-ons and extensions, covering popular open source projects and third-party providers commonly used with Kubernetes.

By incorporating these add-ons, AKS simplifies management and reduces operational overhead, allowing users to focus on their core applications. It also enhances productivity by saving time and effort in setting up additional functionalities. With pre-integrated add-ons, developers and operations teams can quickly adopt various tools and frameworks without compatibility concerns. The ecosystem integration with third-party providers expands options for storage, networking, CI/CD tools, and more. These add-ons benefit from the active Kubernetes community, ensuring ongoing support and updates.

The add-ons' installation, configuration, and life cycle are managed by AKS. You can install an add-on or manage add-ons using the **az aks enable-addon** command. You can get a full list of add-ons and open source and third-party integrations supported by AKS here: `https://learn.microsoft.com/en-us/azure/aks/integrations#available-add-ons`.

All those add-ons, extensions, and third-party integrations are of good service in deploying your modern application workloads. We'll now take a look at how to deploy applications on AKS.

Deploying applications on AKS

You have learned that Kubernetes serves as a state manager, specifically designed for deploying and efficiently managing containers.

Developers interact with Kubernetes using tools such as kubectl, a **command-line interface** (**CLI**). Kubernetes objects, such as Pods, are used to define and configure workloads. The process of deploying an application and understanding the communication between end users and Kubernetes clusters is the same whether you are working on managed Kubernetes or other Kubernetes flavors.

Pods represent running processes and are defined in YAML or JSON files, specifying container images, resource requirements, and network settings. Developers use kubectl to create, manage, and inspect

Pods. Kubernetes objects such as Services, Deployments, ConfigMaps, and Secrets are also used for various aspects of application configuration. Using kubectl commands, developers create, update, and delete these objects, ensuring the desired configurations and behaviors for their workloads.

All operations and communications between components, as well as external user commands, within Kubernetes are facilitated through REST API calls expertly handled by the API server. In Kubernetes, every entity is treated as an API object, enabling seamless interaction and management throughout the system.

Kubernetes objects, also referred to as Kubernetes API primitives, serve as the fundamental building blocks for running containerized workloads within the Kubernetes cluster. These objects play a crucial role in defining and configuring various aspects of the workload, ensuring its smooth deployment and operation.

Kubernetes primitives

The following are the main Kubernetes objects we're going to use in our daily life working with Kubernetes clusters.

Pod

The foundational building block in Kubernetes is a Pod. It represents the smallest deployable unit within the system. Pods are hosted on worker nodes and encapsulate the actual application workload. Applications are packaged and deployed within containers, with a single Pod being capable of containing one or more containers.

The following is an example of a Pod YAML definition:

```
apiVersion: v1
kind: Pod
metadata:
  name: nginx
spec:
  containers:
  - name: nginx
    image: nginx:alpine
    ports:
    - containerPort: 80
```

You can use the following command to deploy a YAML definition to your Kubernetes clusters:

```
kubectl apply -f <your-spec>.yaml
```

ReplicaSet

A ReplicaSet ensures the high availability of Pods by defining a desired number of replicas. It guarantees that the cluster maintains the specified number of replicas at all times. In the event of failure, the ReplicaSet automatically deploys new replicas to replace any that are lost.

DaemonSet

Similar to a ReplicaSet, a DaemonSet ensures that at least one copy of a specific Pod is distributed evenly across each node in the Kubernetes cluster. Whenever a new node is added, a replica of the Pod is automatically assigned to that node. Likewise, when a node is removed, the associated Pod is automatically terminated.

StatefulSet

A StatefulSet is utilized to manage stateful applications that require persistent storage volumes to maintain their data. It enables users to ensure data persistence and the ordered deployment and scaling of stateful workloads.

Job

Jobs are employed for executing workloads reliably and defining completion criteria. Typically, a Job creates one or more Pods to carry out the specified task. Once the Job is finished, the containers within the Pods exit, and the Pods transition into the "Completed" status. Jobs are ideal when running a workload that needs to be executed once and succeed without interruption.

CronJob

CronJobs extend the capabilities of Jobs by enabling users to schedule their execution based on a predefined cron expression. A cron expression is a string that defines a schedule for executing recurring tasks in software systems. This allows for executing Jobs at specific intervals or on a recurring schedule tailored to specific requirements.

Deployment

A Deployment provides a convenient way to define the desired state of a deployment, such as specifying the number of replicas within a ReplicaSet. It simplifies the process of rolling out and rolling back updates to the application, ensuring seamless management of the desired deployment state. With Deployments, you gain the ability to easily undo changes, pause and resume deployments as needed, and ensure a smooth rollout and rollback process. Deploying a ReplicaSet with a specific number of replicas and effectively managing updates becomes simpler and more effective with the capabilities provided by Deployments.

ConfigMap

A ConfigMap is a Kubernetes object designed to store configuration data in the form of key-value pairs. This data is then readily accessible to configure software running within a container. By configuring a Pod to consume configMaps, you can conveniently utilize this configuration data through environment variables, command-line arguments, or by mounting a volume containing configuration files. ConfigMaps provide a flexible and efficient means of managing and injecting configuration data into your containerized applications.

Secrets

Secrets in Kubernetes are essential objects that securely store sensitive data, such as passwords, API tokens, or keys. Rather than storing this confidential information directly within a Pod spec or container, Secrets are used to pass and manage the data within a Pod. This approach ensures a higher level of security and protects sensitive information from being exposed or inadvertently stored within the container itself. Secrets play a crucial role in maintaining the confidentiality and integrity of sensitive data within the Kubernetes ecosystem.

It's important to remember that both ConfigMaps and Secrets data can be easily accessed within Pods, either as environment variables or through volumes. To make these resources available, the Pod definition needs to include a reference to the desired ConfigMaps or Secrets. By referencing them, you enable the Pod to use the configuration data or sensitive information stored within these objects.

We have now covered the Kubernetes primitives and the roles of each of the building blocks. Next, you will be learning about some common application deployment strategies on Kubernetes.

Application life cycle management

In Kubernetes, there are many approaches to communicating with API servers, all of which can be classified into one of two high-level categories: imperative management and declarative management. Both methods are employed for managing Kubernetes objects, and they involve using tools such as kubectl and YAML definitions.

Imperative management versus declarative management

Imperative management allows you to interact with Kubernetes by executing specific kubectl commands. These commands directly manipulate the current state of the cluster, enabling you to make immediate changes to the workload. On the other hand, declarative management aligns with the desired state management philosophy of Kubernetes. When working declaratively, you define the desired state of the workload using YAML-defined specifications or command-line parameters. Upon executing a kubectl command, Kubernetes seamlessly transitions the current state of the workload to match the desired state you have specified.

Utilizing the power of kubectl, you can employ both imperative and declarative management techniques to effectively manage and control Kubernetes objects. This flexibility empowers you to dynamically adapt and shape the state of your Kubernetes cluster, ensuring it aligns with your desired configurations and requirements.

Helm

Besides the Kubernetes-native way, we can also use package management tools such as Helm. Helm serves as a management tool specifically designed for handling packages of pre-configured Kubernetes objects, known as Helm charts. These charts encompass a collection of predefined configurations and resources, making it easier to deploy and manage complex applications within a Kubernetes environment. With Helm, you can efficiently package, distribute, and deploy these charts, simplifying the process of managing Kubernetes objects and accelerating application development and deployment workflows. This makes Helm a great tool to streamline the application life cycle on Kubernetes, including installation and management.

You can find popular Helm charts from the community or share your own application with the Helm community from here: `https://artifacthub.io/packages/search`.

Understanding AKS networking

Kubernetes is designed to facilitate desired state management for hosting containerized workloads, leveraging shared compute resources. However, ensuring smooth communication between Kubernetes components and external services can present challenges. This is where Kubernetes networking plays a crucial role.

Kubernetes networking basics

Kubernetes networking resolves the complexities of facilitating communication between different components within a cluster. It enables applications on Kubernetes to seamlessly interact with each other and with services outside of the cluster. By effectively managing networking configurations and implementing reliable networking solutions, Kubernetes establishes secure and efficient connectivity, fostering a cohesive ecosystem for running distributed applications.

Let's start with the following important concept to help you understand Kubernetes networking better.

Services

Kubernetes networking enables communication between different components within the cluster, facilitates connectivity with external services, and ensures that applications can interact seamlessly. The Pods in Kubernetes clusters should be reachable from any Pod or node within a cluster. It is possible to use the IP address of a Pod directly and access the Pod. However, it is important to know that

Pods are ephemeral, and they might get a new IP address if the previous Pod has gone down. In such cases, the application will break. Kubernetes provides Services, which decouple Pod instances from their clients. Pods may be created and torn down, but the IP address of a Kubernetes Service remains constant and stable. Clients can connect to the Service IP address, which in turn has one endpoint for each Pod it can send requests to. If there are multiple Pod instances, each of their IP addresses will be available to the Service as an endpoint object. When a Pod goes down, the endpoints are updated to reflect the current Pod instances along with their IP addresses.

A Service provides multiple types of IP address schemes. There are four types of Services: ClusterIP, NodePort, LoadBalancer, and Ingress controller using Application Gateway.

ClusterIP

The most fundamental scheme is known as ClusterIP, and it is an internal IP address that can be reached only from within the cluster. The ClusterIP scheme is shown in *Figure 8.3*:

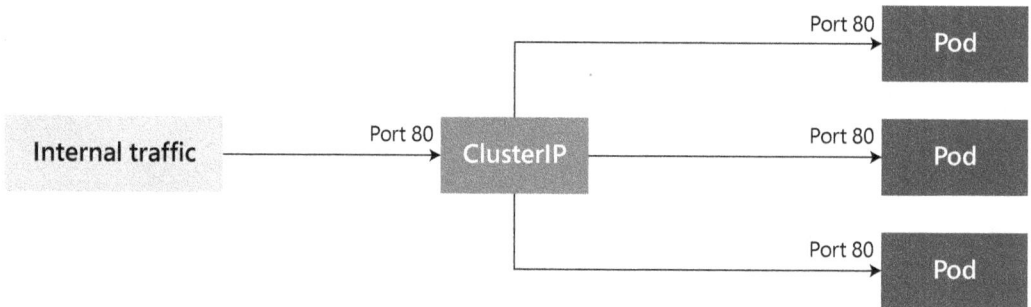

Figure 8.3: The workings of ClusterIP

NodePort

ClusterIP also allows the creation of NodePort instances, using which it gets a ClusterIP. However, it can also open a port on each of the nodes within a cluster. The Pods can be reached using ClusterIP addresses as well as by using a combination of the node IP and node port, as shown in *Figure 8.4*:

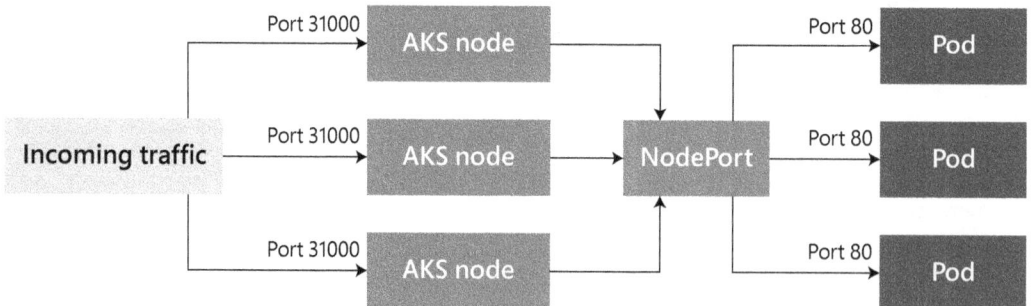

Figure 8.4: The workings of NodePort

LoadBalancer

Services can refer not only to Pods but to external endpoints as well. Finally, Services also allow the creation of a load-balancer-based Service that is capable of receiving requests externally and redirecting them to a Pod instance using ClusterIP and NodePort internally, as shown in *Figure 8.5*:

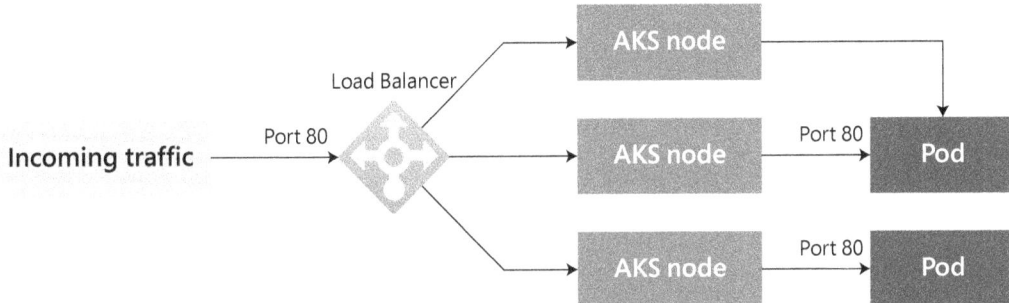

Figure 8.5: The workings of LoadBalancer

Ingress controller

There is one final type of Service known as the Ingress controller. In Kubernetes, Ingress is a vital component that efficiently routes incoming network traffic to services within the cluster. Ingress acts as a router, enabling multiple services in the Kubernetes cluster to be exposed externally using a single IP address.

As applications grow in complexity, Ingress becomes essential for handling advanced traffic routing scenarios, including subdomain and wildcard domain redirection. Ingress helps you gain precise control over routing rules, TLS termination, session affinity, and traffic splitting, ensuring enhanced security, performance, and resource utilization. The Ingress controller provides advanced functionalities such as URL-based routing, as shown in *Figure 8.6*:

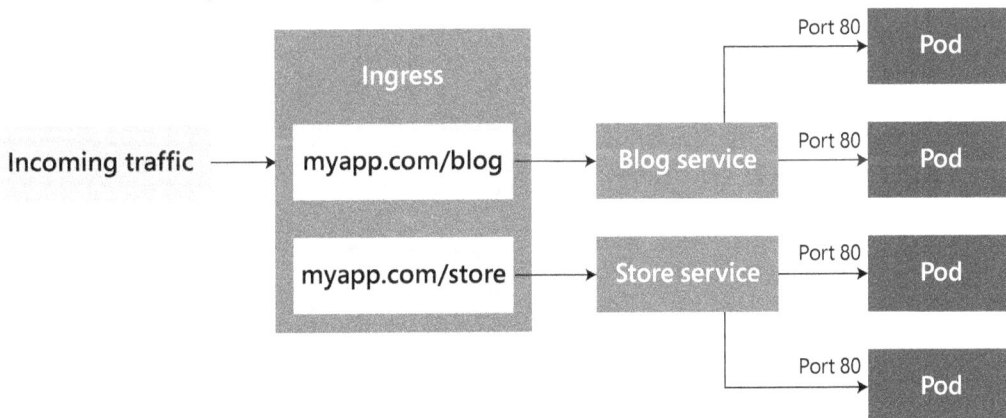

Figure 8.6: The workings of the Ingress controller

In order to establish seamless communication within a Kubernetes cluster, it is essential for the control plane to have connectivity with the worker nodes and the Pods residing on them. Similarly, worker nodes should be able to communicate with each other and maintain connectivity with the control plane.

Interestingly, it might be surprising to learn that the core Kubernetes itself does not directly manage the networking stack. Rather, this responsibility falls upon the container runtime present on the individual nodes. The container runtime takes charge of managing the networking stack, ensuring efficient network communication between components within the cluster. Now let's take a look at how Kubernetes networking works.

Demystifying Kubernetes' networking models

Kubernetes sets forth three important principles that a container runtime must adhere to. These principles are as follows:

- Pods should be able to communicate with other Pods without requiring any changes to their source or destination addresses. This is achieved through **Network Address Translation (NAT)** mechanisms.

- Agents, such as kubelets, should have direct communication with Pods residing on the nodes, enabling efficient interaction.

- Pods hosted directly on the host network should maintain the ability to communicate with all other Pods within the cluster.

When it comes to AKS, Microsoft provides two distinct networking models for managing network communication within the cluster:

- **Kubernet**: This model utilizes a simple and straightforward network implementation, relying on basic network configuration for communication between Pods

- **Azure CNI**: In this model, Azure **Container Networking Interface (CNI)** is used to provide advanced networking capabilities, leveraging Azure's networking infrastructure for efficient communication between Pods

By understanding these networking models, AKS users can make informed decisions tailored to their specific requirements and networking preferences. Let's take a look at each of them in the next section.

kubenet

In AKS, the default networking framework is kubenet. Under kubenet, each node within the cluster receives an IP address from the connected virtual network's subnet. However, Pods do not directly obtain IP addresses from the subnet. Instead, a separate addressing scheme is employed to assign IP addresses to Pods and Kubernetes Services.

When setting up an AKS instance, it is crucial to define the IP address range for Pods and Services to avoid IP conflicts. Since Pods exist on a different network than the nodes, requests originating from Pods or targeting Pods undergo NAT or routing to replace the source Pod IP with the node's IP address and vice versa.

It's important to note that in user-defined routing, Azure supports a maximum of 400 routes and imposes a limit of 400 nodes for the cluster. The following figure illustrates the scenario where an AKS node acquires an IP address from the virtual network, while the Pods created within the node do not directly obtain IP addresses from the network.

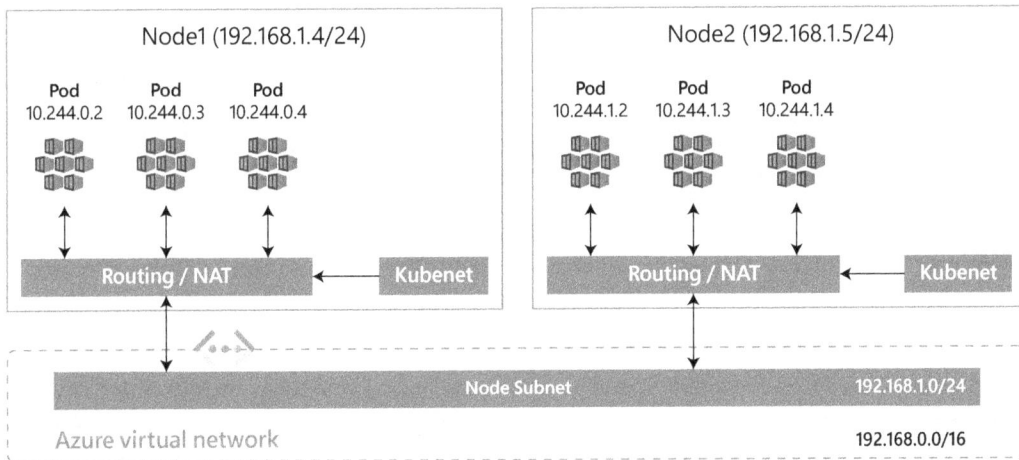

Figure 8.7: Networking in AKS

By default, this kubenet networking model is configured with 110 Pods per node. This means there can be a maximum of 110 * 400 Pods in a Kubernetes cluster by default. The maximum number of Pods per node is 250. This limit ensures optimal performance and resource allocation within each node. However, if you need more Pods, you can add more worker nodes to accommodate larger workloads when necessary. Proper planning and consideration of resource utilization are crucial when determining the optimal Pod-to-node ratio to maintain an efficient and stable Kubernetes environment.

This scheme should be used when IP address availability and user-defined routing are not a constraint.

CNI

Azure CNI provides a networking approach where both Nodes and Pods are assigned IP addresses directly from the network subnet. This allows for the flexible allocation of IP addresses, enabling as many Pods as there are available unique IP addresses on the subnet. Consequently, meticulous planning of the IP address range becomes crucial when adopting this networking strategy.

It's worth noting that Windows hosting is exclusively supported by the Azure CNI networking stack. Additionally, certain AKS components, including virtual nodes and virtual kubelet, rely on the Azure CNI stack. We can reserve IP addresses in advance based on the expected number of Pods. Sufficient extra IP addresses should always be reserved on the subnet to prevent IP address exhaustion and avoid the need for cluster reconstruction due to increased application demand.

By default, the Azure CNI networking stack is configured to support 30 Pods per node, but this can be bumped up to a maximum of 250 Pods per node, providing the flexibility required to accommodate varying workload requirements.

Network policy

When running modern, microservices-based applications in Kubernetes, controlling the communication between components is essential for security and compliance. In an AKS cluster, all Pods have unrestricted communication by default. To enhance security, you can define network policies to regulate traffic flow.

Network policy is a Kubernetes specification that allows you to define rules for Pod-to-Pod communication. By leveraging network policies, you can enforce access control between Pods based on label selectors. An example of this is that you can restrict access to backend applications, only allowing connectivity from specific frontend services or limiting database access to authorized application tiers.

Network policies are defined as YAML manifests and can be included in wider manifests that create deployments or services. Azure provides two options for implementing network policies in AKS: Azure Network Policy Manager and Calico Network Policies. When creating an AKS cluster, you choose the policy option, and it cannot be changed later.

Azure Network Policy Manager uses Linux IPTables for Linux nodes and **Host Network Service (HNS)** ACLPolicies for Windows nodes to enforce policies. These policies are translated into allowed and disallowed IP pairs, which are then programmed as IPTable/HNS ACLPolicy filter rules. Calico Network Policies, on the other hand, is an open source network and security solution provided by Tigera.

By utilizing network policies in AKS, you have fine-grained control over the communication between Pods, enabling you to enforce secure access and protect your microservices architecture.

To learn more about network policy and the differences between kubenet and Azure CNI, please check the following documentation article: `https://learn.microsoft.com/en-us/azure/aks/concepts-network`.

Understanding AKS cluster security

Container security ensures comprehensive protection throughout the entire end-to-end pipeline for application workloads within AKS. At a high level, it includes the following four categories.

Build security

Build security is crucial as the entry point of the supply chain. It involves conducting static analysis, vulnerability assessment, and compliance checks on image builds. Rather than failing a build for vulnerabilities, it focuses on segmenting vulnerabilities actionable by development teams and allowing grace periods for issue remediation.

Registry security

Registry security involves assessing image vulnerability states and detecting drift or unauthorized images. Utilizing Notary V2 to attach signatures ensures that deployments come from trusted sources, maintaining the integrity of the registry.

Cluster security

Cluster security in AKS involves the management and maintenance of Kubernetes master components by Microsoft. Each AKS cluster has a dedicated Kubernetes master providing the API server, scheduler, and other essential services. Access to the API server can be limited using authorized IP ranges, and fully private clusters can restrict API server access to the virtual network.

Node security

Node security is an essential aspect of AKS ensuring a secure environment for running containerized application workloads. AKS utilizes Azure **Virtual Machines** (**VMs**) (or Virtual Machine Scale Sets) known as nodes. Those nodes are managed and maintained by users.

When creating or scaling out an AKS cluster, nodes are automatically provisioned with the latest OS security updates and configurations, prioritizing a secure foundation. Besides the OS level, we also need to ensure the Kubernetes cluster upgrades to maintain security and compliance for those security-sensitive upgrades. In addition, getting the latest Kubernetes version ensures access to the latest and greatest features from the Kubernetes community.

To optimize security when transferring data across different servers within a data center –that is, to ensure East-West or lateral movement attack protection – Kubernetes and thus AKS rely on Kubernetes node authorization. This is a special-purpose authorization mode that specifically authorizes API requests made by kubelets. Kubelets that are outside of the node group are not authorized to perform actions within the cluster.

Nodes are securely deployed within a private virtual network subnet that is devoid of any public IP addresses, so as to achieve enhanced protection against external threats. SSH access, essential for management and troubleshooting purposes, is restricted solely to the internal IP address, ensuring controlled and secure access.

To address storage requirements, AKS uses Azure Managed Disks, which provide high-performance SSD-backed storage. The data stored on these disks is automatically encrypted at rest within the Azure platform, reinforcing data security measures. Furthermore, Azure Managed Disks employ secure replication mechanisms within the Azure data center, bolstering data redundancy and protection.

These comprehensive security measures within the AKS node environment offer a professional framework for running containerized workloads and maintaining a secure and controlled operational environment.

Network security

Network security in AKS is a crucial aspect to ensure secure connectivity and control over traffic flow. By deploying AKS clusters within existing Azure virtual network subnets, seamless connectivity with on-premises networks is achieved through Azure Site-to-Site VPN or ExpressRoute. To limit access to services within the internal network, Kubernetes Ingress controllers can be defined with private, internal IP addresses.

When using a custom subnet for the AKS cluster, whether Azure CNI or Kubenet, it is important not to modify the NIC-level network security group managed by AKS. Instead, subnet-level network security groups can be created to control traffic flow, ensuring that they do not interfere with essential cluster management functions such as load balancer access, communication with the control plane, and egress.

AKS offers support for Kubernetes network policies to enforce restrictions on network traffic between Pods within the cluster. By utilizing network policies, specific network paths can be allowed or denied based on namespaces and label selectors, enabling granular control over network communication within the AKS cluster.

Application security

To ensure application security in AKS, Microsoft Defender for Containers can be utilized to detect and prevent cyberattacks targeting applications running within Pods. Continuous scanning helps identify vulnerabilities and maintain the desired state of application security.

Kubernetes Secrets play a crucial role in securing sensitive data within Pods. By creating Secrets using the Kubernetes API, access credentials and keys can be injected securely. Secrets are provided only to nodes with scheduled Pods that require them and are stored in tmpfs, ensuring that they are not written to disk. The deletion of Pods removes associated Secrets from the node's tmpfs. Secrets are stored within a specific namespace and are accessible only by Pods within the same namespace. This approach reduces the exposure of sensitive information in YAML manifests, as access to Secrets is requested from the Kubernetes API server. It is important to handle the raw secret manifest files, which contain base64-encoded data, as sensitive information and avoid committing them to source control. AKS effectively manages the storage of Kubernetes secrets in etcd, ensuring encryption at rest within the secure Azure platform.

Demystifying managed AKS – Azure Container Apps

Many users who are new to Kubernetes and seek a simplified approach to working with containerized workloads on Microsoft Azure are turning to Azure Container Apps as an alternative to AKS.

Azure Container Apps offers a compelling solution for deploying applications and microservices without the need to manage complex infrastructure. As a fully managed Kubernetes-based application platform, it provides a seamless experience for deploying apps from code or containers.

Before diving into Azure Container Apps, it's important to understand two essential components that contribute to its functionality: Dapr and KEDA. By incorporating Dapr and KEDA into Azure Container Apps, developers are provided with powerful tools that significantly enhance the scalability, reliability, and performance of their containerized applications. Now, let's take a look at each of them in the following sections.

Dapr – Distributed Application Runtime

Dapr is a powerful and practical runtime system designed for building distributed applications. It offers a range of APIs that simplify microservice connectivity, making it easier for developers to create resilient and secure microservices. Dapr follows a building block approach, providing APIs for common distributed application capabilities such as state management, service-to-service invocation, and pub/sub messaging. Licensed under the MIT License and hosted on GitHub, Dapr is written in the Go programming language, ensuring a solid foundation for its functionality. By leveraging Dapr, developers can seamlessly handle state, invoke services, and implement publish-subscribe messaging in their applications, simplifying the complexities of distributed systems and enabling cloud-native and serverless computing.

The following diagram describes how Dapr fits into Azure Container Apps.

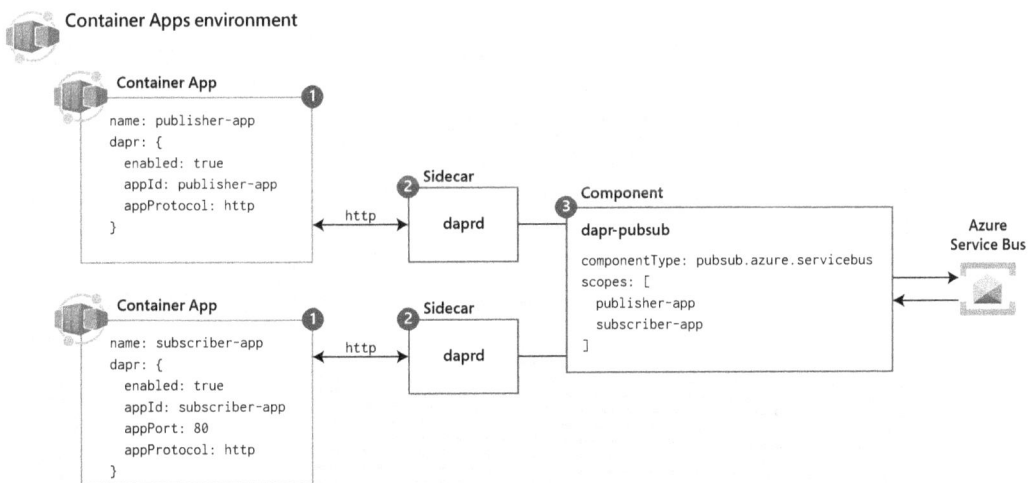

Figure 8.8: Dapr and Azure Container Apps

With Azure Container Apps, you can build diverse modern applications and microservices while benefiting from centralized networking, observability, dynamic scaling, and streamlined configuration management. The platform also supports the resilient design of microservices through comprehensive integration with Dapr, enabling efficient event-driven processing.

KEDA – Kubernetes Event-Driven Autoscaling

Kubernetes Event-Driven Autoscaling (**KEDA**) is a lightweight component that enables you to scale Kubernetes workloads based on events. It can be seamlessly added to any Kubernetes cluster and works alongside standard Kubernetes features such as the **Horizontal Pod Autoscaler** (**HPA**).

KEDA can scale Deployments, Jobs, StatefulSets, and custom resources with ease and with support for various event sources, such as AWS SQS, Kafka, and RabbitMQ. It offers flexibility in scaling based on metrics such as event count, payload size, and time intervals. Additionally, KEDA allows scaling workloads down to zero instances during inactivity, reducing costs and environmental impact. By using KEDA, you can achieve improved cost-efficiency, performance, and reliability for your Kubernetes workloads.

The following diagram shows Azure Container Apps being used in a scaling scenario with KEDA to deal with increasing demands to process messages in an Azure Service Bus queue:

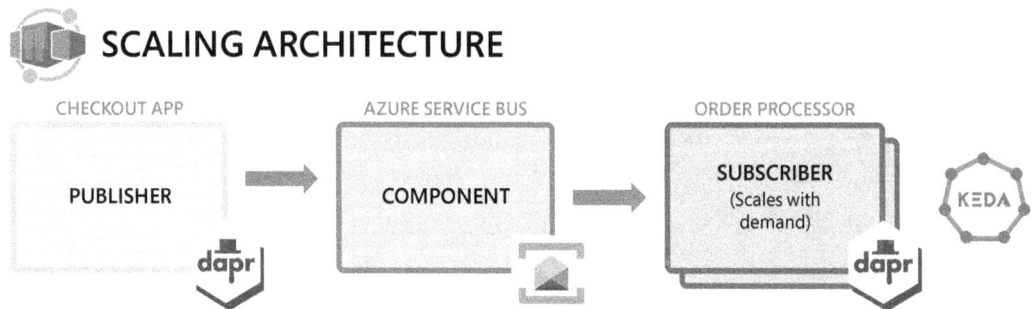

Figure 8.9: Azure Container Apps in a scaling scenario with KEDA

Azure Container Apps utilizes the power of KEDA to enable dynamic scaling, ensuring optimal resource allocation based on workload demands. To fully harness the potential of Dapr and KEDA, it is vital to grasp their practical implications in real-world scenarios. Let's explore the key use cases where these powerful components deliver substantial value and showcase their practical applications.

Key scenarios

Azure Container Apps provides a versatile solution that caters to a wide range of use cases. These include deploying API endpoints, hosting background processing applications, and enabling event-driven processing. See the following figure for a visual representation of these capabilities.

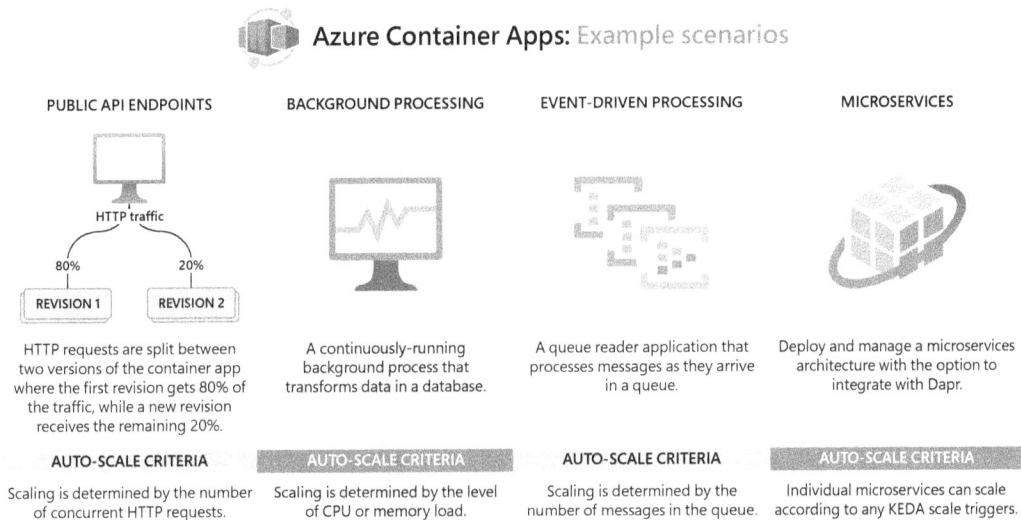

Azure Container Apps: Example scenarios

PUBLIC API ENDPOINTS	BACKGROUND PROCESSING	EVENT-DRIVEN PROCESSING	MICROSERVICES
HTTP traffic — 80% REVISION 1 / 20% REVISION 2			
HTTP requests are split between two versions of the container app where the first revision gets 80% of the traffic, while a new revision receives the remaining 20%.	A continuously-running background process that transforms data in a database.	A queue reader application that processes messages as they arrive in a queue.	Deploy and manage a microservices architecture with the option to integrate with Dapr.
AUTO-SCALE CRITERIA	**AUTO-SCALE CRITERIA**	**AUTO-SCALE CRITERIA**	**AUTO-SCALE CRITERIA**
Scaling is determined by the number of concurrent HTTP requests.	Scaling is determined by the level of CPU or memory load.	Scaling is determined by the number of messages in the queue.	Individual microservices can scale according to any KEDA scale triggers.

Figure 8.10: Key scenarios of Azure Container Apps

By using Azure Container Apps, developers can focus on application development and innovation, as the platform takes care of the underlying infrastructure complexities. Azure Container Apps enables executing application code packaged in any container, providing flexibility and allowing developers to use their preferred runtime or programming model. With Azure Container Apps, you can enjoy the benefits of running containers while leaving behind the concerns of managing cloud infrastructure and complex container orchestrators. This seamless integration empowers developers to build and deploy containerized applications with ease and efficiency, unlocking the full potential of their applications.

Simplifying container deployment with Azure Container Instances

In addition to AKS and Azure Container Apps, **Azure Container Instances (ACI)** offers a direct and efficient approach to running containers in Azure, removing the burden of managing virtual machines or relying on higher-level services.

Use cases and scenarios

ACI proves advantageous for diverse scenarios, primarily the following.

Standalone containerized applications

When you have a microservice-based architecture or a single-container application, ACI provides a hassle-free experience for running and managing your containers. For instance, ACI enables easy scaling and independent management of microservices, ensuring optimal resource allocation. Developers can containerize applications, such as Python web frameworks (Flask, for example), for seamless scalability and high availability. ACI abstracts away infrastructure concerns, allowing data analytics companies to deploy and manage containerized applications without the need for manual resource provisioning. ACI's scalability and parallel computing capabilities make it ideal for processing large datasets. Overall, ACI simplifies container deployment and scaling, empowering developers to focus on core functionalities.

Efficient task automation with ACI

ACI offers a streamlined approach to task automation. With ACI, you can package and execute discrete tasks within containers, leveraging the lightweight and isolated runtime environment provided by containers. This enables you to automate various workflows, such as data processing, batch jobs, or periodic tasks. ACI's ability to start containers in seconds and its pay-as-you-go billing model based on actual usage make it a cost-effective choice for running automated tasks, eliminating the need to provision and manage virtual machines.

Optimized build jobs with ACI

ACI provides an efficient environment for executing build jobs. Whether you are building software applications, running CI/CD pipelines, or performing build and test processes, ACI can help streamline your build workflows. ACI's ability to start containers quickly allows you to scale up your build capacity on-demand, reducing the time required for compiling code, running tests, or packaging artifacts. By decoupling the build process from virtual machine management, ACI simplifies the setup and execution of build jobs, enhancing productivity and reducing infrastructure overhead.

Advantages

ACI offers a range of advantages when it comes to flexibility, scalability, security, and cost-efficiency in deploying and managing containerized applications:

- **Fast startup times**: ACI offers rapid container startup, starting containers in seconds without the need to provision and manage virtual machines. This makes the deployment of applications quick and efficient, hence reducing time to market.

- **Container access**: ACI enables the exposure of container groups with public IP addresses and assigns them a **Fully Qualified Domain Name (FQDN)**, simplifying accessibility and making applications easily reachable for users.

- **Compliant deployments**: ACI ensures application isolation and security comparable to virtual machines, making them suitable for hostile multi-tenant usage. This guarantees that your applications remain isolated and protected within the container environment.

- **Custom sizes**: ACI allows for the precise specification of CPU cores and memory, enabling optimal utilization and cost-efficiency. You can tailor the container resources to match the exact needs of your applications, paying only for what you require.

- **Persistent storage**: ACI supports the direct mounting of Azure file shares backed by Azure Storage, enabling the retrieval and persistence of application state. This ensures that your containers can access and utilize storage resources effectively.

- **Support for both Linux and Windows containers**: ACI can schedule both Linux and Windows containers, providing flexibility and compatibility across different OSs. You can choose the OS type preference while creating your container groups.

- **Co-scheduled groups**: ACI supports the scheduling of multi-container groups, allowing you to combine your main application container with supporting role containers. This facilitates the deployment and management of interconnected containerized applications.

- **Azure virtual network deployment**: ACI enables deployment into an Azure virtual network. This provides secure communication with other resources within the network in the public cloud and possible seamless integration with on-premises resources. It also enhances network security.

- **Confidential container deployment**: ACI offers the capability to run containers in a **Trusted Execution Environment (TEE)**, ensuring hardware-based confidentiality and integrity protection for container workloads. This enhances security and protects sensitive data.

- **Spot container deployment**: ACI provides the option to run spot containers for unused Azure capacity at a significantly discounted price. Spot containers are suitable for non-mission-critical workloads and allow you to save up to 70% compared to regular-priority containers.

Hopefully, the information provided here has given you a better understanding of the benefits and features of ACI. ACI serves as an easy and lightweight platform to meet your containerization requirements. By embracing the simplicity and power of containerization with ACI, you can unlock exciting new possibilities for your applications.

Summary

By now, you should have a solid understanding of building and scaling applications on AKS clusters and Azure Container Apps. You should now be confident in migrating your Kubernetes workloads using AKS on Azure. In the next chapter, we'll have a look at the capabilities and tools available when designing big data solutions with Microsoft Azure.

Designing Big Data Solutions with Azure

The previous chapter explored container hosting and orchestration with Azure Kubernetes Service. Now we can change gears a bit and explore big data solutions.

In today's data-driven world, the ability to harness the vast amounts of information produced daily is more than just an advantage—it's a necessity. Data has become the lifeblood of organizations, providing the foundation for decisions and strategies. However, the sheer volume of data generated today—dubbed *big data*—presents unique challenges.

In this chapter, we will discuss big data in the context of data warehousing and advanced analytics and talk about solutions that allow us to use large amounts of data. With big data analytics, organizations can access more and higher-quality data, leading to better decision-making. It allows companies to base their decisions on hard data rather than intuition or observation.

Businesses can utilize big data to analyze customer behavior and tailor products, services, and advertisements to better meet customer needs and improve their overall experience. It can identify bottlenecks in a production process, track performance, help improve quality assurance, increase innovation, and provide a competitive advantage.

In this chapter, we will discuss the following topics:

- Designing big data solutions
- Azure services and tools for big data
- Using AI services for data solutions
- Efficient IoT integrations

This chapter will provide insight into the best Azure tools and services that can be used to design big data and intelligent solutions.

Why do we need big data solutions?

Data refers to raw, unprocessed, unorganized facts, or details that might not make much sense or provide context. For instance, random numbers or statistics, unprocessed observations, or individual pieces of an incomplete dataset are all examples of data.

There are three main aspects of big data, often called the "3Vs," which are volume, velocity, and variety:

- **Volume**: Refers to the massive amounts of data produced by different platforms and devices. These platforms can generate data every second, making it impossible for traditional data processing tools to handle.

- **Velocity**: Refers to the speed at which data is produced and processed. Businesses require real-time or near-real-time information to make informed decisions.

- **Variety**: Indicates the different types of data. Data can be structured, semi-structured (such as JSON), or unstructured (such as free text or video).

Organizations need big data solutions to manage these 3Vs effectively. The ability to store, process, and analyze big data can reveal patterns, trends, and insights that otherwise remain hidden. Big data solutions provide a competitive edge and foster innovation, efficiency, and improved decision-making.

Big data typically involves several steps, including extraction, transformation, and loading. This process is commonly called ETL and ELT.

The letters **E**, **T**, and **L** stand for the following:

- **Extraction**: Gathering data from various sources, such as databases, files, APIs, or streaming platforms. The data can be structured (e.g., relational databases) or unstructured (e.g., documents or activity feeds). This step aims to retrieve and prepare relevant data for further processing.

- **Transformation**: Manipulating and converting the extracted data into a suitable format for analysis and storage. This step involves data cleansing, validation, enrichment, and integration. Common transformations include filtering out irrelevant data, standardizing formats, handling missing values, aggregating data, and creating new derived variables.

- **Load**: Storing the transformed data in a target system such as a data warehouse or a specialized big data platform. An appropriate data schema for efficient querying and analysis is defined here, with optimized storage and partitioning strategies.

In an ETL process, data is extracted from one or more sources, transformed based on predefined rules and structures, and then loaded into a target system. This process is often used with structured data and follows a batch-oriented approach. The transformed data is typically stored in a separate data warehouse for analysis.

The ELT process flips the transformation and load steps. Data is extracted and loaded directly into a target system. Transformation is then performed within the target system using distributed computing frameworks such as Apache Hadoop or Apache Spark. This approach maximizes the power of modern big data platforms to process and analyze data in its raw form. This allows for more flexibility and scalability when dealing with large volumes of unstructured or semi-structured data.

Both approaches have their pros, cons, and use cases. ETL is best used with structured data and when predefined transformations are necessary. Conversely, ELT is more flexible and scalable, allowing for raw data exploration and ad hoc transformations. The choice between ETL and ELT depends on the specific requirements, data characteristics, and the available technology stack.

As the volume of data increases, so does the complexity of managing, storing, processing, and analyzing it. There is also the increasing challenge of ensuring the data's security and privacy.

Proper data management allows you to ensure quality, extract valuable insights for decision-making, and increase operational efficiency. By effectively managing this data, businesses can also ensure compliance with various data protection regulations, reducing the risk of penalties and damage to their reputation.

When considering data management, organizations should design solutions with these best practices in mind:

- **Data governance**: Set clear policies and procedures for data collection, storage, processing, and usage to ensure the data's quality, integrity, and security. This also involves respecting the privacy of individuals. Robust anonymization and pseudonymization techniques can be implemented, as well as obtaining the necessary consent for data collection and processing.

- **Data storage and management**: Use techniques such as storing data based on its usage and value to optimize costs and use technologies such as data lakes and data warehouses to support diverse data types and analytic needs.

- **Data security**: Implement encryption, secure device identification and authentication, and a robust security policy to ensure data stays safe.

- **Data processing and analysis**: Turn raw data into actionable insights using techniques such as edge computing (processing data closer to its source) to reduce latency and network congestion and advanced analytics and machine learning algorithms.

- **Interoperability**: Ensuring that different and unrelated devices can communicate and work with each other is essential. Using standard protocols and data formats helps to ensure interoperability.

Now that you have seen the different reasons big data solutions are developed, let us discuss some key design elements.

Designing big data solutions

Big data refers to copious amounts of incoming data being sourced from several sources. The major challenge here is that we need to aggregate these different representations of data and present them in a meaningful form so that they can be consumed by technical and non-technical persons alike.

We must employ tools and services that specialize in extracting, transforming, loading, and presenting the data for this challenge. When dealing with data from diverse sources with varying formats and velocities, it becomes crucial to establish a systematic approach for storing, integrating, filtering, and refining the data. This ensures we can efficiently work with the data and derive value from it for other operations. A clearly defined data management process is necessary to handle such scenarios effectively.

A typical data transformation process involves four steps:

1. **Ingestion**: Data is acquired and brought into the big data environment. The data originates from various sources, and connectors facilitate its ingestion into the big data platform.

2. **Storage**: Data must be stored in a data pool for long-term retention. The storage solution should accommodate historical and real-time data and handle structured, semi-structured, and unstructured data. Connectors are used to retrieve data from the data sources, or the data sources themselves can directly push the data into storage.

3. **Analysis**: Data retrieved from storage undergoes filtering, grouping, joining, and transforming processes. These operations are performed to extract valuable insights and gain a deeper understanding of the data.

4. **Visualization**: Analysis results are conveyed through reports distributed via various notification platforms. Additionally, the insights can be utilized to create visually appealing dashboards enriched with graphs and charts, enabling intuitive data exploration and interpretation.

Azure provides several tools and services for various stages of big data processing. Here are some prominent Azure tools for each process:

1. **Ingestion**:

    I.   **Azure Event Hubs**: A highly scalable event streaming platform for ingesting and processing large volumes of data from diverse sources.

    II.   **Azure Data Factory**: A data integration service that enables data movement and orchestration across various sources, including on-premises and cloud-based systems.

    III. **Azure IoT Hub**: Specifically designed for handling and ingesting data from **Internet of Things (IoT)** devices at scale.

2. **Storage**:

    I.   **Azure Blob Storage**: A scalable and cost-effective object storage service for storing large amounts of unstructured data, including files, images, and videos.

    II.   **Azure Data Lake Storage**: A fully managed data lake solution that enables storage and analysis of big data. It supports structured, semi-structured, and unstructured data with high scalability.

3. **Analysis**:

    I.   **Azure Synapse Analytics**: An integrated analytics service that combines big data and data warehousing capabilities, providing a unified environment for storage and analysis. It contains several services that work together to deliver big data solutions.

    II.   **Azure Databricks**: A fast, collaborative, and Apache Spark-based analytics platform that supports large-scale data processing, machine learning, and real-time analytics.

    III. **Azure HDInsight**: A fully managed cloud service that provides popular open source frameworks, such as Hadoop, Spark, and Hive, for processing and analyzing big data.

    IV. **Azure Stream Analytics**: A real-time analytics service for processing and gaining insights from streaming data using SQL-like queries.

4. **Visualization**:

    I.   **Power BI**: A powerful **business intelligence** (**BI**) and data visualization tool that allows you to create interactive dashboards, reports, and visualizations to convey data insights.

    II.   **Azure Data Explorer**: A fast and highly scalable data exploration and visualization service for real-time analysis of large datasets.

    III. **Azure Analysis Services**: A fully managed analytics service that enables creating, deploying, and exploring interactive analytical models and visualizations.

These Azure tools offer a wide range of capabilities to support the end-to-end big data processing life cycle, from data ingestion to storage, analysis, and visualization. The choice of tools depends on specific requirements, data characteristics, and the desired outcomes of the big data processing tasks. *Figure 9.1* displays the typical layout of a big data solution.

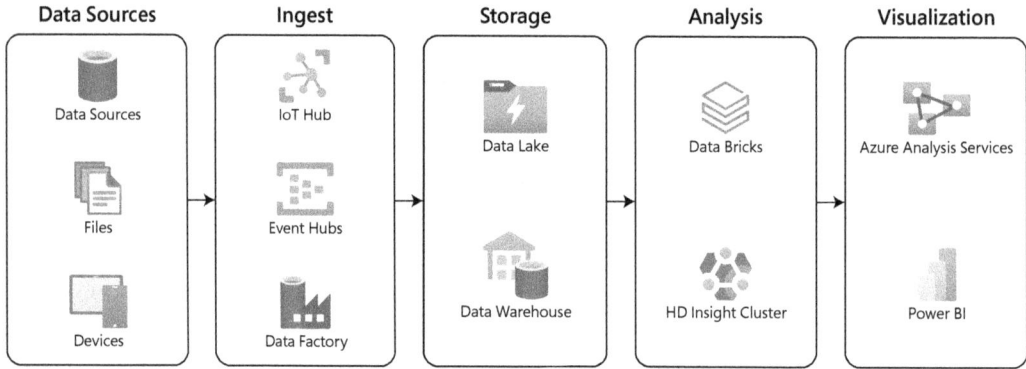

Figure 9.1: Typical big data solution steps

Now that we know why we design big data solutions, let us explore the concept of data warehousing a bit more.

Data warehousing

A data warehouse system is used for reporting and analysis, acting as a central repository of data integrated from one or more data sources. Data warehouses store current and historical data in one place and create analytical reports for knowledge workers throughout the enterprise. Knowledge workers are often the core of an organization, bringing expertise to their daily work, which allows them to lead initiatives and participate in high-level decision-making.

The primary source of the data is cleaned, transformed, cataloged, and made available to managers and other business professionals for data mining, online analytical processing, market research, and decision support. Data warehousing is crucial for data science to have access to the data it needs for creating BI reports, data visualizations, and predictive analytics.

Data warehouses are typically designed with a denormalized schema structure. Let's say, for instance, we have a relational database as a data source. To produce a report from the relational store, we would need several joins to gather data from related tables. This can lead to sub-optimal load times for ad hoc reports. In a data warehouse, we would identify the various data points across this database and create a single representation of these data points, removing the dependencies on foreign keys. This way, we have optimized representations of the data and aggregations for read operations necessary for reporting and analysis. Now let us explore the dynamics of data analytics.

Data analytics

Data analytics is the process of inspecting, cleaning, transforming, and modeling data with the goal of discovering useful information, making conclusions, and supporting decision-making. Multiple techniques and methodologies are used to analyze data from various sources in different sizes and formats, from structured data (such as numbers, dates, and groups) to unstructured data (such as text, images, and voice recordings).

Azure Synapse Analytics is a limitless analytics service that combines enterprise data warehousing and big data analytics. It provides a unified experience to ingest, explore, prepare, manage, and serve data for immediate BI and machine learning needs.

Azure Synapse combines SQL, Apache Spark big data, log and time series analytics and exploration, and data integration pipeline (ETL/ELT) technologies. With this service, the following benefits can be realized:

- **On-demand or provisioned resources**: You can query data on your terms. It allows you to use serverless (on-demand) or provisioned resources.

- **Integrations**: It is deeply integrated with other services in the Azure ecosystem, such as Power BI for visualization and Azure Machine Learning for building predictive models.

- **Real-time analytics**: It has native connectivity with Azure Stream Analytics, allowing you to bring in real-time data for live dashboards and alerts.

- **Data security and privacy**: It provides always-on data encryption, automated threat detection, and virtual network service endpoints.

- **Scalability**: It is designed to scale compute and storage independently. You can pause compute capacity while leaving data storage intact, leading to significant cost savings potential.

- **Workload isolation**: This allows you to isolate workloads logically. Here, you can support diverse analytic capabilities within the same analytic system.

The data typically passes through a series of stages:

1. **Data ingestion**: Data is ingested into Azure Synapse Analytics from a data source such as Azure Data Lake, Azure Blob Storage, relational databases, and even real-time data for live dashboards and alerts with native connectivity to Azure Event Hubs and Azure IoT Hub.

2. **Data preparation**: Ingested data can be prepared using on-demand or provisioned resources. This includes cleaning the data and transforming it into an optimized format for analysis.

3. **Data analysis**: Prepared data can be analyzed using a built-in serverless SQL pool or provisioned resources, depending on your business needs.

4. **Data serving and visualization**: Data can then be served to end users and visualized using Power BI or other visualization tools.

Azure Synapse Analytics is a powerful tool that aids businesses in efficiently managing, analyzing, and visualizing their data in a scalable, secure, and cost-effective manner.

One of the possible data sources is event hubs or data streams, which are suitable for smart devices to generate data streams, and we need to understand how to connect to and monitor data from these devices properly.

Let us look at how IoT and telemetry play a part in big data processing.

IoT and telemetry

IoT is a network of devices, called "things," embedded with sensors, software, and other technologies to connect and exchange data with other devices and systems over the internet. These "things" can be anything from everyday household items, such as refrigerators and thermostats, to industrial machinery and sensors in various sectors, such as healthcare, transportation, and agriculture.

Telemetry is the automatic recording and wireless transmission of data from remote or inaccessible sources to an IT system in a central location for monitoring and analysis. In the context of IoT, telemetry data is the stream of data that these IoT devices generate and send back to the central system.

IoT and telemetry contribute significantly to the phenomenon we call "big data." As IoT devices become more ubiquitous, the volume, velocity, and variety of the data generated increase exponentially. IoT devices incessantly stream telemetry data, creating vast amounts of unstructured data every second. When processed and analyzed, this data provides valuable insights that can lead to significant efficiency improvements, cost reductions, and new revenue opportunities.

Figure 9.2 conceptualizes a practical pipeline and shows where each technology would fit in.

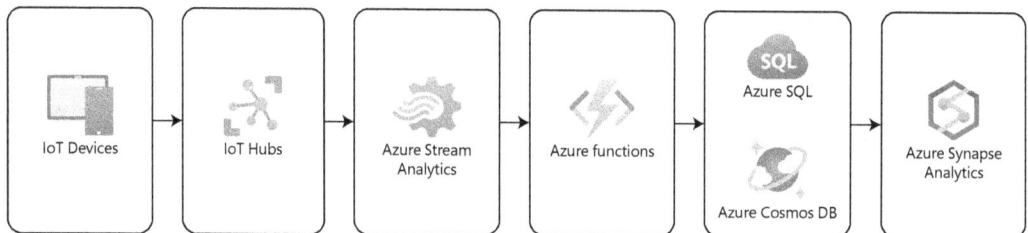

Figure 9.2 – IoT solution with Azure services

The stages are as follows:

1. IoT devices send data to Azure IoT Hub.

2. Azure IoT Hub provides bi-directional communication between IoT devices and the cloud.

3. Azure Stream Analytics processes the data in real time as it arrives from IoT Hub. Data can be interrogated with to filters, sorting logic, and aggregations. Data can also be joined from multiple data streams, depending on your business requirements.

4. Azure Functions can be used for event-driven processing, triggered based on the incoming telemetry data.

5. Azure Cosmos DB or Azure SQL Database can be used to store the processed data for further analysis. Azure Cosmos DB is better for unstructured data and Azure SQL Database for relational data.

6. Azure Synapse Analytics or Azure Data Lake Storage can provide big data analytics and AI capabilities for data processing.

7. Power BI can be used to visualize the analytics results. You can create real-time dashboards and reports to monitor the telemetry data and gain insights.

This is a simple outline of how a system could be architected, so bear in mind that the architecture can vary significantly depending on the specific requirements of your IoT solution. Use the appropriate Azure services and features depending on your needs.

Now that we know how to aggregate an influx of data from various sources, let us explore integrating intelligent technologies and machine learning into the fold.

Utilizing AI for intelligent solutions

Artificial Intelligence (**AI**) can be used for intelligent solutions in various sectors because it can analyze large amounts of data, learn from it, and make predictions or decisions. This can remove some errors associated with the manual human element and improve efficiency, effectiveness, and personalization. As AI continues to improve, we can expect to see even more innovative uses of AI in various sectors.

AI and big data are two revolutionary technologies transforming how we conduct business and live our lives. As we know, big data refers to large and diverse datasets of information that grow ever-increasingly. Conversely, AI refers to machines that can perform tasks that normally require human intelligence. When integrated, AI and big data provide powerful capabilities to extract meaningful insights and make informed decisions.

Integrating AI with big data produces opportunities for the following:

- **Predictive analytics**: Machine learning, a subset of AI, can analyze vast amounts of data to find patterns and make predictions. Businesses use these predictive models to assess market trends, predict customer behavior, and identify potential risks. Predictive analytics can help detect fraudulent transactions in financial applications or be used to predict disease outbreaks or patient readmissions in healthcare. Marketing companies can use predictive analytics to anticipate customer behavior and implement targeted marketing strategies.

- **Natural Language Processing (NLP)**: NLP enables machines to understand human language. This means that a computer can more effectively analyze unstructured data generated by human beings, such as social media posts or customer reviews. NLP aims to read, decipher, understand, and make sense of human language in a valuable way. Therefore, it is sometimes employed to analyze human language for sentiment analysis, general information extraction, or content censoring and recommendations. Despite the many benefits of NLP, there are several challenges involved in implementing NLP since it requires large amounts of data and computing resources, and language is complex and nuanced.

- **Data mining**: AI algorithms can sift through large volumes of data to identify patterns or correlations that humans may overlook. In this process, machine learning algorithms, statistical models, and other AI techniques are applied to analyze data and discover hidden patterns. The discovered knowledge can then be evaluated and interpreted to make decisions or predictions. Despite these advantages, ethical and privacy concerns may arise when data mining involves personal data. Handling such data responsibly and complying with relevant laws and regulations is crucial.

Microsoft Azure offers several AI and machine learning solutions that can be integrated into different data pipeline stages to provide intelligent, scalable, and cost-effective solutions.

Azure Machine Learning

Azure Machine Learning is a cloud-based predictive analytics service that makes it possible to create and deploy predictive models as analytics solutions quickly. It provides a complete workbench for data scientists to experiment, develop, and deploy models using various tools and languages, including Python, R, PyTorch, and TensorFlow.

This service offers the following features:

- **Automated machine learning**: This allows you to automate time-consuming, iterative machine learning model development tasks

- **Azure Machine Learning designer**: This provides a drag-and-drop interface for building, testing, and deploying machine learning models

- **MLOps (DevOps for machine learning)**: This helps you to manage the life cycle of your machine learning models effectively

Azure Machine Learning pricing depends on the resources used and the region. It follows a pay-as-you-go model, where you pay for the computing and storage resources you use. More details can be found here: `https://azure.microsoft.com/en-us/pricing/details/machine-learning/#pricing`.

Of course, with great technology comes great power, so you want to ensure that you clearly understand the business problem and what you want your model to predict. Preprocess your data appropriately, and do not hesitate to try the various machine learning algorithms to find the best model. Always look for opportunities to refine and update your model to reflect changes in the data over time.

Azure Cognitive Services

Azure Cognitive Services is a collection of pre-built AI services that help to build intelligent applications without requiring machine learning expertise. These services are categorized into five groups:

- **Decision**: Help in anomaly detection and content moderation. These algorithms can check for content within images, videos, and text and detect patterns that should be highlighted.

- **Language**: Based on NLP to extract information about the intent of user-submitted text along with entity detection. Also helps with text analytics and translation to different languages.

- **Speech**: Has features that help with speech-to-text, text-to-speech, and in-speech translation. It can be used to ingest audio files and take actions based on the content on behalf of users.

- **Vision**: These services are used for image classification and help in image processing by providing meaningful information. Computer vision can provide various information from images of objects, people, characters, emotions, and so on.

- **Web search**: Helps to implement comprehensive search operations based on text, images, and video and provides custom search options.

From this suite of services, we can access services such as Computer Vision for image processing, a Face API to detect and recognize faces, and even Video Indexer for extracting insights from videos. Speech services include speech-to-text, text-to-speech, and speaker recognition, among others. The following is a breakdown of the services.

Vision	Web search (Bing)	Language	Speech	Decision
Computer Vision Face Video Indexer Custom Vision Form Recognizer (Preview) Ink Recognizer (Preview)	Autosuggest Custom Search Entity Search Image Search News Search Spell Check Video Search Web Search	Immersive Reader (Preview) Language Understanding QnA Maker Text Analytics Translator	Speech to Text Text to Speech Speech Translation Speaker Recognition (Preview)	Anomaly Detector (Preview) Content Moderator Personalizer

Table 8.1: Azure Cognitive Services breakdown

Cognitive Services can be consumed through RESTful HTTP endpoints. In this case, the endpoint is invoked directly by crafting the header and body with appropriate values. The response is then interrogated for the return results of the API call. All the AI services in Cognitive Services are REST APIs that accept HTTP requests in JSON and other formats. You can also use an Azure-provided **software development kit** (SDK). SDKs are available for .NET, Python, Node.js, Java, and Go.

The pricing for Azure Cognitive Services varies depending on the service and the number of transactions. It typically follows a tiered pricing model, where you pay for the number of transactions. You can get more details here: https://azure.microsoft.com/en-us/pricing/details/cognitive-services/#pricing.

Free tiers are available for each service, making it cost-effective to start experimenting. Be sure to choose the most suitable service based on your requirements and monitor your usage carefully to ensure cost-effectiveness.

Azure Bot Service

Azure Bot Service enables developers to create, deploy, and manage intelligent bots that interact naturally with users. It uses the Microsoft Bot Framework and can be integrated with other AI services, such as Azure Cognitive Services.

The pricing for Azure Bot Service includes Standard (free tier) and Premium channels, and the provisioned instance can be run as a standard Azure App Service web app. You can get more pricing details here: https://azure.microsoft.com/pricing/details/bot-services/#pricing.

Ensure you define your bot's purpose clearly before developing a solution using this service. Azure Bot Service allows you to implement **Language Understanding** (**LUIS**). This state-of-the-art language modeling service can build natural language into apps, bots, and IoT devices.

Microsoft Azure provides a comprehensive and robust platform for integrating AI and machine learning into your applications. It offers flexible pricing options that scale with your needs. Whether you're an experienced data scientist or a developer looking to integrate intelligent features, Azure has tools and services to help you succeed.

Now, let us explore a hands-on approach to developing an intelligent solution that makes the most of Azure's AI services and a big data pipeline.

Designing intelligent solutions

Every intelligent or AI-based project requires proper scoping and understanding of the problem being solved. Typically, they go through these seven phases:

1. **Data ingestion**: This is the data preparation step, where data is extracted from various sources and cleaned, and any deviations from the norm are disregarded. Data can come from relational, semi-structured, or unstructured databases, such as documents and event hubs.

2. **Data transformation**: Using either an ETL or ELT process, the data is transformed into a consumable format. Azure Synapse Analytics can handle the transformation and data warehousing activities for this phase.

3. **Analysis**: In this phase, the transformed data is assessed thoroughly for patterns and insights are generated from it. Azure Cognitive Services can be used to assess the data and generate meaningful insights accordingly.

4. **Data modeling**: Post analysis, the data is cleaned and stored in a central area for AI algorithms to generate a model. AI model generation can be done through Azure Machine Learning, and it is an iterative process. It involves experimentation by using various combinations of data (feature engineering) to ensure that the data model is robust. Data is fed into learning algorithms to identify patterns and train the model. The data is then tested to check its effectiveness and efficiency.

5. **Validating the model**: This step involves constantly testing and refining the model to find its effectiveness. The closer the result is to reality, the sounder and more usable the model.

6. **Deployment**: When the model meets a minimum threshold, it can be deployed to production so that real-time data can be fed into it to get the predicted output. Azure Functions is a good candidate for moving data between the sources and analysis services. After deployment, the model can be accessed and used in applications.

7. **Monitoring**: The deployed model is monitored for future analysis of all incoming data and to retrain and improve the effectiveness of models.

These phases can be long-running and time-consuming and resource intensive. You also run the risk of cost and time overruns. Based on the data at hand, and the solution being sought, there is also a risk of failure. This is why using Azure services can assist in quick validations of the ideas while keeping costs relatively low, as Azure costs only amount to what is consumed. *Figure 9.3* displays an architectural solution for an intelligent solution.

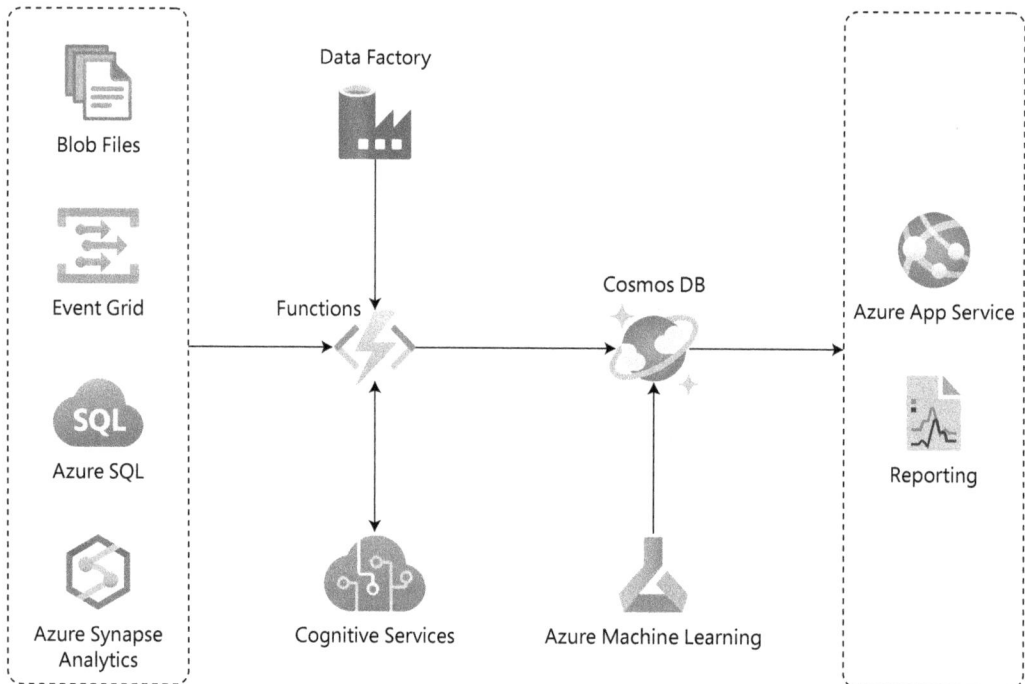

Figure 9.3 – Core components in the solution are Azure Functions,
Azure Cognitive Services, and Cosmos DB

Out-of-the-box AI solutions are provided by Azure and can be used by developers for efficiency and effectiveness. The final AI solution should be easily consumable for third-party applications and should be consumable by any application that runs on any operating system. Generally, these services can be made available as platform-agnostic HTTP RESTful API endpoints.

Summary

In this chapter, you gained an understanding of the application architecture for creating big data and intelligent solutions using Azure technologies. Azure provides several services and integrations that assist in developing big data pipelines that can ingest data in various forms and from different sources, consolidate the data, and ultimately convert it into a more acceptable form for human consumption. We can then build dashboards and visualizations using powerful tools, such as Power BI.

We then must consider that data might not always be from static sources, such as databases or files, but it might come in varied volumes and velocities from smart devices. These devices can send data based on different parameters, and the data might not be standardized or structured. In this case, we use IoT solutions and messaging systems to handle and react to the incoming event data from these devices.

After figuring out how to collate and aggregate big data, we need to apply some intelligence to assist with deciphering the data and identifying possibly elusive trends. This is where we employ AI services and algorithms to sift through the data and introduce speedy assessments and pattern recognition. While some services, such as Cognitive Services, can provide instant intelligent feedback on the data, we might need to use other services, such as Azure Machine Learning, for ongoing analysis and training.

Now that we understand big data and AI solutions a bit more, let us explore architecting applications on a trusted platform.

Architecting Secure Applications on a Trusted Platform

In the dynamic world of cloud computing, secure applications form the foundation of maintaining business integrity and data safety. Microsoft Azure offers several security features designed to cater to modern security needs. This chapter delves into the intricacies of architecting secure applications on Azure.

We will explore various ways to secure applications, such as understanding Azure's built-in security services—Azure **Active Directory** (**AD**) and **Azure Key Vault**. Additionally, we will uncover the advantages and techniques of implementing a layered security model, commonly referred to as "defense-in-depth," and examine the roles of firewalls, **network security groups** (**NSGs**), access controls, and permission restrictions.

This chapter is a blueprint for your secure cloud journey, outlining Azure tools, services, and best practices for building resilient and secure applications. It will help you navigate the complex security landscape in Azure, ensuring your applications stand against evolving threats in the digital landscape. Whether you're new to Azure or an experienced professional seeking to enhance your security skills, this chapter will provide invaluable insights into secure application architecture on Azure.

We'll start by discussing the cloud adoption framework in Azure.

The Cloud Adoption Framework for Azure

The Cloud Adoption Framework for Azure is a set of best practices for securely, efficiently, and cost-effectively implementing cloud solutions. This framework provides security best practices, guidelines, and tools for all phases of the cloud journey, from initial planning and implementation to the management of the solution. The framework provides a structured approach for designing, migrating, or building new applications on Azure, and it covers all aspects of cloud adoption, from initial planning to ongoing operation.

It is a robust set of guidelines that Microsoft has designed to streamline the cloud adoption process. It facilitates the strategic, technical, and business planning decisions organizations must make when migrating to the cloud. The framework offers proven methodologies, best practices, and tools to accelerate the adoption process while mitigating risk.

The Cloud Adoption Framework for Azure is divided into six key phases, each with its specific purpose and focus:

1. **Strategy**: This is the preliminary phase where you define your business motivations, specific outcomes you wish to achieve, and potential obstacles. The aim is to establish a clear business case for cloud adoption.

2. **Plan**: Post-strategy, organizations must align their technical capabilities with the business objectives. This phase involves identifying potential applications or workloads for migration and creating a comprehensive skills-readiness plan.

3. **Ready**: This phase is about preparing the Azure environment for the planned adoption. It focuses on setting up the cloud environment, governance structures, and landing zones.

4. **Migrate or innovate**: Organizations either migrate existing applications to the cloud (rehosting, refactoring, rearchitecting, or rebuilding) or create new applications using cloud-native technologies. Decisions here are driven by the business case established in the strategy phase.

5. **Manage**: Organizations must manage resources effectively once applications are migrated or created in the cloud. This phase includes cost management, security management, and performance tracking.

6. **Govern and optimize**: This final phase ensures ongoing compliance with business policies and continuous improvement of the cloud environment. It emphasizes maintaining governance, managing risk, and optimizing resources for cost-effectiveness and performance.

Understanding the Cloud Adoption Framework for Azure is crucial for various reasons:

1. **Streamlined migration**: The Cloud Adoption Framework provides a systematic approach to cloud adoption. It enables you to ensure that all critical areas are covered.

2. **Risk mitigation**: By following Azure's best practices and guidelines, businesses can reduce the risk associated with cloud adoption, including data security and compliance risks.

3. **Achieving business objectives**: The Cloud Adoption Framework aligns cloud adoption with specific business outcomes. It helps organizations realize cost reduction, increased agility, or improved service delivery goals.

4. **Continuous improvement**: The Cloud Adoption Framework is about getting to the cloud and optimizing your cloud environment post-migration. This focus on continuous improvement ensures businesses can adapt to changing needs and take full advantage of their cloud investment.

Essentially, the Cloud Adoption Framework for Azure is a compass that navigates organizations through the cloud adoption journey. It is a must-understand for any organization looking to harness the full potential of cloud technologies, particularly those utilizing Microsoft Azure. As with any complex process, understanding and following a well-structured, proven methodology can differentiate between success and failure. Learn more about the Cloud Adoption Framework here: `https://aka.ms/caf`.

Now let us review some key Azure security services and how they can be best employed.

Azure security services

As enterprises around the globe migrate their workloads to the cloud, security remains a top priority. Microsoft Azure provides a comprehensive portfolio of security tools and services designed to protect, detect, and respond to security threats in your cloud environment. Azure security services protect your applications and data, including service offerings such as Azure AD and Azure Key Vault. They provide authentication and encryption, facilitate policy compliance, and more. Let us review Azure AD and how its offerings assist us in application development and security.

Azure AD

Azure AD is Microsoft's multi-tenant, cloud-based directory and identity management service. It combines core directory services, application access management, and identity protection into an integrated solution. Azure AD is not just an identity provider; it's also a complete platform that provides robust capabilities for identity management, application access control, and security. It is used to manage identities (users and groups), secure access to applications, and provide a framework for developers to build identity-aware applications.

With Azure AD, organizations can provide their users with a **single sign-on** (**SSO**) experience so that they can access multiple applications with a single set of credentials. It also integrates seamlessly with on-premises Active Directory, extending the latter's capabilities to the cloud.

Azure AD can be implemented in various ways based on organizational needs:

- **Cloud-only mode**: This mode is suitable for organizations without an existing on-premises Active Directory. All user management tasks are performed in Azure AD, and all identities are stored in the cloud.

- **Synchronized identity mode**: This hybrid mode suits organizations with an on-premises Active Directory. Identities are synchronized from the on-premises Active Directory to Azure AD using Azure AD Connect.

- **Federated identity mode**: This mode is another type of hybrid identity where on-premises identities are extended to Azure AD using federation. It's used when organizations require more advanced scenarios, such as enforcing their Active Directory sign-in policy or smart-card-based authentication.

Being a cloud-based service, Azure AD can scale to accommodate any number of users and groups without requiring additional infrastructure. While using Azure AD, the following additional features can be added to its offerings and capabilities:

- **Multifactor authentication (MFA)**: MFA adds an extra layer of security by requiring users to present two or more factors to authenticate their identity. These factors are generally described as "something you know" and "something you have."

- **Conditional Access policies**: These policies help to provide fine-grained control over how and when resources are accessed. These policies are simple if-then statements that determine what action a user must complete to access a resource. For example, an HR manager must complete MFA to access the payroll application.

- **Role assignments**: **Azure role-based access control** (**Azure RBAC**) allows you to manage which users can access what Azure resources and what areas they can access. For example, one user can manage virtual machines in a subscription, and another can manage virtual networks, while neither can access the SQL databases.

- **Activity Log Monitor**: This feature allows you to monitor activity logs regularly to detect suspicious activities and mitigate potential threats.

The Azure AD feature set has existed for as long as Microsoft Azure has and has expanded its feature set gradually. As it grows, the different components and moving parts spread across screens and blades in the Azure portal. Microsoft Entra has been introduced as an all-in-one management portal for Azure AD.

Microsoft Entra Permissions Management operates as a **Cloud Infrastructure Entitlement Management** (**CIEM**) solution, delivering a framework for minimum access privileges. It enables users to run with a basic permission set and necessitates an approval process for temporary, need-based permission escalation. Microsoft Entra provides a single interface for overseeing access across the big three cloud providers—Azure, AWS, and Google Cloud—enabling users to tackle what Microsoft refers to as the "permissions gap," which is the discrepancy between assigned and used permissions.

Microsoft Entra also offers Verified ID, a decentralized identity system leveraging the distributed blockchain to generate user credentials. These credentials, stored in the Microsoft Authenticator app, enable hassle-free, reliable identity verification. What sets this system apart is the shift in credential ownership from the identity provider to the user, giving the user control over the verification process and the content within the digital credentials.

Several benefits can be realized when using Azure AD, and one of the most beneficial ones in application development is the ability to assign an identity to an Azure resource. This allows for easy communication between services, and we will discuss this next.

Managed identities and service principals

Managed identities for Azure resources are a feature that provides Azure services with an automatically managed identity in Azure AD. This service simplifies managing credentials for applications that need to authenticate to other services on Azure. Essentially, Azure takes care of rolling credentials and managing the identity lifecycle.

There are two types of managed identities:

- **System-assigned**: This identity is tied directly to a specific Azure resource. When the resource is deleted, Azure automatically cleans up the credentials and the identity. For example, when an Azure app service is created, it is automatically assigned a managed identity that can be used to request tokens from Azure AD, and the name will be the same as the name of the service.

- **User-assigned**: It is also possible to create an identity as a standalone Azure resource that can be assigned to one or more instances of an Azure service. Unlike system-assigned, this identity isn't automatically deleted when the associated resource is deleted. In this case, multiple resources can share the same permissions as assigned to this identity.

Azure AD and managed identities can significantly enhance both Azure and on-premises applications' security and management. Managed identities can authenticate to any Azure service that supports Azure AD authentication, eliminating the need to store credentials in code or elsewhere. Azure AD is an all-encompassing **identity and access management (IAM)** solution that provides a wide range of capabilities. Its advanced security features and seamless integration with other Microsoft services make it an excellent choice for organizations seeking to enhance their identity management and authentication mechanisms.

A service principal is a backbone concept of Azure AD and application and service interactivity. The service principal defines an access policy and permissions for a user or application. It enables core features such as authentication during sign-in and authorization during resource access. When a managed identity is enabled, a service principal representing that managed identity is created in your tenant. A service principal can also be a global application object instance in a single tenant or directory. A service principal is created in each tenant where the application is present and references the globally unique app object. A service principal object is created when an application is permitted to access resources in a tenant (upon registration or consent).

Service principals can also be used for connections to third-party applications, for instance, when connecting a GitHub action to an Azure web app service. A service principal can be created with the appropriate permissions that the tasks need. GitHub can then use this service principal to connect to Azure during deployment activities. GitHub is a simple example, but any application that allows for integration or interaction with Azure resources can benefit from the presence and use of service principals.

Another significant benefit of using managed identities is that they can be used across different applications and services. When applications need to share secrets, they can be stored centrally in a key vault, and managed identities can be granted access. Let us explore Azure Key Vault and how it helps secure application secrets.

Azure Key Vault

Azure Key Vault is a service provided by Microsoft Azure to safeguard cryptographic keys, secrets (such as passwords, database connection strings, etc.), and certificates used by cloud applications and services. It acts as a secure repository where organizations can store these confidential items, mitigating the risk of inadvertent or malicious exposure. Using Azure Key Vault, developers can centrally manage cryptographic keys, secrets, and certificates and share these secrets across several applications that share these dependencies.

Applications do not have direct access to the key vault; instead, they request the Azure Key Vault service to perform encryption, decryption, or signing of data on their behalf. This feature ensures that the application doesn't store or handle sensitive data, reducing potential exposure. The Azure service hosting the application must be given access to the key vault, and the most convenient way to facilitate this access is by granting the managed identity of the application access.

Some features and benefits of using Azure Key Vault include the following:

- **Security and compliance**: Azure Key Vault enables organizations to comply with security standards and certifications. It ensures that only authorized services and applications have access to sensitive data.

- **Access policies**: Key Vault provides granular access policies for keys, secrets, and certificates separately. Access policies in Azure Key Vault define who has what type of permissions to access the secrets in the key vault. As a best practice, implement the principle of least privilege when assigning permissions. Use Azure managed identities for applications to authenticate to Azure Key Vault. It eliminates the need to store credentials in your code.

- **Audit trails and versioning**: All operations in Azure Key Vault are logged in Azure Monitor, allowing for complete auditing and transparency. It also supports versioning for secrets, which allows you to have multiple versions of a secret as backups against accidental changes or deletions and roll back to previous versions when needed.

Azure Key Vault is a powerful service for securely managing secrets and certificates. It plays a vital role in developing secure applications on Microsoft Azure. Azure Key Vault helps organizations protect sensitive information and meet regulatory compliance obligations. The service has a Standard tier, which encrypts secrets with a software key, and a Premium tier, which includes **hardware security module (HSM)**-protected keys. You can read more about the pricing and features here: `https://azure.microsoft.com/pricing/details/key-vault/`.

There are a few considerations to make when implementing this service:

- **Complexity**: It might add complexity to the application architecture as developers need to handle the additional layer for secret management. Azure Key Vault also does not have a folder or hierarchical structure to organize keys, secrets, and certificates. As a result, managing these can become complicated if the number of stored items grows large.

- **Dependency**: Applications become dependent on the availability of Azure Key Vault. If there's an issue with Azure Key Vault, applications may be unable to retrieve the keys or secrets. Applications might also face latency when retrieving secrets from the vault, especially if the application and Key Vault are in different regions. This could have an impact on the application's performance.

To secure your applications, you also need internal security and resource restrictions. This will ensure that inadvertent changes are not made to resources while they are in use. We will discuss these next.

Azure security policies and locks

Security policies in Azure define rules and configurations to manage and mitigate risk in the Azure environment. They provide a robust set of default policies out of the box and allow for custom policy creation, thus ensuring that an organization's specific security and compliance requirements are met.

Security policies help you ensure all resources are configured according to the organization's security requirements and standards. This consistency reduces the chances of security gaps and vulnerabilities. They also help in enforcing specific configurations and settings. Security policies help organizations to meet industry standards and regulatory requirements.

When using Azure security policies, you should avoid creating broad policies. Instead, focus on creating granular policies that can be applied to specific resources or resource groups. You should review and update your policies to ensure they reflect changes in your organization's security requirements. Fortunately, Azure provides built-in policies that can be used as a starting point and create custom policies only when necessary.

Sometimes the biggest threat to your Azure resources is from within, and it is important to set parameters around how the team can interact with resources. This is where Azure resource locks can help.

Azure resource locks

Azure resource locks add a layer of protection to prevent accidental deletion or modification of resources. There are two types of locks:

- Delete locks, which prevent the resource from being deleted
- Read-only locks, which prevent all changes to the resource

By preventing accidental deletions or modifications, locks can help maintain continuity of services.

When implementing Azure resource locks, consider that locks should be applied to resources requiring high protection. However, be cautious about where and when you use read-only locks, as they can interfere with some operations. Apply locks at different levels (resource, resource group, or subscription) based on the sensitivity and criticality of the resources. As a contingency, ensure a procedure is in place to remove locks in case emergency resource changes are needed quickly.

Essentially, Azure security policies and locks are crucial tools for ensuring the safety and integrity of resources within the Azure environment. When appropriately used, they provide a reliable and automated way to protect resources from unwanted changes and maintain compliance with various security standards and regulations.

Now let us explore how Azure policies work, how they help establish rules around them, and how resources should be secured.

How does Azure Policy work?

Azure Policy is a service in Azure that is used to create, assign, and manage different rules over resources, ensuring they stay compliant with corporate standards and service-level agreements. To be clear, Azure Policy is a service that facilitates setting up security rules around resources to ensure the early detection of breaches and vulnerabilities. As explored in the previous section, Azure security policies allow organizations to establish rules around how Azure resources can be created and managed by the organization in accordance with compliance.

Azure policies are rules that govern and regulate the properties and activities of resources deployed in the Azure environment. They enforce different rules and effects over resources, ensuring compliance with corporate standards and service-level agreements. Policies can control the types of resources that are allowed to be created. You can specify attributes such as location, SKU, or any property in the resource's schema; enforce specific configuration settings on resources, ensuring they align with the required standards; and manage resources by ensuring they remain compliant with external regulations or internal policies. Azure Defender for Cloud or Azure Sentinel can manage these moving parts. The following is an example of the Defender for Cloud dashboard and how it shows an overview of the resources and the cloud platforms they are on.

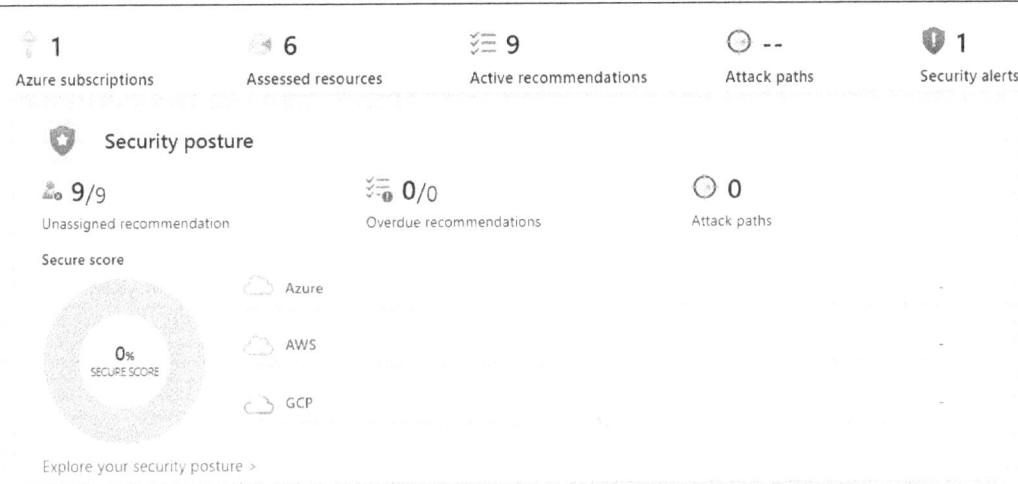

1
Azure subscriptions

6
Assessed resources

9
Active recommendations

--
Attack paths

1
Security alerts

Security posture

9/9
Unassigned recommendation

0/0
Overdue recommendations

0
Attack paths

Secure score

0%
SECURE SCORE

Azure

AWS

GCP

Explore your security posture >

Figure 10.1: Microsoft Defender for Cloud in the Azure portal, showing a
high-level summary of Azure resources and the overall security posture

A warning is issued when a resource doesn't comply with a policy, allowing you to address the issue. They are integral to maintaining the security of resources in the Azure environment. They ensure compliance with organizational and regulatory requirements, enhancing the security posture and streamlining resource management.

A good reference for recommended policies is the Microsoft cloud security benchmark. It provides detailed best practices to improve the security of workloads, data, and services in Azure and multi-cloud environments. You can monitor these baseline recommendations on the Microsoft Defender dashboard, and Azure policy definitions can be found under the Regulatory Compliance section. The information from the benchmark guidelines offers relevant advice to Microsoft Sentinel and ensures the implementation of robust security measures.

Let us explore Azure Sentinel next.

Azure Sentinel

Azure Sentinel is a cloud-native and scalable SIEM/SOAR solution from Azure. SIEM and SOAR are two critical concepts in the field of cybersecurity that deal with threat detection, analysis, and mitigation:

- **Security information and event management (SIEM)**: Refers to software solutions that aggregate and analyze activity from various resources across an IT environment. SIEM tools collect security data from network devices, servers, and domain controllers, consolidate the monitored data to detect abnormal activity, and provide real-time analysis of security alerts generated by applications and network hardware.

- **Security orchestration, automation, and response (SOAR)**: Describes a collection of software and tools that collect data about security threats from multiple sources and respond to low-level security events without human intervention. These tools improve the efficiency of physical and digital security operations and support case management, automation, orchestration, and reporting features.

Azure Sentinel is designed to help security teams work smarter and react faster. It uses built-in **artificial intelligence (AI)** to analyze massive volumes of data across an enterprise quickly. It seamlessly integrates with devices, applications, servers, and other cloud provider environments. With it, you can ingest, filter, and sort security data efficiently, and with built-in machine learning models and anomaly detection algorithms, Azure Sentinel helps identify potentially harmful behavior and unusual patterns across your data, alerting you to threats that might otherwise go unnoticed.

Azure Sentinel can automate common tasks and responses, freeing your team to focus on complex threats. With its SOAR capabilities, Azure Sentinel can automate responses to specific threats. Alongside Azure Policy, Sentinel can trigger remediation actions based on defined policies, ensuring the swift mitigation of threats and a return to compliance.

Essentially, Azure Sentinel and Azure Policy work in tandem to provide a comprehensive security solution for your Azure environment. While Azure Policy ensure your resources align with your organizational and regulatory requirements, Azure Sentinel enhances these security measures through advanced threat detection, investigation, and automated responses. Together, they provide a robust, comprehensive security system that protects your resources and helps maintain a strong compliance posture.

Another key strategy for effective resource management is tagging. With tags, we can label our resources for easier grouping and identification. We will discuss this next.

Why tag resources?

Tagging resources in Azure is crucial for managing them effectively. Tags allow you to categorize resources based on purpose, owner, environment, or other criteria that suit our business needs. This simplifies cost tracking, security, governance, and management across the resources.

In the simplest terms, tags are name/value pairs that can be attached to resources and resource groups in Azure. Despite their simplicity, tags serve several crucial functions contributing to effective, efficient, and economical cloud management. With potentially thousands of resources, running, managing, and keeping track of them can be difficult. One of the significant challenges in cloud computing is controlling costs. By tagging resources, you can track costs on a more granular level. For example, you can track costs by department, project, or environment, which aids in budgeting and chargeback scenarios.

While tagging is an excellent resource management tool, effective tagging requires thoughtful strategizing and execution. Consider the following:

- Establishing and following a consistent naming convention for your tags. This will make understanding and managing them easier as your resource count grows.

- Managing tags throughout a resource's lifecycle, meaning tags should be added when the resource is created, updated as needed during the life of the resource, and removed when no longer needed.

- Using bulk tools to simultaneously apply, update, or remove tags from multiple resources. Use Azure Policy, the Azure CLI, or PowerShell to perform these operations.

- Avoiding storing and exposing sensitive information such as personally identifiable data in the tags.

Now that we have seen how we implement infrastructure and networking security, let us explore RBAC and how it aids us in securing our infrastructure.

Exploring RBAC protections

RBAC is a policy-neutral access control mechanism around roles and privileges. RBAC allows you to define role-permission relationships, user-role relationships, and role-role relationships. RBAC facilitates duty segregation within a team so that users can be granted the exact access that they need to perform their jobs. Responsibilities are typically organized into roles that have common skill sets and career profiles, such as the following:

- **Security leadership**: Persons in this role ensure that other teams coordinate with each other. They also set cultural norms, policies, and standards for security.

- **Security architect**: This role type provides a key governance capability to ensure all the technical functions work harmoniously within a consistent architecture.

- **Security posture and compliance**: A role type that embodies the fusion of compliance reporting and classic security domains such as vulnerability management and configuration baselines. Although the reach and target groups for security and compliance reporting vary, they both assess the organization's security level.

- **Platform security engineer**: These tech-centric positions concentrate on platforms that accommodate various workloads, including access control and asset safeguarding. These roles are typically classified into teams possessing specific technical expertise in areas such as network security, infrastructure and endpoints, identity, and key management. These teams operate on both preventative and detective controls, where detective controls involve collaboration with SecOps, and preventative controls mainly involve working with IT operations.

- **Application security engineer**: This is another tech-focused set of positions that are dedicated to security controls for distinct workloads, catering to both traditional development models and contemporary DevOps/DevSecOps frameworks. They incorporate a mix of application and development security expertise for unique code, along with infrastructure capabilities for standard technical elements such as VMs, databases, and containers. The placement of these roles, whether within central IT or security organizations or embedded in business and development teams, is contingent upon specific organizational parameters.

Azure has over 100 built-in roles that can be assigned to users, groups, and services. They are categorized based on the job role that will be carried out. The general category roles include Owner, Contributor, Reader, and User Access Administrator, and where the built-in roles don't meet your needs, Azure allows you to create custom roles.

Roles can be accessed through the **Access Control (IAM)** blade underneath any Azure service, and they can be assigned accordingly. The configuration screen is as depicted in *Figure 10.2*.

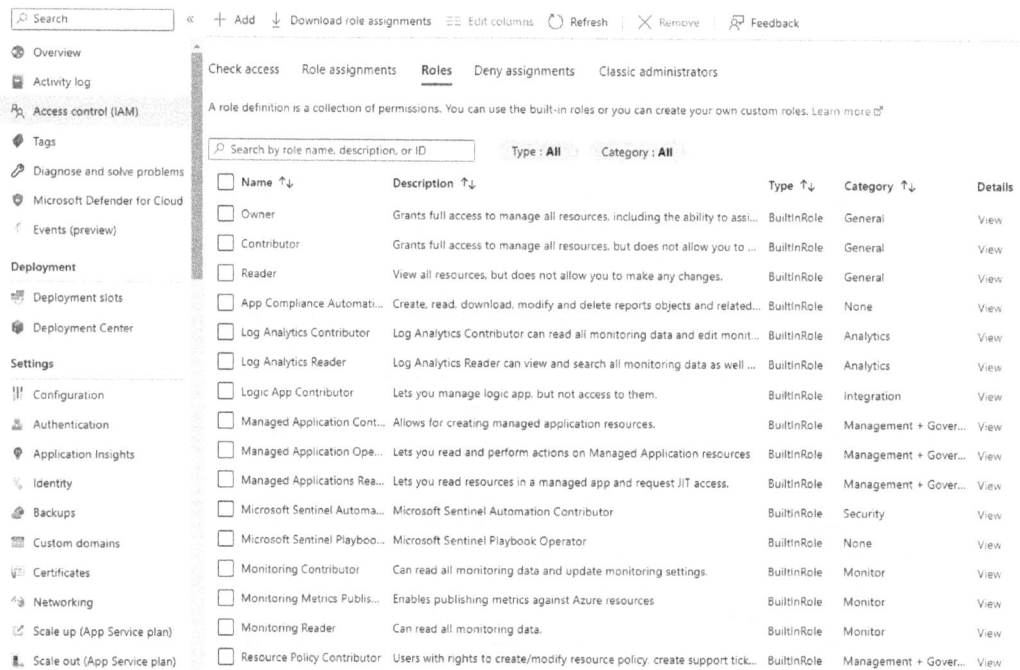

Figure 10.2: Azure portal blade displaying the roles that can be assigned to an Azure resource

Recall that you can define your custom roles if you cannot use one of the built-in roles for your solution. A custom role is a collection of permissions you can tailor to your needs. The role definition is a JSON file that includes the role name, description, assignable scopes, and a list of actions the role can perform. After the role is defined and created, you can assign it to users, groups, service principals, and managed identities.

Do note that custom roles add complexity to access control management, as you need to maintain and keep track of what each custom role does. In using custom role definitions, always follow the principle of least privilege, granting only the permissions necessary to perform the associated tasks.

Azure has several services that can be used to manage RBAC operations:

- **Azure activity log**: As an auditing tool, administrators can view who made changes, when, and what was changed. This helps in tracking all the assignments and activities performed by different roles.

- **Azure Privileged Identity Management (PIM)**: An excellent tool for maintaining minimum privilege access. It helps manage, control, and monitor access within Azure AD, Azure, and other Microsoft Online Services products.

- **Defender for Cloud**: Provides several tools to monitor security configurations, including RBAC assignments, and will alert people of suspicious activities.

RBAC should be implemented with careful planning and regular maintenance. You can effectively use RBAC to secure your Azure environment.

Now that we have a better understanding of some of the tools and services that help us secure our infrastructure and give real-time analytics and auditing of activity, let us explore cybersecurity and how we can implement best practices in our architecture. Learn more about Azure RBAC here: `https://learn.microsoft.com/en-us/azure/role-based-access-control/overview`.

Microsoft Cybersecurity Reference Architecture

Cybersecurity comprises a set of best practices to protect internet-connected systems, including hardware, software, and data, from digital attacks. It is designed to prevent the unauthorized access, use, disclosure, disruption, modification, or destruction of information. Cybersecurity strategies encompass various measures to ensure data confidentiality, integrity, and availability.

The **Microsoft Cybersecurity Reference Architecture** (MCRA) delineates the layers of security control and best practices around Microsoft's array of services and products. It showcases how components combine and should interact to create a secure enterprise environment. MCRA answers the following questions:

- What security features exist in the Azure platform?

- How are users and resources validated and authenticated, and what authorizations do persons have?

- What native tools does Azure provide for security management?

- What other cloud platforms does Microsoft protect?

- What are the appropriate protocols for rapid incident responses?

- How does **Shared Access Service Edge (SASE)** compare to Zero Trust policies?

MCRA aligns with the Zero Trust security model, which teaches us to "never trust, always verify." The Zero Trust model requires you to authenticate and authorize based on all available data points, including user identity, location, device health, service or workload, data classification, and anomalies. It also strongly recommends following the least privilege access principles and limiting user access with **just-in-time** and **just-enough-access** (**JIT/JEA**), risk-based adaptive policies, and data protection to prevent lateral movement and data exfiltration. It is structured around several key aspects of cybersecurity:

- **IAM**: Ensures that only authenticated and authorized users and devices can access the system or network. IAM utilizes Azure AD for identity management and implementing Conditional Access policies.

- **Threat protection**: Emphasizes the need to detect and respond to threats in real time. Defender for Cloud and Microsoft 365 Defender all offer advanced threat analytics, endpoint detection and response, and network traffic analytics features.

- **Information protection**: Involves classifying, labeling, and protecting sensitive data. This is implemented through **Microsoft Information Protection** (**MIP**) and **Azure Information Protection** (**AIP**). This aspect also makes use of **Data Loss Prevention** (**DLP**) capabilities to prevent unauthorized data sharing.

- **Security management**: Focuses on unifying security management across platforms. In Azure, we can use tools such as Microsoft 365 Security Center and Defender for Cloud.

- **Privacy and compliance**: Focuses on meeting regulatory compliance requirements and maintaining privacy principles. Tools such as Compliance Manager and Microsoft 365 compliance center help perform risk assessments and compliance checks. **Microsoft Priva** helps you meet these challenges so you can achieve your privacy goals. It works in tandem with **Microsoft Purview Compliance Manager** to provide data protection and privacy assessment templates that correspond to compliance regulations and industry standards worldwide.

MCRA is designed to work seamlessly with various Microsoft products, such as Microsoft 365 and Microsoft Azure, and has integration support for third-party apps such as ServiceNow and Salesforce and other cloud platforms such as **Amazon Web Services** (**AWS**) and **Google Cloud Platform** (**GCP**). This facilitates an integrated approach to security, ensuring that all components of the IT environment are adequately protected and security policies are uniformly enforced.

You can access detailed MCRA documents, diagrams, and starter templates at the official documentation website: `https://learn.microsoft.com/security/cybersecurity-reference-architecture/mcra`.

Let us explore the concept of compliance management with Azure Purview.

Microsoft Purview

Microsoft Purview, an enhancement of the Azure Data Catalog service, makes it easy for data users to locate reliable and valuable data. It acts as an integrated data governance platform that aids in managing and administrating your data, whether on-premises, across multiple cloud services, or within **software as a service (SaaS)** applications. Its automated data discovery feature can effortlessly generate comprehensive and current maps of a data environment.

It also has data classification and complete data lineage tools that ensure data security. With it, you can do the following:

- Create a unified data landscape map to build a solid foundation for effective data management and governance across hybrid sources.

- Automate and manage metadata with built-in and custom classifiers and MIP sensitivity labels for data classification.

- Ensure consistent labeling of sensitive data across platforms such as SQL Server, Azure, Microsoft 365, and Power BI.

- Use Apache Atlas APIs for easy integration of all your data systems.

- Facilitate the seamless discovery of reliable data while maximizing consumer data using Purview Data Catalog.

- Search data using technical or business terminologies by examining related technical, business, semantic, and operational metadata.

- Unearth data for business insights and identify existing analytics and reports to avoid redundant work.

Microsoft Purview is designed to allow enterprises to maximize their existing data assets as the catalog aids in making data sources easily discoverable and comprehensible for data managers. It offers a cloud-based service where you can register data sources. During this registration process, the data stays at its original location. At the same time, a replica of its metadata and a reference to the data source location is incorporated into Microsoft Purview. This metadata is then indexed to enhance the discoverability and understandability of each data source.

Following the registration of a data source, its metadata can be further enriched by adding more metadata. Users annotate a data source by offering descriptions, tags, or other metadata to request access. This descriptive metadata complements the structural metadata, such as column names and data types registered from the data source.

The main objective of registering sources is to aid the discovery and understanding of data sources and their usage. Enterprise users may require data for various tasks such as business intelligence, app development, data science, or any other task demanding specific data. They can utilize the data catalog discovery experience to locate data that suits their needs swiftly, understand the data to assess its appropriateness, and consume the data by accessing the data source with their preferred tool.

Now that we see how Microsoft Purview helps with our data governance and integrations, let us review some infrastructure security features of Microsoft Azure.

Azure infrastructure security

Microsoft Azure is a cloud hosting platform with physical data centers across the globe. As such, Azure's approach to infrastructure security starts with protecting its physical data centers, network, and hardware. Microsoft designs data centers with multiple layers of physical and logical security controls to comply with a broad range of international standards, such as ISO 27001 and PCI DSS Level 1, to name a few. These measures secure their physical investments and ensure that their clientele can remain confident that their data and infrastructure are secured from external parties.

Beyond the physical hardware in the data centers, we begin to think about our virtualized solution infrastructure. A solution's components, such as virtual networks, machines, and other Azure services, must implement the best and most flexible security measures to balance compliance and usability.

Azure provides built-in security controls across data, applications, compute, networking, and identity to help protect information and systems on the cloud and on-premises. For access control, we can use the previously discussed RBAC features, and you can use various networking controls to prevent unauthorized access, such as **Distributed Denial of Service (DDoS)** protection, NSGs, and **Application Security Groups (ASGs)**.

Let us review how NSGs and firewalls work in more detail.

Network security groups

NSGs in Azure provide security at the subnet level. An NSG is a set of security rules that allow or deny inbound and outbound network traffic for several Azure resources. They act as a virtual firewall for your network, providing granular inbound and outbound security rule control. Each rule specifies the following:

- **Direction**: Whether the rule applies to inbound or outbound traffic.
- **Protocol**: The network protocol (TCP, UDP, or ICMP) this rule applies to.
- **Source and destination**: The rule's source and destination IP address ranges and ports.
- **Action**: Specifies whether to allow or deny the matching traffic.
- **Priority**: The order in which rules are applied. The lower the number, the higher the priority.

NSG rules are required when configuring a virtual machine; for example, to enable access to the virtual machine via RDP, we first need to enable access to port 3389 for both TCP and UDP traffic. We could also have a rule that allows HTTP internet traffic on port 80 and another rule that blocks all other inbound internet traffic. *Figure 10.3* shows how inbound rules can be configured for an NSG in the Azure portal.

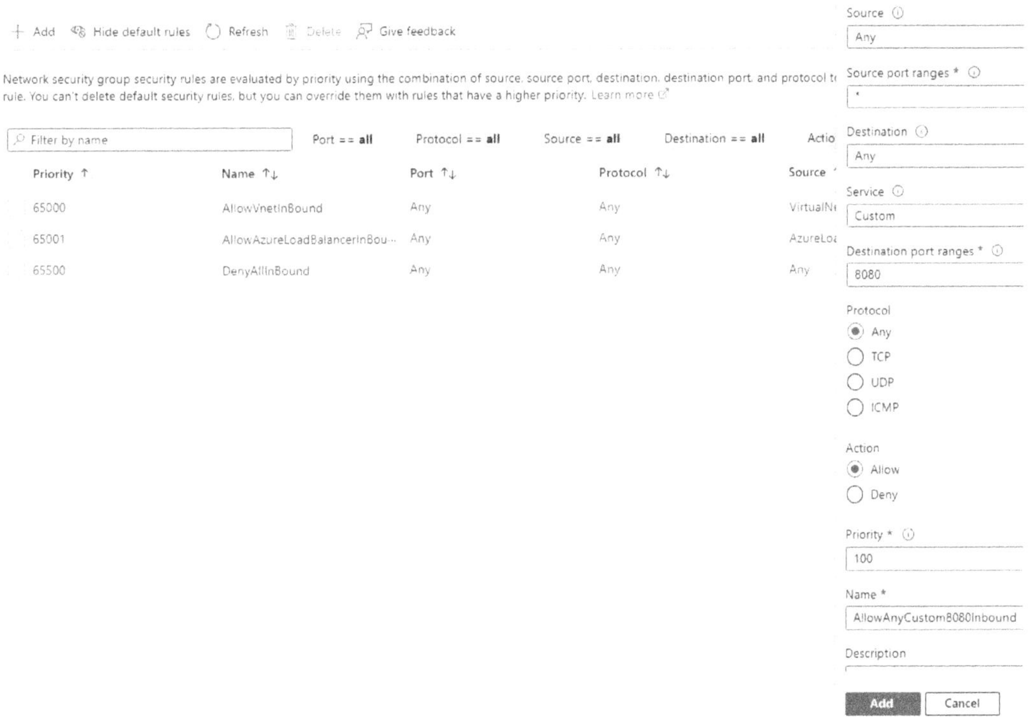

Figure 10.3: Inbound security rules can be added to an NSG to control the traffic that is allowed into the network

An NSG is more targeted to protecting networks or subnets, but there is also Azure Firewall, which can be used to monitor a broader scope of network traffic. We will explore this next.

Azure Firewall

Azure Firewall is a fully stateful firewall as a service with built-in high availability and unrestricted cloud scalability. It analyzes the complete context of a network connection and not just individual packets, unlike NSG rules, and scales up and down relative to changing network traffic volume, which can lead to significant cost savings during low-peak periods.

Firewall rules can be set up to filter outbound traffic, limit outbound traffic to specified lists of **fully qualified domain names** (**FQDNs**), and restrict traffic to specific ports and protocols. This service can also be configured to fire alerts and deny traffic to and from known malicious IPs and domains based on threat intelligence sourced from Microsoft. You can control user access to website categories such as social networking, search engines, and gambling.

Azure Firewall and NSGs complement each other to provide layered defense-in-depth security in your Azure environment. NSGs act as a basic firewall providing a first level of defense. At the same time, Azure Firewall provides a more complex and intelligent service offering more advanced and granular controls.

Beyond setting up basic rules around how web traffic should flow in and out of our system, we need to be able to view, in real time, any policy or rule violations that occur across our cloud-based ecosystem. For this kind of data, visualization, and control, we use Azure Monitor and Security Center. We will discuss these next.

Azure Monitor

Azure Monitor maximizes the availability and performance of your applications and services by delivering a comprehensive solution for collecting, analyzing, and acting on telemetry from your cloud and on-premises environments. It helps you understand how your applications are performing and proactively identifies issues affecting them and the resources they depend on.

Azure Monitor collects data for both the application and infrastructure level from several sources, including application logs, operating system logs, and performance data; it analyzes it for insights using Azure Log Analytics; and it includes powerful visualization tools, including Azure dashboards and Workbooks, which allow you to create complex, interactive reports and visualizations of your data. You can also configure alert rules based on specified conditions to automate responses to these alerts. An example of an action could be running a runbook or triggering a logic app.

Azure Monitor and Defender for Cloud are designed to work in harmony, providing an encompassing view of the security and performance of your resources. Defender for Cloud provides security recommendations based on its assessment and monitoring of the security state of Azure resources. When a threat is detected, it creates a security alert directly integrated into Azure Monitor. So, you can view and manage security alerts and other operational issues in a unified interface.

Defender for Cloud uses policies to monitor security configurations and provide a score reflecting your organization's security posture. It includes a set of more than 90 built-in Azure policies (as discussed earlier) that assess resources for security issues, flagging potential vulnerabilities and risks. It is a comprehensive and integrated solution that helps secure network, identity, data, and applications across your Azure environment. Its primary functions include the following:

- **Threat protection**: Advanced analytics and global threat intelligence are built in to detect incoming threats and post-breach activity

- **Security assessment**: Provides a security score to evaluate your security posture, helping organizations to assess their resource configuration and security settings

- **Regulatory compliance**: Helps ensure your workloads comply with regulatory standards by providing detailed insights into your compliance status

- **Security recommendations**: Offers recommendations to improve security across identity, compute, networking, and data services

Azure Policy works in the background to enforce and manage security policies across your Azure resources. When a subscription is added to Defender for Cloud, a default policy is automatically assigned to the subscription and inherited by all resources under it. Security Center starts evaluating the resources in that scope for compliance when these policies are assigned to a specific scope. The result of this assessment is reflected in your Secure Score, a quantifiable measure of your security posture.

You can also customize these policies or create new ones as needed. Defender for Cloud continuously assesses the state of your resources to provide visibility into your compliance against the policies in place, and automatic remediation can be configured for policies should non-compliant resources be detected.

Now let us focus on Azure **Web Application Firewall** (**WAF**), a robust service designed to shield our web applications from exploits and vulnerabilities.

Azure Web Application Firewall (WAF)

Azure WAF is a powerful tool for protecting web applications from threats. It can be provisioned as a feature of Azure Application Gateway and it provides centralized, scalable, and robust protection from malicious attacks on web applications, including centralized protection of your web applications from common exploits and vulnerabilities, such as SQL injection and cross-site scripting.

It operates on layer 7 (the application layer) of the **Open Systems Interconnection** (**OSI**) model by inspecting the contents of the data packets in more detail. This model categorizes and groups computing functions into a universal set of rules and requirements.

These rules are based on the **Open Web Application Security Project** (**OWASP**) standard and can be customized and extended based on your needs. OWASP is a foundation that works to improve software security through a community-led and open-source software project. The project focuses on strategies and solutions to mitigate the vulnerabilities and security risks of web applications. The OWASP Top 10 is a document for developers about web application security. It outlines the most critical security risks to web applications and forms a basis for the configuration rules for the WAF.

When traffic comes into a web application, it passes through Azure WAF before it reaches the application. Azure WAF then analyzes cookies, headers, and other parts of the incoming web request, using rules to identify and filter out malicious traffic. The request is allowed, blocked, or logged for further inspection depending on the defined rules. *Figure 10.4* depicts how user requests are handled when WAF protection has been applied to the applications.

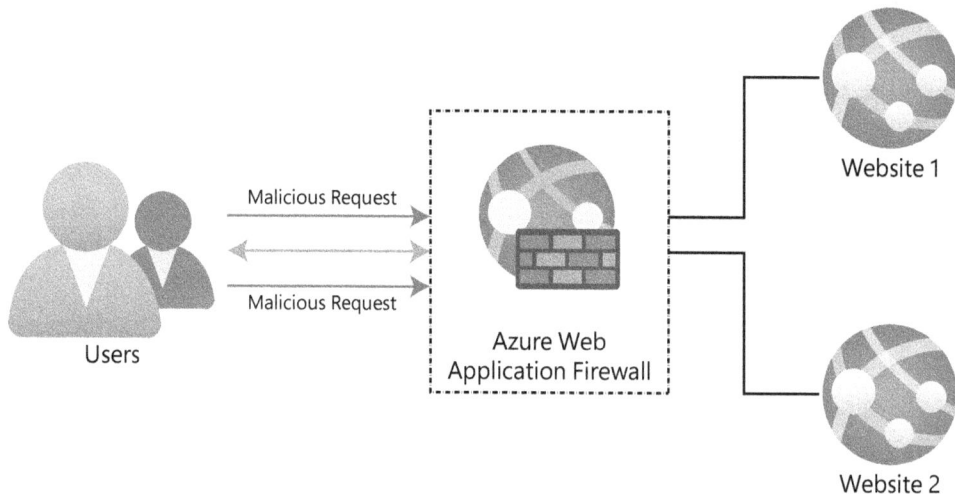

Figure 10.4: WAF protecting Azure App Service-hosted websites

Azure WAF can protect any Azure App Service implementation, including Web Apps, mobile app backends, and RESTful APIs. It can also be applied at the network's edge before traffic reaches the web application. It also integrates with Azure Monitor and Azure Log Analytics to provide insights into your application's traffic patterns.

Now let us review Azure landing zones and how they solidify an application's security features.

Azure landing zones

An Azure landing zone is an operational blueprint for a cloud environment, offering scalable, modular, enterprise-grade building blocks that facilitate successful cloud deployments. It ensures your deployments align with the Microsoft Cloud Adoption Framework for Azure best practices, promoting secure and regulatory-compliant multi-account environments.

Azure landing zones are preconfigured templates designed to set a baseline environment within the cloud, allowing for the deployment of multiple resources in a structured and coordinated manner. They emphasize governance, security, and compliance at scale and provide a consolidated set of design guidelines that simplify and accelerate the adoption of Azure. The landing zone approach gives businesses a clear roadmap when transitioning to Azure. It is essential in setting up a secure, scalable cloud environment with well-defined network security boundaries, RBAC, and data sovereignty.

Two main strategies are chosen based on the aptitude of the implementation team:

- Using the Azure landing zone accelerator:

  - Ideal when a business needs an initial comprehensive implementation of landing zones that include governance, security, and operations right from the beginning

  - If needed, you can alter the setup using **infrastructure as code (IaC)** to establish and configure an environment that suits your needs

  - For IaC, skills in using Azure Resource Manager templates and GitHub are valuable assets

- Customization:

  - This strategy is used when it's crucial to construct your environment to fulfill specific demands or foster internal skills

  - Concentrates on the fundamental landing zone aspects needed to commence cloud adoption

  - Technical and business requirements are deemed fulfilled when the environment's configuration aligns with the Azure landing zone conceptual architecture

The Azure landing zone results from multi-subscription Azure environments that account for scale, identity, governance, security, and networking. Landing zones allow companies to provide greenfield development and application migrations at an enterprise scale in Azure.

Summary

Understanding the cloud security services that are available is very important. A useful guide for best practices in designing a secure infrastructure is the Cloud Adoption Framework. Azure AD provides a managed authentication and authorization solution for users and Azure resources. Azure resources are assigned a managed identity at creation, and this can be used for easy authentication and access control between the different services in your cloud environment. It is also possible to create service principals, which can be assigned to multiple services and facilitate third-party integration.

It is also important to properly secure your resources by defining access control restrictions. You can restrict your cloud users and administrators to confined roles and permissible actions using resource locks and RBAC rules. This will limit the changes that they can make in the environment and contribute to greater uptime and infrastructural continuity.

Azure Policy defines security policies based on your organization's risk profile and appetite. Azure Sentinel and Defender for Cloud will implement these policies and allow you to manage threats and rules surrounding these definitions. Azure Monitor is another powerful tool that helps us to gather insights from different parts of the infrastructure. Defender for Cloud also allows you to monitor hybrid and heterogenous cloud solutions for threats.

You can use Azure Firewall and Azure NSGs to define rules around traffic to and from Azure resources in an Azure virtual network, and Azure WAF to secure web applications in keeping with industry-standard threats and mitigations.

Now let us move on to the next chapter and discuss cost governance on Azure.

11
Cost Governance on Azure

Cost governance on Azure is critical in today's highly competitive market. It enables enterprises to strike a balance between promoting digital transformation and adhering to financial restraints.

Azure cost governance is a strategic method that allows businesses to maximize their cloud investments while maintaining strict financial control. Furthermore, it allows organizations to prioritize performance and innovation while aligning their cloud usage with their financial goals. As a result, organizations can keep their cloud spending predictable and under control.

Organizations can reduce the risks associated with unexpected expenses and budget overruns by implementing effective cost governance strategies. This, in turn, gives organizations the confidence to allocate their resources strategically and fuel their growth ambitions.

Let's start by looking at the various Azure subscription options and the cost-cutting offerings that Azure provides.

Understanding Azure subscription plans and offers

Azure offers various subscription options that cater to a range of customer needs. They each play a crucial role in billing.

The main Azure subscription models are as follows:

- **Pay-as-you-go**: This is one of the most popular licensing models in Azure. Customers are invoiced based on their actual Azure resource utilization, with no upfront fees or long-term commitments. Customers are billed monthly based on their usage. Credit cards and other invoice payment options are accepted. Please see the following for further details on pay-as-you-go pricing: https://azure.microsoft.com/pricing/purchase-options/pay-as-you-go/.

- **Enterprise Agreements (EAs):** EAs involve a financial commitment between organizations and Microsoft. Organizations agree to use a specified amount of Azure resources under an EA. If their usage exceeds the agreed-upon amount, customers receive an overage invoice. EAs allow the creation of multiple accounts and subscriptions. There are two types of EAs: direct EAs, in which customers have a direct billing relationship with Microsoft, and indirect EAs, where billing is managed by a partner. EAs offer superior discounts and benefits due to the commitment made by Microsoft. For more information on EAs, please see `https://www.microsoft.com/licensing/licensing-programs/enterprise`.

- **Azure in Cloud Solution Provider (CSP):** Azure in CSP enables customers to work with a CSP partner who provisions a subscription on their behalf. Customers do not have a direct billing relationship with Microsoft because invoicing is fully managed by the CSP partner. In a nutshell, Microsoft invoices the CSP partner, who will then invoice the customer, including their margin. For more information on Azure in CSP, please read this article: `https://azure.microsoft.com/pricing/offers/ms-azr-0145p/`.

- **Azure free account:** Azure offers a free account that allows customers to explore and test Azure services within predefined usage limits. It is a great way to get started with Azure at no cost. For the first 30 days, this free account provides $200 (USD) in Azure credits. For more information on Azure free accounts, please review this page: `https://azure.microsoft.com/free/`.

The aforementioned offerings are only a subset of the complete range offered by Azure. You can find a comprehensive list, including offerings such as Azure Sponsorship, Azure for Students, Azure Pass, and Dev/Test subscriptions, at `https://azure.microsoft.com/support/legal/offer-details`.

Cost optimization features

For additional savings, consider the following cost optimization features:

- **Azure Reservations:** Customers can save money by committing to one-year or three-year plans for various Azure products and services. Azure Reservations are available for a wide range of Azure offerings, including VMs, storage, SQL databases, and Cosmos DB. Customers who commit to a longer-term contract can receive considerable discounts of up to 72% off pay-as-you-go pricing. This makes it an ideal option for workloads with predictable and consistent usage patterns. For more information on Azure Reservations, please see `https://azure.microsoft.com/reservations/`.

- **Azure Hybrid Benefit (AHB):** AHB allows customers to use their existing on-premises Windows Server, SQL Server license, or Linux subscription to reduce the cost of operating those workloads in Azure. Customers can save money on Azure VMs and Azure SQL Database by bringing their own licenses. For more information on AHB, please see `https://azure.microsoft.com/pricing/hybrid-benefit`.

- **Azure Spot VMs:** Spot VMs offer significant cost savings by using spare Azure capacity. Customers can bid on unused Azure VM capacity and run workloads at a reduced cost. However, there is a possibility of service interruption if the capacity is needed by paying customers. Spot VMs are suitable for fault-tolerant workloads or those with flexible timing requirements. For more information on Azure Spot VMs, please see `https://azure.microsoft.com/products/virtual-machines/spot`.

- **Azure savings plans for compute:** This cost-saving option offers a flexible pricing model. Customers can save up to 65% off pay-as-you-go pricing on compute services by committing to a fixed hourly amount for one or three years. For more information on Azure savings plans for compute, please see `https://learn.microsoft.com/azure/cost-management-billing/savings-plan/savings-plan-compute-overview`.

The aforementioned licensing models and cost optimization features allow customers to choose the most suitable solution based on their requirements, budget, and workload characteristics. It is important to evaluate and compare the features and cost implications of each licensing model to make informed decisions.

Now that we have gained a comprehensive understanding of Azure's offerings, let's shift our focus to the important aspects of Cost Management + Billing on the Azure platform.

Understanding Cost Management + Billing on Azure

Unlike traditional infrastructure, there is no upper limit on Azure consumption. However, Azure imposes certain limits on the number of resources that can be deployed, in the form of both hard limits and soft limits. Resources that have "hard limits" would have specific maximum thresholds imposed on their usage. To determine these limits, please refer to the official Microsoft documentation at `https://learn.microsoft.com/azure/azure-resource-manager/management/azure-subscription-service-limits`.

It is important to note that the default limit can vary depending on the type of subscription you have for Azure services. Should the need arise, it is possible to request an increase in soft limits by contacting Azure Support.

Companies must closely monitor their Azure consumption and usage to effectively manage costs. While creating policies, it is important to establish organizational standards and conventions. Also, it is equally crucial to track billing and consumption data. Furthermore, adopting best practices for resource utilization in Azure is essential to maximize returns on investment. To achieve this, architects must possess knowledge about Azure resources, features, and associated costs, and conduct cost/benefit analyses of various features and solutions.

> **Note**
>
> Data transfers going into Azure are free of charge. However, data transfers coming out of Azure to other locations, such as the internet or other Azure regions, will incur a fee.
>
> Always refer to the official Azure pricing documentation for each individual service you use as a best practice.

The **Cost Management + Billing** feature (see *Figure 11.1: Cost Management + Billing service in the Azure portal*) provides detailed billing and usage information within the Azure portal. To access this feature, users can navigate to the master navigation blade.

Management and administrators can use the **Cost Management + Billing** tools to keep track of expenses, analyze usage patterns, and make resource allocation and optimization decisions.

> **Note**
>
> The **Cost Management + Billing** feature is enforced by **Role-Based Access Control (RBAC)**. This means only users with the appropriate RBAC roles and permissions are permitted to see the cost and consumption details.

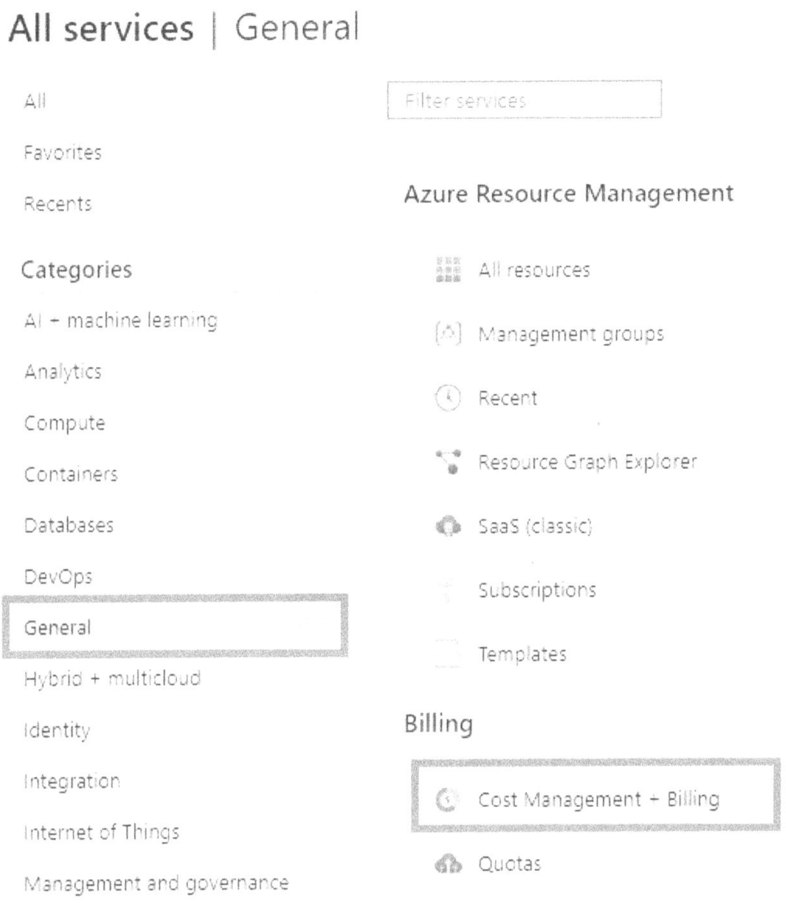

All services | General

All

Favorites

Recents

Categories

AI – machine learning

Analytics

Compute

Containers

Databases

DevOps

General

Hybrid + multicloud

Identity

Integration

Internet of Things

Management and governance

Filter services

Azure Resource Management

▦ All resources

[^] Management groups

⏱ Recent

⁑ Resource Graph Explorer

☁ SaaS (classic)

Subscriptions

Templates

Billing

💲 Cost Management + Billing

☁ Quotas

Figure 11.1: Cost Management + Billing service in the Azure portal

Cost management encompasses a suite of **Financial Operations (FinOps)** tools that empower customers to analyze, manage, and optimize their costs effectively.

The Billing feature provides comprehensive tools to handle a customer's billing account and facilitate invoice payments.

The cost management tools are accessible in the Azure portal from any management group, subscription, or resource group. This gives stakeholders the ability to see the costs within the scope to which they have been granted access.

To learn more about **Cost Management + Billing**, go to the following web page: `https://learn.microsoft.com/azure/cost-management-billing/cost-management-billing-overview`.

In the next section, we will have a look at some of the cost-calculating tools that Azure offers.

Azure cost calculators

One of the main benefits of cloud computing is the ability to scale and architect different platform characteristics based on your needs, which can lead to cost savings. To ensure that you are making good ROI from your cloud investments, it is important to have a clear understanding of your cloud expenses.

Here are two useful tools from Azure to help optimize and manage your cloud expenses:

- **Azure Pricing Calculator**: The Azure Pricing Calculator (see *Figure 11.2: Azure Pricing Calculator*) allows you to estimate the cost of running your workloads in Azure. The calculator provides an estimated cost breakdown by entering parameters such as the services you plan to use, desired configurations, and projected usage. This enables you to assess the financial impact of your choices and make smart resource allocation decisions. The Azure Pricing Calculator can be found at `https://azure.microsoft.com/pricing/calculator/`.

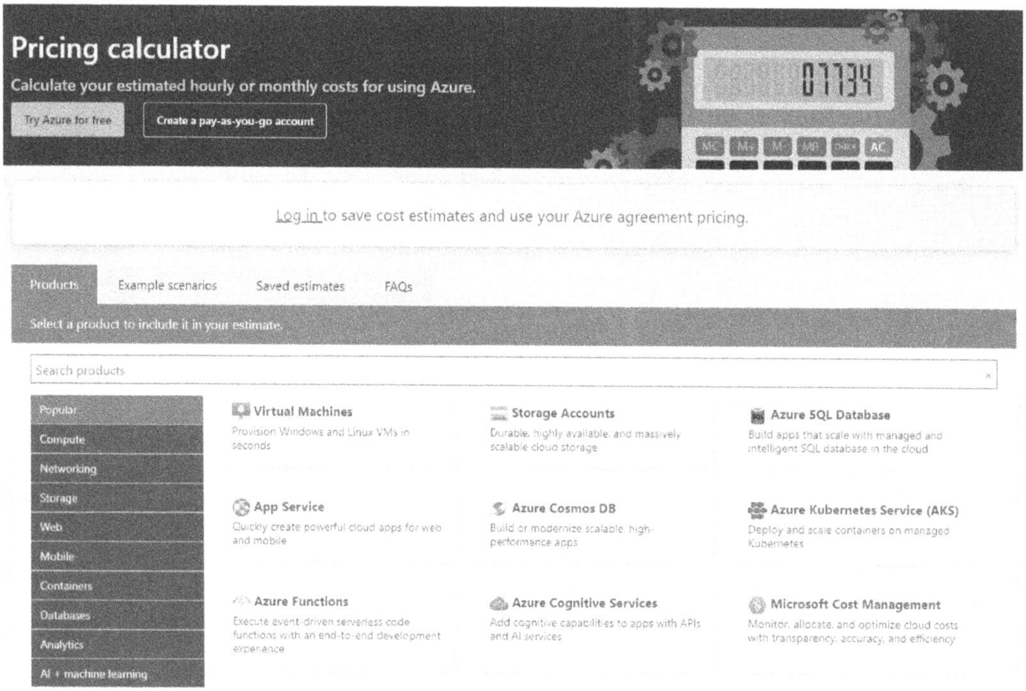

Figure 11.2: Azure Pricing Calculator

- **Azure Total Cost of Ownership (TCO) Calculator**: The Azure TCO Calculator (see *Figure 11.3: Azure Total Cost of Ownership (TCO) Calculator*) helps you understand the potential cost savings of running workloads in Azure versus maintaining on-premises infrastructure. The TCO Calculator provides a complete comparison to help you evaluate the financial benefits of migrating to Azure by taking into consideration factors such as hardware, software, labor, and energy costs. This tool assists in assessing the long-term cost-effectiveness of adopting Azure in your firm. The Azure TCO Calculator can be found at `https://azure.microsoft.com/pricing/tco/calculator/`.

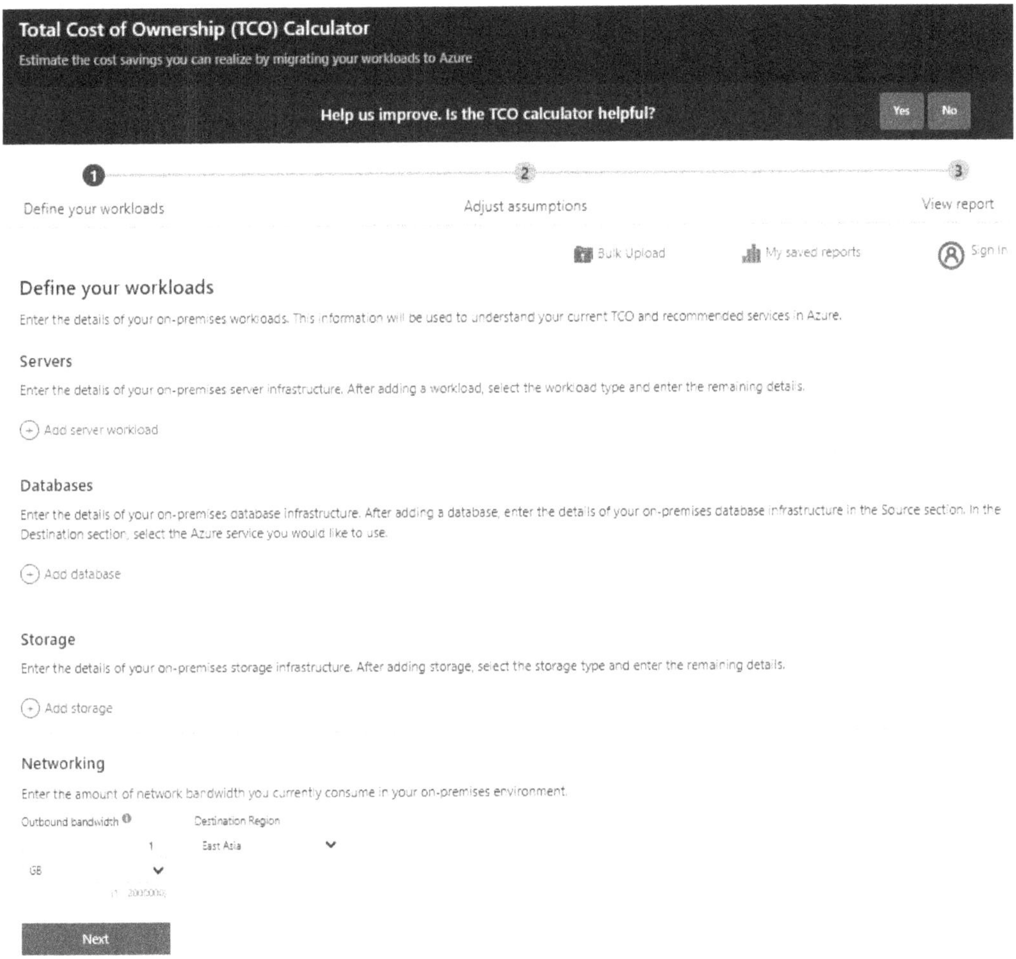

Figure 11.3: Azure Total Cost of Ownership (TCO) Calculator

These cost calculators help you gain insights into your cloud consumption and make data-driven decisions to optimize your cloud resources for both cost efficiency and performance.

In the next section, we will look at some of the best techniques for optimizing your costs on Azure.

Best practices for cost optimization and governance

To achieve cost optimization in Azure, architects must have a solid perspective of their architecture as well as the specific Azure components that are being used. Architects can make the most informed decisions regarding the best offerings from Microsoft in terms of **Stock Keeping Unit (SKU)**, size, and features by continually monitoring, conducting audits, and analyzing usage patterns.

Here are some common cost optimization best practices:

- **Right-size resources**: Analyze resource usage to ensure that resources are provisioned with suitable sizes based on workload requirements. Over-provisioning resources can lead to unnecessary costs.

- **Use cost-effective pricing options**: To save money, explore various pricing options, such as reserved instances or spot VM instances. Determine the most cost-effective pricing model by evaluating the workload's characteristics.

- **Use Azure Cost Management + Billing**: Use the Azure Cost Management + Billing feature to gain insights into resource costs and consumption. Monitor spending trends, create budgets, and set up alerts to help manage costs more effectively.

- **Create budgets in Cost Management**: Budgets in cost management allow customers to plan and manage costs efficiently. Organizations can ensure that their spending remains within the predetermined organizational limits by configuring alerts based on actual or forecasted costs. When the defined budget criteria are exceeded, notifications are sent to allow for timely interventions and remedial actions.

- **Use Azure Advisor**: Utilize Azure Advisor, which uses machine learning and AI to analyze usage patterns and provide cost-saving recommendations for resources. These insights play a crucial role in cost optimization. For more details, see the upcoming *Azure Advisor* section.

- **Use Azure Migrate to do cost analysis before migrating**: Azure Migrate is a valuable tool that can help organizations save money when migrating their workloads to the Azure cloud. Azure Migrate gives insights into resource utilization and performance by accurately assessing on-premises infrastructure and workloads. This information allows organizations to right-size their Azure infrastructure and select the most cost-effective instance sizes while avoiding over-provisioning.

- **Implement resource tagging**: Tag Azure resources consistently to enable effective cost allocation, resource grouping, and filtering. Tags can be used to track costs for specific departments, projects, or initiatives.

- **Automate resource management**: Use automation tools, such as Azure Automation or Azure Logic Apps, to streamline resource provisioning, scaling, and deprovisioning. Unnecessary resource usage and costs can be avoided by using automated resource management.

- **Optimize data storage**: Assess the data storage needs of your applications and select the most suitable Azure storage services, such as Blob Storage, File Storage, or Managed Disks, based on performance and cost considerations.

- **Monitor and optimize network traffic**: Analyze network traffic patterns and reduce data transfer costs by utilizing Azure Virtual Network service endpoints, peering, or Content Delivery Networks (CDNs) where applicable.

- **Regularly review and optimize resource usage**: Conduct regular resource consumption audits to discover areas for optimization. To eliminate wasteful costs, unused or underutilized resources should be identified and either rightsized or decommissioned.

Architects can maximize the value of their Azure investments while keeping costs under control by implementing these cost optimization best practices.

Azure Advisor

Azure Advisor (see *Figure 11.4: Azure Advisor*) is a tool designed to offer actionable recommendations for optimizing cloud usage based on best practices and historical usage patterns. It provides guidance in various areas, including cost optimization, security, performance, and availability.

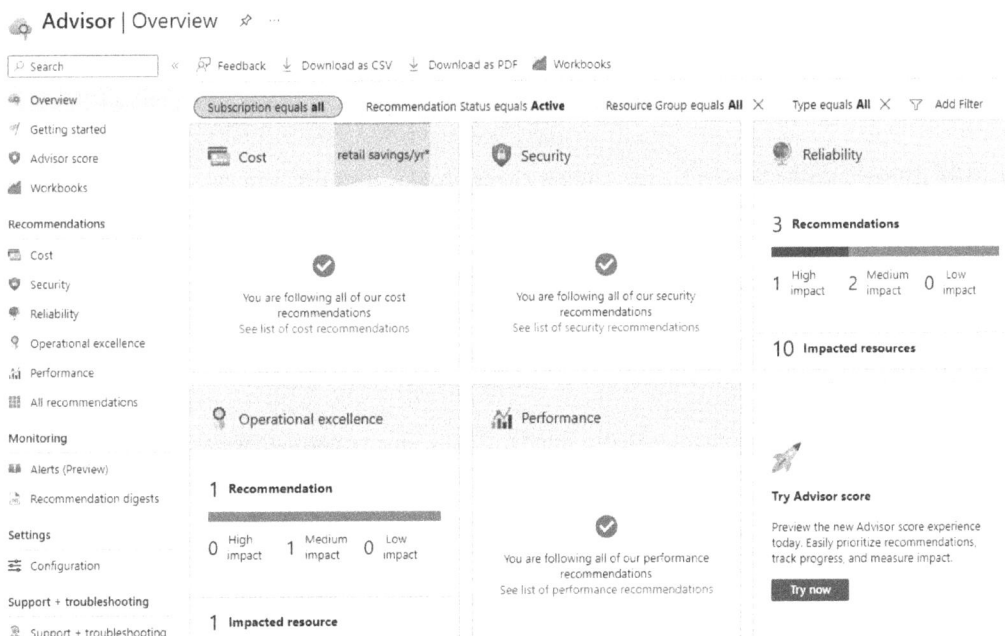

Figure 11.4: Azure Advisor

To learn more about Azure Advisor, please visit https://learn.microsoft.com/azure/advisor/advisor-overview.

Azure Governance

Azure Governance encompasses a range of processes and mechanisms designed to maintain complete control over resources deployed in Azure. With Azure Governance, organizations can establish guardrails within their Azure subscriptions using predefined and custom policies. Additionally, organizations can gain valuable insights into their cloud spending to effectively manage costs and optimize their cloud investments.

Here are some key points to consider:

- **Implement logical organization and tagging**: Apply tags to resources, resource groups, and subscriptions to create logical categorizations. Tags not only help with resource organization but also enable cost evaluations from different perspectives. Azure policies can be employed to enforce tagging requirements, and multiple policies can be combined into initiatives for compliance checks and reporting purposes.

- **Establish a naming convention**: Set up a consistent naming convention for all resource types and resource groups to ensure clarity and organization across resources. Azure policies can be used to efficiently enforce and maintain this naming convention.

- **Use Azure Blueprints**: Azure Blueprints standardizes resource provisioning, resource group setup, and environment deployments in compliance with corporate standards, including naming conventions and tag use. Check out the following documentation to learn more about Azure Blueprints: https://learn.microsoft.com/azure/governance/blueprints/overview.

- **Use Azure landing zones**: Azure landing zones provide a strong framework for deploying workloads in Azure with best practices, guidelines, and essential components such as security, networking, and governance. Azure landing zones enable organizations to accelerate their cloud adoption journey while adhering to industry standards. They help businesses to optimize the performance, cost-effectiveness, and security of their cloud resources. To learn more about Azure landing zones, please visit https://learn.microsoft.com/azure/cloud-adoption-framework/ready/landing-zone/.

Organizations can maintain control, enforce standards, and ensure consistency across their Azure resources by following these Azure governance principles.

Optimizing Infrastructure as a Service (IaaS) costs

When using **Infrastructure as a Service (IaaS)** resources (such as VMs) in your solution, compute costs are typically the largest portion of your expenses, followed by storage costs.

Consider applying the following best practices to reduce compute and storage costs in your Azure environment to achieve cost optimization.

Compute best practices

In addition to the previously listed common best practices, the following best practices for compute services can help optimize resource use and enhance cost efficiency:

- **Consider shutting down or deallocating unused compute services**: To stop resource usage and reduce costs, consider shutting down or deallocating any idle resources (such as VMs).

- **Select optimal compute locations**: Select the best location for your compute services, such as VMs, while ensuring that all essential Azure features are available in the same region. This helps to reduce egress traffic.

- **Dynamically resize VMs**: Scale up or down VMs based on demand. Evaluate newly released SKUs on a regular basis to determine whether a different size better meets your requirements.

- **Make use of Azure Virtual Machine Scale Sets (VMSS)**: Begin with a modest number of VMs in a scale set and scale out when demand grows. This allows you to adjust resources dynamically based on workload requirements. Consider using predictive autoscaling to help manage and scale VMSS. This feature predicts when to scale out using machine learning. To learn more about the VMSS predictive autoscale feature, please see `https://learn.microsoft.com/azure/azure-monitor/autoscale/autoscale-predictive`.

- **Use Azure DevTest Labs**: Use Azure DevTest Labs for development and testing purposes. These labs provide essential features, such as policies, auto-shutdown, and autostart, which help to reduce costs. For more information on Azure DevTest Labs, please see `https://azure.microsoft.com/products/devtest-lab`.

- **Reduce network traffic between Azure regions**: You can reduce costs by minimizing data transfers between Azure regions. In most cases, inbound data transfers to Azure are free of charge. However, outbound data transfers from Azure to other destinations, such as the internet or different Azure regions, may incur data transfer fees. Always reference the official Azure price documentation for each specific service you use to understand the fees associated with data transfers as a best practice.

- **Use load balancers**: Use a load balancer with a public IP address to access multiple VMs, rather than assigning a public IP to each individual VM, resulting in cost savings.

- **Monitor and adjust VM performance**: Continuously monitor VMs, assess performance metrics, and adjust resources as needed. This can involve scaling up or down VMs or even reducing their quantity to optimize costs.

Customers can effectively cut expenses and maximize the value of their Azure resources by applying these compute best practices.

Next, we will look at similar recommended practices for storage.

Storage best practices

In addition to the previously mentioned common best practices, when it comes to using Azure Storage to host applications and store data, it is important to follow best practices to ensure efficiency and cost-effectiveness.

Consider the following recommendations for storage optimization:

- **Choose appropriate storage redundancy**: Select the right redundancy type for your storage needs, such as **Geo-Redundant Storage (GRS)**, **Locally Redundant Storage (LRS)**, or **Read-Access Geo-Redundant Storage (RA-GRS)**. Keep in mind that GRS has higher costs compared to LRS.

- **Optimize storage tiers**: Use different storage access tiers based on data usage patterns. Infrequently accessed data should be archived in the cool or archive tier, whereas frequently accessed data should be kept in the hot tier. This helps reduce costs by aligning storage costs with data access frequency.

- **Remove unnecessary blobs**: Review and remove blobs that are no longer needed on a regular basis to free up storage space and save money.

- **Delete unused OS disks**: When deleting VMs, be sure to delete the associated OS disks as well. This saves money on storage costs.

- **Monitor and optimize storage account usage**: Understand how storage accounts are metered based on their size, write/read/list operations, and container operations. This knowledge can help you optimize resource usage and costs.

- **Prefer standard disks over premium disks**: Unless your business requires the specific performance characteristics of premium disks, opt for standard disks to save costs. For example, Standard SSD (E30) costs $77 (USD)/month while Premium SSD (P30) costs $135 (USD)/month. By choosing SSD disks over Premium SSD, you can potentially save 57% on disk costs.

- **Consider Azure Premium SSD v2 disk storage**: Determine whether Premium SSD v2 disk storage meets your solution needs. Premium SSD v2 storage decouples disk performance (IOPS) from disk size (GB). This means that a high-performance (IOPS) disk can be specified without requiring the use of large disks. This scenario can result in storage cost reductions of up to 90%. For more information on Premium SSD v2, refer to this article: `https://learn. microsoft.com/azure/virtual-machines/disks-types#premium-ssd-v2`.

- **Use CDN and caching**: Use CDNs and caching mechanisms for static files to eliminate the need for frequent storage retrieval, enhancing performance and lowering storage costs.

- **Use reserved capacity**: Azure offers reserved capacity for blob data, which allows you to save money by committing to a specific quantity of storage in advance.

You can architect cost-effective storage solutions that suit the needs of your application by following these storage best practices.

In the next section, we will discuss cost optimization for **Platform as a Service (PaaS)** solutions.

Optimizing Platform as a Service (PaaS) costs

When provisioning and using PaaS resources, it is important to be mindful of the cost implications. In addition to the previously listed common best practices, consider the following best practices to optimize costs for solutions that make use of PaaS services:

- **Choose the appropriate Azure SQL tier**: Select the appropriate tier and performance levels for Azure SQL databases based on the requirements of your application. Right-sizing the tier ensures cost savings without sacrificing performance.

- **Consider elastic databases**: If your application requires several databases, elastic databases may be less expensive than single databases. Elastic databases provide resource sharing as well as efficient scaling.

- **Re-architect for PaaS solutions**: Evaluate the possibility of migrating from IaaS solutions to PaaS solutions. PaaS offerings, such as serverless or microservices with containers, reduce maintenance costs and operate on a consumption-based pricing model. This allows for cost savings by only paying for services that are actively used and reducing expenses when services are not actively used.

It should be noted that each Azure resource may have different cost optimization considerations. Consult the documentation for each feature to learn more about its cost and usage implications.

General best practices

In addition to the previously described service-specific best practices, here are some general guidelines to bear in mind for cost optimization in Azure:

- **Consider alternate regions**: Resource costs may be different across regions. If performance, latency, and regulatory governance allow, consider the option of using an alternate region that offers cheaper pricing for your specific resource needs.

- **Explore EAs**: EAs provide better discounts than other offers. Engage with the Microsoft account team to learn more about the benefits and potential cost savings you can obtain by signing up for an EA.

- **Use Azure Prepayment to prevent overspending**: Azure Prepayment is an upfront payment option that helps organizations to control their Azure costs and avoid overspending. It is especially beneficial for organizations with predictable usage patterns. It allows them to purchase the required prepayment amount in advance and use Azure services without fear of overspending.

- **Delete unused resources**: Review your Azure resources on a regular basis to identify those that are no longer needed or underutilized. To save money, consider downsizing their SKU or size. If resources are no longer required, delete them to avoid incurring expenses.

While these are general recommendations, best practices may differ depending on your individual use cases and requirements. As you gain experience and architect more solutions in Azure, you can establish your own set of best practices. In addition, consult the official documentation for each Azure component to ensure that you are adopting cost-effective solutions that are based on the most recent guidelines.

Summary

In this chapter, you gained valuable insights into the significance of cost management and optimization on Azure. We've investigated the various pricing options and discussed the services and tools offered by Azure for managing costs.

Effective cost management is critical because while monthly expenses may be low at first, they can quickly grow if resources are not continuously monitored. As cloud architects, it is essential to design applications in a cost-effective manner by using Azure resources with proper SKUs, tiers, and sizes. This involves knowing when to start, stop, scale up, scale out, scale down, scale in, or transfer data to save money.

By implementing proper cost management practices, you can ensure that actual expenses match your budgetary expectations. This allows you to maximize the value of your cloud investments while maintaining cost control throughout the project life cycle.

12
Conclusion

Throughout this book, we've explored different solutions to help architects and business decision makers thrive in the face of limited resources, and showcased the power of Microsoft Azure as a transformative tool for achieving remarkable results. Here, we'll cover the key takeaways from each chapter.

Chapter 1, Unlock New Opportunities with Azure

We gained insights into why numerous decision makers opt for Azure: its cost-effectiveness, robust security measures, governance capabilities, scalability options, reliable performance, high availability, and more. We also discussed the concept of responsibility segregation within various Azure cloud models. This chapter provides business decision makers with a set of fundamental steps to unlock new opportunities with Azure so that organizations can take full advantage of the cloud.

Chapter 2, Achieve Availability, Scalability, and Monitoring with Azure

In this chapter, we delved deep into Azure's capabilities for high availability, scalability, and efficient application monitoring. We explored Azure's inherent flexibility, which enables organizations to effectively manage fluctuations in traffic and demand and allows them to adapt and scale as needed. We learned how Azure equips businesses with invaluable insights for proactive management of applications and infrastructure, ensuring uninterrupted high availability, scalability, and optimal performance.

Chapter 3, Cloud Architecture Design Patterns

This chapter covered the significance of robust architectural design in the development and scoping of cloud solutions. We reviewed the design of Azure Virtual Network and Azure Storage designs, emphasizing their pivotal roles in establishing efficient and secure cloud infrastructures. We explored various design patterns related to messaging, performance, and scalability, shedding light on their practical application for achieving optimal cloud solutions. While we touched upon the subject of virtual networks and their design, a more comprehensive examination of Azure network infrastructure and design was reserved for the next chapter.

Chapter 4, Azure Network Infrastructure and Design

In this chapter, we continued our exploration of networking in Azure. We reviewed several standard design patterns used when configuring and provisioning networking components in Azure. We also examined some common problem areas that often arise in real-world scenarios during network design. This chapter revolved around the exploration of core components such as virtual networks, subnets, and gateways, and how the OSI model's representation of application communication can be applied to various network services. Understanding these aspects aid decision-making processes regarding the selection of appropriate services based on specific requirements. By combining these decisions with insights gained from addressing common problem areas, it becomes possible to develop solutions that effectively meet the unique needs of businesses and organizations.

Chapter 5, Automating Architecture on Azure

In this chapter, we emphasized the immense potential of automation on Azure by using **Infrastructure as Code (IaC)**. By automating key processes on Azure, organizations can free up valuable resources and propel themselves toward greater efficiency and success. Organizations can unlock a multitude of advantages, including streamlined processes, enhanced productivity, and the capacity to drive innovation within a fiercely competitive landscape.

Chapter 6, Optimize Performance with Azure OLTP Solutions

This chapter presented a comprehensive overview of Azure SQL Database, a reliable and robust solution for managing mission-critical databases that appeals to a diverse range of customers. We also discussed the various Azure SQL Database deployment types, including single instance, managed instance, and elastic pools. By conducting a thorough assessment of business requirements, architects can select the most suitable deployment model for their specific needs. Additionally, we explored different pricing strategies, such as DTUs, RUs, and vCPUs, allowing organizations to align their pricing with their unique requirements.

Chapter 7, Designing Serverless Architecture Solutions in Azure

In this chapter, we explored Azure Functions and durable functions, highlighting their fundamental significance in the development of serverless applications. We also saw the implementation of event-driven architectural solutions, which make use of Azure Event Grid and Logic Apps. These technologies enable developers to build scalable and responsive applications while harnessing the power of the serverless paradigm.

Chapter 8, Deploying, Managing, and Scaling Containers with Azure Kubernetes Service

This chapter examined the architecture of AKS clusters and the utilization of add-ons, extensions, and third-party integrations with AKS. We explored application development with a focus on Kubernetes primitives and the management of the application lifecycle. We also reviewed Kubernetes networking, encompassing Kubernetes and CNI models, Ingress controllers, and network policies. Lastly, we provided a brief overview of AKS cluster security and introduced managed AKS through **Azure Container Apps (ACA)**. This chapter equipped you to confidently navigate the Azure ecosystem and harness the power of containers and Kubernetes to drive your application development and deployment efforts to new heights.

Chapter 9, Designing Big Data Solutions with Azure

This chapter provided valuable insights into the application architecture required to build big data and intelligent solutions using Azure services. Azure offers a wide range of services and integrations that facilitate the development of robust big data pipelines, enabling the ingestion of data from diverse sources and formats. This data can then be transformed into compelling dashboards and visualizations using tools such as Power BI. We also explored how to effectively handle and respond to event data using IoT solutions and messaging systems that can efficiently process and analyze the incoming data streams.

We learned how we can harness the power of AI services and algorithms to extract meaningful insights and identify elusive trends from aggregated big data. These tools enable rapid assessments and pattern recognition, with services such as Cognitive Services providing instant intelligent feedback on the data. For ongoing analysis and training, services such as Azure Machine Learning play a key role in enabling continuous refinement and optimization of AI models.

Chapter 10, Architecting Secure Applications on a Trusted Platform

This chapter discussed the various Azure services that safeguard user data, applications, and infrastructure. We learned that defining security policies with Azure Policy based on the organization's risk profile can enhance security. Azure Sentinel and Microsoft Defender for Cloud utilize these policies to manage threats, monitor security states, and provide actionable recommendations. Azure Monitor offers insights for proactive monitoring, while Defender for Cloud addresses threats in hybrid and heterogeneous environments, working alongside Azure Monitor for detection and mitigation. Azure Firewall and Network Security Groups enable precise control over virtual networks. Azure Active Directory provides authentication and authorization support, seamlessly integrating with managed identities. Organizations can establish a robust security posture in the Azure environment by implementing the security services mentioned in this chapter.

Chapter 11, Cost Governance on Azure

In the final chapter, we discussed the importance of cost management and optimization on Azure. We emphasized the need to closely monitor resources to prevent unexpected escalations in expenses. As cloud architects, it is crucial to design applications with cost-effectiveness in mind by selecting appropriate Azure resources, SKUs, tiers, and sizes.

Proper cost management enables architects and business decision makers to maintain control over costs throughout the entire project lifecycle. By closely monitoring and optimizing costs, we can maximize the value derived from Azure and ensure that our cloud investments align with our budgetary requirements.

Summary

Throughout this book, we have explored features and functionalities provided by Azure, enabling architects and business decision makers to harness the limitless potential of the cloud. We have also examined how Azure can enhance operational efficiency, scale businesses seamlessly, strengthen security measures, and stimulate innovation across organizations.

With Azure as a powerful tool at their disposal, architects and decision makers can confidently navigate the cloud landscape and propel their enterprises toward a future defined by success and growth.

Index

A

accounts: 5, 39, 41, 52-53, 56, 60, 79, 99, 121, 165, 224, 234

ACID: 111, 121, 125

ACLPolicies: 176

ACLs: 127

add-ons: 161, 167, 239

Advisor: 2, 9-10, 35-36, 230-231

Agents: 166, 174

aggregate: 59, 150, 152, 188, 193, 199, 209

agility: 11, 83, 101, 135, 202

AI-based: 197

AI-driven: 8, 123

Alto: 76-77

ALZ-Bicep: 96

Amazon: 163, 214

Apache: 127, 187, 189, 191, 215

APIs: 7, 27, 45, 58, 64, 91, 123, 137, 139-140, 151, 179, 186, 196, 215, 220

ASGs: 70, 216

asynchronous: 109, 151

Atlas: 215

atomicity: 111, 121

azure-portal: 39

azurerm: 91, 96

azure-sql: 8, 115, 119, 130

B

backend: 16-17, 19, 50-51, 71-72, 130, 153, 176

Bicep: 85, 88-89, 92-94, 96-97, 99, 103, 105, 107

blockchain: 204Blueprints: 43, 232

budget: 10, 12, 61, 139, 223, 225, 230

C

cache: 53, 60, 71

Cassandra: 121, 123

CDNs: 231, 234

cloud-native: 44, 57, 138, 160, 179, 202, 209

ClusterIP: 172-173

clusters: 161, 163, 165-168, 171, 177-178, 184, 239

Cognitive: 195-199, 239

ConfigMaps: 165, 168, 170

Contoso: 158-160

Cosmos: 9, 53, 57, 109, 112, 121-123, 128, 132-133, 137, 142, 193, 198, 224

cross-region: 78-79, 121

cross-site: 219

cyberattacks: 63, 178

‹packt›

Subscribe to our online digital library for full access to over 7,000 books and videos, as well as industry leading tools to help you plan your personal development and advance your career. For more information, please visit our website.

Why subscribe?

- Spend less time learning and more time coding with practical eBooks and Videos from over 4,000 industry professionals

- Improve your learning with Skill Plans built especially for you

- Get a free eBook or video every month

- Fully searchable for easy access to vital information

- Copy and paste, print, and bookmark content

Did you know that Packt offers eBook versions of every book published, with PDF and ePub files available? You can upgrade to the eBook version at packtpub.com and as a print book customer, you are entitled to a discount on the eBook copy. Get in touch with us at customercare@packtpub.com for more details.

At www.packtpub.com, you can also read a collection of free technical articles, sign up for a range of free newsletters, and receive exclusive discounts and offers on Packt books and eBooks.

Other Books You May Enjoy

If you enjoyed this book, you may be interested in these other books by Packt:

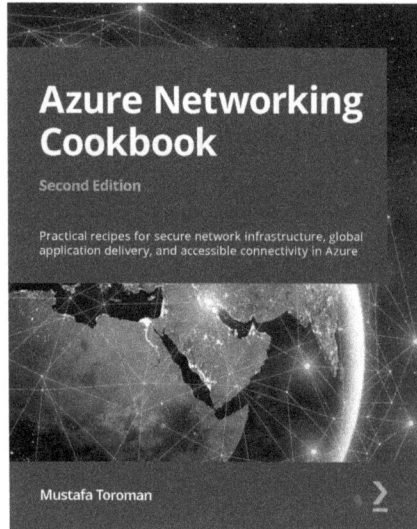

Azure Networking Cookbook - Second Edition

Mustafa Toroman

ISBN: 978-1-80056-375-9

- Learn to create Azure networking services
- Understand how to create and work on hybrid connections
- Configure and manage Azure network services
- Learn ways to design high availability network solutions in Azure
- Discover how to monitor and troubleshoot Azure network resources
- Learn different methods of connecting local networks to Azure virtual networks

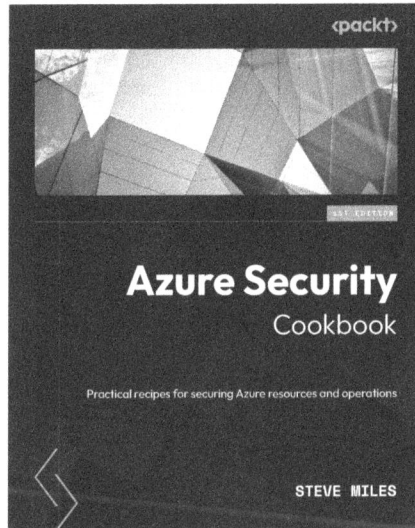

Azure Security Cookbook - Second Edition

Steve Miles

ISBN: 978-1-80461-796-0

- Find out how to implement Azure security features and tools
- Understand how to provide actionable insights into security incidents
- Gain confidence in securing Azure resources and operations
- Shorten your time to value for applying learned skills in real-world cases
- Follow best practices and choices based on informed decisions
- Better prepare for Microsoft certification with a security element

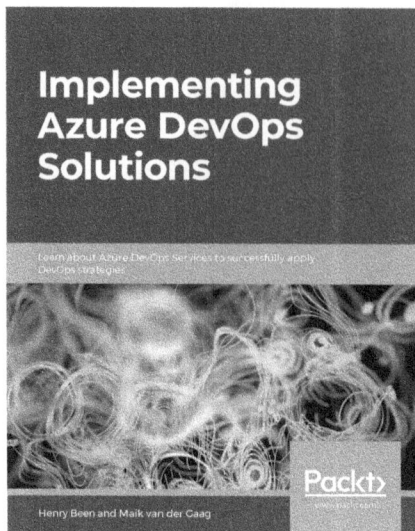

Implementing Azure DevOps Solutions

Henry Been and Mark van der Gaag

ISBN: 978-1-78961-969-0

- Get acquainted with Azure DevOps Services and DevOps practices
- Implement CI/CD processes
- Build and deploy a CI/CD pipeline with automated testing on Azure
- Integrate security and compliance in pipelines
- Understand and implement Azure Container Services
- Become well versed in closing the loop from production back to development.

Packt is searching for authors like you

If you're interested in becoming an author for Packt, please visit authors.packtpub.com and apply today. We have worked with thousands of developers and tech professionals, just like you, to help them share their insight with the global tech community. You can make a general application, apply for a specific hot topic that we are recruiting an author for, or submit your own idea.

Download a free PDF copy of this book

Thanks for purchasing this book!

Do you like to read on the go but are unable to carry your print books everywhere?

Is your eBook purchase not compatible with the device of your choice?

Don't worry, now with every Packt book you get a DRM-free PDF version of that book at no cost.

Read anywhere, any place, on any device. Search, copy, and paste code from your favorite technical books directly into your application.

The perks don't stop there, you can get exclusive access to discounts, newsletters, and great free content in your inbox daily

Follow these simple steps to get the benefits:

1. Scan the QR code or visit the link below

https://packt.link/free-ebook/9781837639144

2. Submit your proof of purchase
3. That's it! We'll send your free PDF and other benefits to your email directly